Cram101 Textbook Outlines to accompany:

Human Development

Papalia, Olds and Feldman, 9th Edition

An Academic Internet Publishers (AIPI) publication (c) 2007.

With Cram101.com online, you also have access to extensive reference material.

You will nail those essays and papers. Here is an example from a Cram101 Biology text:

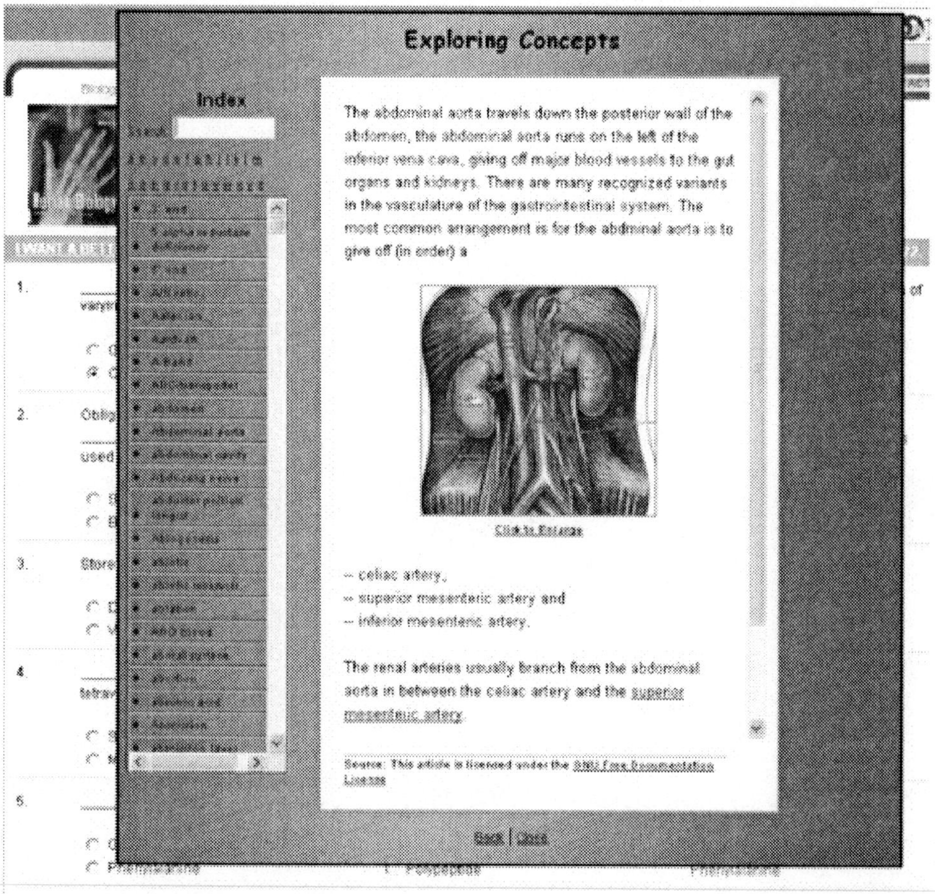

Visit **www.Cram101.com**, click Sign Up at the top of the screen, and enter DK73DW in the promo code box on the registration screen. Access to www.Cram101.com is normally $9.95, but because you have purchased this book, your access fee is only $4.95. Sign up and stop highlighting textbooks forever.

Learning System

Cram101 Textbook Outlines is a learning system. The notes in this book are the highlights of your textbook, you will never have to highlight a book again.

How to use this book. Take this book to class, it is your notebook for the lecture. The notes and highlights on the left hand side of the pages follow the outline and order of the textbook. All you have to do is follow along while your intructor presents the lecture. Circle the items emphasized in class and add other important information on the right side. With Cram101 Textbook Outlines you'll spend less time writing and more time listening. Learning becomes more efficient.

Cram101.com Online

Increase your studying efficiency by using Cram101.com's practice tests and online reference material. It is the perfect complement to Cram101 Textbook Outlines. Use self-teaching matching tests or simulate in-class testing with comprehensive multiple choice tests, or simply use Cram's true and false tests for quick review. Cram101.com even allows you to enter your in-class notes for an integrated studying format combining the textbook notes with your class notes.

Visit **www.Cram101.com**, click Sign Up at the top of the screen, and enter **DK73DW2925** in the promo code box on the registration screen. Access to www.Cram101.com is normally $9.95, but because you have purchased this book, your access fee is only $4.95. Sign up and stop highlighting textbooks forever.

 ISBN: 1-4288-0242-8

Human Development
Papalia, Olds and Feldman, 9th

CONTENTS

Evolution	Commonly used to refer to gradual change, evolution is the change in the frequency of alleles within a population from one generation to the next. This change may be caused by different mechanisms, including natural selection, genetic drift, or changes in population (gene flow).
Darwin	Darwin achieved lasting fame as originator of the theory of evolution through natural selection. His book Expression of Emotions in Man and Animals is generally considered the first text on comparative psychology.
Infancy	The developmental period that extends from birth to 18 or 24 months is called infancy.
Nurture	Nurture refers to the environmental influences on behavior due to nutrition, culture, socioeconomic status, and learning.
Life span	Life span refers to the upper boundary of life, the maximum number of years an individual can live. The maximum life span of human beings is about 120 years of age. Females live an average of 6 years longer than males.
Learning	Learning is a relatively permanent change in behavior that results from experience. Thus, to attribute a behavioral change to learning, the change must be relatively permanent and must result from experience.
Scientific research	Research that is objective, systematic, and testable is called scientific research.
Terman	Terman revised the Stanford-Binet Intelligence Scale in 1916, commonly used to measure intelligence (or I.Q.) in the United States. William Stern's suggestion that mental age/chronological age times 100 (to get rid of the decimal) be made the "intelligence quotient" or I.Q. This apparent mathematization of the measurement gave it an air of scientific accuracy and detachment which contributed greatly to its acceptance among educators and the broad public.
Norms	In testing, standards of test performance that permit the comparison of one person's score on the test to the scores of others who have taken the same test are referred to as norms.
Emotion	An emotion is a mental states that arise spontaneously, rather than through conscious effort. They are often accompanied by physiological changes.
Logical thought	Drawing conclusions on the basis of formal principles of reasoning is referred to as logical thought.
Brain imaging	Brain imaging is a fairly recent discipline within medicine and neuroscience. Brain imaging falls into two broad categories -- structural imaging and functional imaging.
Neuroscience	A field that combines the work of psychologists, biologists, biochemists, medical researchers, and others in the study of the structure and function of the nervous system is neuroscience.
Temperament	Temperament refers to a basic, innate disposition to change behavior. The activity level is an important dimension of temperament.
Dementia	Dementia is progressive decline in cognitive function due to damage or disease in the brain beyond what might be expected from normal aging.
Brain	The brain controls and coordinates most movement, behavior and homeostatic body functions such as heartbeat, blood pressure, fluid balance and body temperature. Functions of the brain are responsible for cognition, emotion, memory, motor learning and other sorts of learning. The brain is primarily made up of two types of cells: glia and neurons.
Social policy	Social policy is the study of the welfare state, and the range of responses to social need.
Human factors	Human factors refers to the study of the interaction of people and machines. It is a technology that applies knowledge of human behavior, cognition, physical capabilities and dimensions to the design of products, equipment, or large-scale systems that can be used easily, effectively and safely by human operators.

Quantitative change	Quantitative change refers to change in number or amount, such as in height, weight, or size of vocabulary.
Qualitative change	A qualitative change refers to a change in kind, structure, or organization, such as the change from nonverbal to verbal communication.
Embryo	A developed zygote that has a rudimentary heart, brain, and other organs is referred to as an embryo.
Personality	Personality refers to the pattern of enduring characteristics that differentiates a person, the patterns of behaviors that make each individual unique.
Cognitive development	The process by which a child's understanding of the world changes as a function of age and experience is called cognitive development.
Affect	A subjective feeling or emotional tone often accompanied by bodily expressions noticeable to others is called affect.
Puberty	Puberty refers to the process of physical changes by which a child's body becomes an adult body capable of reproduction.
Creativity	Creativity is the ability to think about something in novel and unusual ways and come up with unique solutions to problems. It involves divergent thinking, having many solutions or views to a problem.
Attention	Attention is the cognitive process of selectively concentrating on one thing while ignoring other things. Psychologists have labeled three types of attention: sustained attention, selective attention, and divided attention.
Reasoning	Reasoning is the act of using reason to derive a conclusion from certain premises. There are two main methods to reach a conclusion,deductive reasoning and inductive reasoning.
Psychosocial development	Erikson's psychosocial development describe eight developmental stages through which a healthily developing human should pass from infancy to late adulthood. In each stage the person confronts, and hopefully masters, new challenges.
Social construction	Concept about the nature of reality, based on societally shared perceptions or assumptions is a social construction.
Perception	Perception is the process of acquiring, interpreting, selecting, and organizing sensory information.
Society	The social sciences use the term society to mean a group of people that form a semi-closed (or semi-open) social system, in which most interactions are with other individuals belonging to the group.
Toddler	A toddler is a child between the ages of one and three years old. During this period, the child learns a great deal about social roles and develops motor skills; to toddle is to walk unsteadily.
Autonomy	Autonomy is the condition of something that does not depend on anything else.
Early childhood	Early childhood refers to the developmental period extending from the end of infancy to about 5 or 6 years of age; sometimes called the preschool years.
Adolescence	The period of life bounded by puberty and the assumption of adult responsibilities is adolescence.
Middle Adulthood	Middle adulthood refers to the developmental period beginning at approximately 40 years of age and extending to about 60. Maximum bone density occurs by the late thirties and begins to degrade.
Late adulthood	The developmental period that lasts from about 60 to 70 years of age until death is referred to as late adulthood.
Friendship	The essentials of friendship are reciprocity and commitment between individuals who see themselves more or less as equals. Interaction between friends rests on a more equal power base than the interaction between children and adults.
Individual	Individual differences psychology studies the ways in which individual people differ in their behavior.

differences	This is distinguished from other aspects of psychology in that although psychology is ostensibly a study of individuals, modern psychologists invariably study groups.
Senses	The senses are systems that consist of a sensory cell type that respond to a specific kind of physical energy, and that correspond to a defined region within the brain where the signals are received and interpreted.
Gross motor skills	Gross motor skills refer to motor skills that involve large muscle activities, such as walking.
Handedness	A preference for the right or left hand in most activities is referred to as handedness. Right-handedness is dominant in all cultures, and it appears before culture can influence the child.
Self-concept	Self-concept refers to domain-specific evaluations of the self where a domain may be academics, athletics, etc.
Self-esteem	Self-esteem refers to a person's subjective appraisal of himself or herself as intrinsically positive or negative to some degree.
Altruism	Altruism is being helpful to other people with little or no interest in being rewarded for one's efforts. This is distinct from merely helping others.
Coregulation	A gradual transferring of control from parent to child, beginning in middle childhood is referred to as coregulation.
Heredity	Heredity is the transfer of characteristics from parent to offspring through their genes.
Maturation	The orderly unfolding of traits, as regulated by the genetic code is called maturation.
Innate	Innate behavior is not learned or influenced by the environment, rather, it is present or predisposed at birth.
Eating disorders	Psychological disorders characterized by distortion of the body image and gross disturbances in eating patterns are called eating disorders.
Reaction time	The amount of time required to respond to a stimulus is referred to as reaction time.
Scientific reasoning	A type of reasoning that involves the generation of hypotheses and the systematic testing of those hypotheses is scientific reasoning.
Attitude	An enduring mental representation of a person, place, or thing that evokes an emotional response and related behavior is called attitude.
Personality trait	According to the Diagnostic and Statistical Manual of the American Psychiatric Association, a personality trait is a "prominent aspect of personality that is exhibited in a wide range of important social and personal contexts. ...".
Life stages	Widely recognized periods of life corresponding to broad phases of development are called life stages. They may cross-culturally or socially defined.
Midlife transition	Levinson's term for the ages from 40 to 45, which are characterized by a shift in psychological perspective from viewing ourselves in terms of years lived to viewing ourselves in terms of the years we have left is called the midlife transition.
Lesbian	A lesbian is a homosexual woman. They are women who are sexually and romantically attracted to other women.
Socioeconomic Status	A family's socioeconomic status is based on family income, parental education level, parental occupation, and social status in the community. Those with high status often have more success in preparing their children for school because they have access to a wide range of resources.
Social role	Social role refers to expected behavior patterns associated with particular social positions.

Population	Population refers to all members of a well-defined group of organisms, events, or things.
Social support	Social Support is the physical and emotional comfort given by family, friends, co-workers and others. Research has identified three main types of social support: emotional, practical, sharing points of view.
Prenatal	Prenatal period refers to the time from conception to birth.
Subculture	As understood in sociology, anthropology and cultural studies, a subculture is a set of people with a distinct set of behavior and beliefs that differentiate them from a larger culture of which they are a part.
Ethnic group	An ethnic group is a culture or subculture whose members are readily distinguishable by outsiders based on traits originating from a common racial, national, linguistic, or religious source. Members of an ethnic group are often presumed to be culturally or biologically similar, although this is not in fact necessarily the case.
Ethnicity	Ethnicity refers to a characteristic based on cultural heritage, nationality characteristics, race, religion, and language.
Discrimination	In Learning theory, discrimination refers the ability to distinguish between a conditioned stimulus and other stimuli. It can be brought about by extensive training or differential reinforcement. In social terms, it is the denial of privileges to a person or a group on the basis of prejudice.
Prejudice	Prejudice in general, implies coming to a judgment on the subject before learning where the preponderance of the evidence actually lies, or formation of a judgement without direct experience.
Depression	In everyday language depression refers to any downturn in mood, which may be relatively transitory and perhaps due to something trivial. This is differentiated from Clinical depression which is marked by symptoms that last two weeks or more and are so severe that they interfere with daily living.
Longitudinal study	Longitudinal study is a type of developmental study in which the same group of participants is followed and measured for an extended period of time, often years.
Sensitive period	A sensitive period is a developmental window in which a predisposed behavior is most likely to develop given appropriate stimulation. In linguistic theory, the period from about 18 months to puberty is when the brain is thought to be primed for learning language because of plasticity of the brain.
Critical thinking	Critical thinking is a mental process of analyzing or evaluating information, particularly statements or propositions that are offered as true.
Cohort	A cohort is a group of individuals defined by their date of birth.
Normative	The term normative is used to describe the effects of those structures of culture which regulate the function of social activity.
Menopause	Menopause is a stage of the human female reproductive cycle that occurs as the ovaries stop producing estrogen, causing the reproductive system to gradually shut down.
Critical period	A period of time when an innate response can be elicited by a particular stimulus is referred to as the critical period.
Imprinting	Imprinting describes any kind of critical period sensitive learning (learning occurring at a particular age or a particular life stage) that is rapid and apparently independent of the consequences of behavior.
Attachment	Attachment is the tendency to seek closeness to another person and feel secure when that person is present.
Lorenz	Lorenz demonstrated how incubator-hatched geese would imprint on the first suitable moving stimulus they saw within what he called a "critical period" of about 36 hours shortly after hatching. Most famously, the goslings would imprint on Lorenz himself .

Species	Species refers to a reproductively isolated breeding population.
Nervous system	The body's electrochemical communication circuitry, made up of billions of neurons is a nervous system.
Acquisition	Acquisition is the process of adapting to the environment, learning or becoming conditioned. In classical conditoning terms, it is the initial learning of the stimulus response link, which involves a neutral stimulus being associated with a unconditioned stimulus and becoming a conditioned stimulus.
Hypothesis	A specific statement about behavior or mental processes that is testable through research is a hypothesis.
Plasticity	The capacity for modification and change is referred to as plasticity.
Theories	Theories are logically self-consistent models or frameworks describing the behavior of a certain natural or social phenomenon. They are broad explanations and predictions concerning phenomena of interest.
Quantitative	A quantitative property is one that exists in a range of magnitudes, and can therefore be measured. Measurements of any particular quantitative property are expressed as as a specific quantity, referred to as a unit, multiplied by a number.
Baltes	Baltes describes the life-span perspective as one that sees hurman development as lifelong, multidimensional, multidirectional, plastic, contextual, and multidisciplinary, and as involving growth, maintenance, and regulation.
Adolescent rebellion	Pattern of emotional turmoil, characteristic of a minority of adolescents, which may involve conflict with family, alienation from adult society, reckless behavior, and rejection of adult values is an adolescent rebellion.
Stages	Stages represent relatively discrete periods of time in which functioning is qualitatively different from functioning at other periods.
Trait	An enduring personality characteristic that tends to lead to certain behaviors is called a trait. The term trait also means a genetically inherited feature of an organism.

Mechanistic model	The mechanistic model views development as a passive, predictable response to stimuli.
Stages	Stages represent relatively discrete periods of time in which functioning is qualitatively different from functioning at other periods.
Population	Population refers to all members of a well-defined group of organisms, events, or things.
Heredity	Heredity is the transfer of characteristics from parent to offspring through their genes.
Trait	An enduring personality characteristic that tends to lead to certain behaviors is called a trait. The term trait also means a genetically inherited feature of an organism.
Rousseau	Rousseau rejected the idea of the blank slate. He believed that learning was a natural consequence of human existence. Further, he thought socialization unimportant in development. Because of his insistence that childhood was different than adulthood and his creation of stages of development, he is known as the father of developmental psychology.
Society	The social sciences use the term society to mean a group of people that form a semi-closed (or semi-open) social system, in which most interactions are with other individuals belonging to the group.
Locke	In 1690, Locke wrote his Essay Concerning Human Understanding. The essay arugued for empiricism, that ideas come only from experience. In other words, there are no innate ideas. The tabula rasa or blank slate was his metaphor.
Quantitative change	Quantitative change refers to change in number or amount, such as in height, weight, or size of vocabulary.
Qualitative change	A qualitative change refers to a change in kind, structure, or organization, such as the change from nonverbal to verbal communication.
Sigmund Freud	Sigmund Freud was the founder of the psychoanalytic school, based on his theory that unconscious motives control much behavior, that particular kinds of unconscious thoughts and memories are the source of neurosis, and that neurosis could be treated through bringing these unconscious thoughts and memories to consciousness in psychoanalytic treatment.
Erik Erikson	Erik Erikson conceived eight stages of development, each confronting the individual with its own psychosocial demands, that continued into old age. Personality development, according to Erikson, takes place through a series of crises that must be overcome and internalized by the individual in preparation for the next developmental stage. Such crisis are not catastrophes but vulnerabilities.
Piaget	Piaget argued that young children's answers were qualitatively different than older children rather than quantitative. There are two major aspects to his theory: the process of coming to know and the stages we move through as we gradually acquire this ability.
Theories	Theories are logically self-consistent models or frameworks describing the behavior of a certain natural or social phenomenon. They are broad explanations and predictions concerning phenomena of interest.
Psychoanalytic	Freud's theory that unconscious forces act as determinants of personality is called psychoanalytic theory. The theory is a developmental theory characterized by critical stages of development.
Psychoanalysis	Psychoanalysis refers to the school of psychology that emphasizes the importance of unconscious motives and conflicts as determinants of human behavior. It was Freud's method of exploring human personality.
Insight	Insight refers to a sudden awareness of the relationships among various elements that had previously appeared to be independent of one another.

Personality	Personality refers to the pattern of enduring characteristics that differentiates a person, the patterns of behaviors that make each individual unique.
Adolescence	The period of life bounded by puberty and the assumption of adult responsibilities is adolescence.
Infancy	The developmental period that extends from birth to 18 or 24 months is called infancy.
Sensitive period	A sensitive period is a developmental window in which a predisposed behavior is most likely to develop given appropriate stimulation. In linguistic theory, the period from about 18 months to puberty is when the brain is thought to be primed for learning language because of plasticity of the brain.
Predisposition	Predisposition refers to an inclination or diathesis to respond in a certain way, either inborn or acquired. In abnormal psychology, it is a factor that lowers the ability to withstand stress and inclines the individual toward pathology.
Learning	Learning is a relatively permanent change in behavior that results from experience. Thus, to attribute a behavioral change to learning, the change must be relatively permanent and must result from experience.
Chronosystem	A chronosystem refers to the patterning of environmental events and transitions over the life course and their sociohistorical contexts.
Microsystem	The setting or context in which an individual lives, including the person's family, peers, school, and neighborhood is a microsystem.
Anal stage	The anal stage in psychology is the term used by Sigmund Freud to describe the development during the second year of life, in which a child's pleasure and conflict centers are in the anal area.
Toddler	A toddler is a child between the ages of one and three years old. During this period, the child learns a great deal about social roles and develops motor skills; to toddle is to walk unsteadily.
Psychosexual development	In psychodynamic theory, the process by which libidinal energy is expressed through different erogenous zones during different stages of development is called psychosexual development.
Early childhood	Early childhood refers to the developmental period extending from the end of infancy to about 5 or 6 years of age; sometimes called the preschool years.
Phallic stage	The phallic stage is the 3rd of Freud's psychosexual stages, when awareness of and manipulation of the genitals is supposed to be a primary source of pleasure. In this stage the child deals with the Oedipus complex, if male, or the Electra Complex, if female.
Attachment	Attachment is the tendency to seek closeness to another person and feel secure when that person is present.
Latency stage	Sigmund Freud suggested that the latency stage, age 6-10, this was a time of sexual latency, when the healthy child ceased all sexual interest and was vulnerable to trauma if he or she experienced sexuality.
Anxiety	Anxiety is a complex combination of the feeling of fear, apprehension and worry often accompanied by physical sensations such as palpitations, chest pain and/or shortness of breath.
Genital stage	The genital stage in psychology is the term used by Sigmund Freud to describe the final stage of human psychosexual development. It is characterized by the expression of libido through intercourse with an adult of the other gender.
Latency	In child development, latency refers to a phase of psychosexual development characterized by

	repression of sexual impulses. In learning theory, latency is the delay between stimulus (S) and response (R), which according to Hull depends on the strength of the association.
Superego	Frued's third psychic structure, which functions as a moral guardian and sets forth high standards for behavior is the superego.
Ego	In Freud's view the Ego serves to balance our primitive needs and our moral beliefs and taboos. Relying on experience, a healthy Ego provides the ability to adapt to reality and interact with the outside world.
Pleasure principle	The pleasure principle is the tendency to seek pleasure and avoid pain. In Freud's theory, this principle rules the Id, but is at least partly repressed by the reality principle.
Reality principle	The reality principle tells us to subordinate pleasure to what needs to be done. Subordinating the pleasure principle to the reality principle is done through a psychological process Freud calls sublimation, where you take desires that can't be fulfilled, or shouldn't be fulfilled, and turn their energy into something useful and productive.
Unconscious thought	Unconscious thought is Freud's concept of a reservoir of unacceptable wishes, feelings, and thoughts that are beyond conscious awareness.
Ambivalence	The simultaneous holding of strong positive and negative emotional attitudes toward the same situation or person is called ambivalence.
Motivation	In psychology, motivation is the driving force (desire) behind all actions of an organism.
Affect	A subjective feeling or emotional tone often accompanied by bodily expressions noticeable to others is called affect.
Psychotherapy	Psychotherapy is a set of techniques based on psychological principles intended to improve mental health, emotional or behavioral issues.
Psychoanalyst	A psychoanalyst is a specially trained therapist who attempts to treat the individual by uncovering and revealing to the individual otherwise subconscious factors that are contributing to some undesirable behavor.
Puberty	Puberty refers to the process of physical changes by which a child's body becomes an adult body capable of reproduction.
Psychosocial stages	Erikson's eight developmental stages through the life span, each defined by a conflict that must be resolved satisfactorily in order for healthy personality development to occur are called psychosocial stages.
Autonomy versus shame and doubt	In Erikson's second stage of development, autonomy versus shame and doubt, which occurs in late infancy and toddlerhood, infants begin to discover that their behavior is their own.
Industry versus inferiority	Erikson's fourth stage of development, industry versus inferiority, develops in the elementary school years. Initiative brings children into contact with a new experiences. They direct their energy toward mastering knowledge and intellectual skills.
Identity versus identity confusion	Identity versus identity confusion is Erikson's fifth developmental stage, which individuals experience during the adolescent years. At this time, individuals are faced with finding out who they are, what they re all about, and where they are going in life.
Intimacy versus isolation	The life crisis of young adulthood, which is characterized by the task of developing binding intimate relationships is referred to as Erikson's intimacy versus isolation stage.
Generativity versus stagnation	Generativity versus stagnation is Erikson's term for the crisis of middle adulthood. The individual is characterized by the task of being productive and contributing to younger generations.
Ego integrity	Erikson's term for the crisis of late adulthood, characterized by the task of maintaining

versus despair	one's sense of identity despite physical deterioration is called ego integrity versus despair.
Late adulthood	The developmental period that lasts from about 60 to 70 years of age until death is referred to as late adulthood.
Concrete operations	In Piaget's theory, the third major stage of cognitive development, in which children can decenter their perception, are less egocentric, and can think logically about concrete objects is called concrete operations.
Formal operations	Formal operations in Piaget's theory is the final stage of cognitive development, in which children are able to apply abstract logical rules. Not everyone reaches the formal operations stage of development.
Initiative versus guilt	Initiative versus guilt is Erikson's third stage of development, which occurs during the preschool years. As preschool children encounter a widening social world, they are challenged more than they were as infants.
Guilt	Guilt describes many concepts related to a negative emotion or condition caused by actions which are believed to be, morally wrong. According to Freud, the avoidance of guilt is the basis for moral behavior.
Psychosocial development	Erikson's psychosocial development describe eight developmental stages through which a healthily developing human should pass from infancy to late adulthood. In each stage the person confronts, and hopefully masters, new challenges.
Life-span perspective	The view that development is lifelong, multidimensional, multidirectional, plastic, contextual, multidisciplinary, and involves growth, maintenance and regulation is referred to as the life-span perspective.
Life span	Life span refers to the upper boundary of life, the maximum number of years an individual can live. The maximum life span of human beings is about 120 years of age. Females live an average of 6 years longer than males.
Adaptation	Adaptation is a lowering of sensitivity to a stimulus following prolonged exposure to that stimulus. Behavioral adaptations are special ways a particular organism behaves to survive in its natural habitat.
Behaviorism	The school of psychology that defines psychology as the study of observable behavior and studies relationships between stimuli and responses is called behaviorism. Behaviorism relied heavily on animal research and stated the same principles governed the behavior of both nonhumans and humans.
Associative learning	A metal connection made between two events is called associative learning.
Classical conditioning	Classical conditioning is a simple form of learning in which an organism comes to associate or anticipate events. A neutral stimulus comes to evoke the response usually evoked by a natural or unconditioned stimulus by being paired repeatedly with the unconditioned stimulus.
Operant Conditioning	A simple form of learning in which an organism learns to engage in behavior because it is reinforced is referred to as operant conditioning. The consequences of a behavior produce changes in the probability of the behavior's occurence.
Pavlov	Pavlov first described the phenomenon now known as classical conditioning in experiments with dogs.
Stimulus	A change in an environmental condition that elicits a response is a stimulus.
Stroke	A stroke occurs when the blood supply to a part of the brain is suddenly interrupted by occlusion, by hemorrhage, or other causes

Attention	Attention is the cognitive process of selectively concentrating on one thing while ignoring other things. Psychologists have labeled three types of attention: sustained attention, selective attention, and divided attention.
Conditioned response	A conditioned response is the response to a stimulus that occurs when an animal has learned to associate the stimulus with a certain positive or negative effect.
Skinner	Skinner conducted research on shaping behavior through positive and negative reinforcement, and demonstrated operant conditioning, a technique which he developed in contrast with classical conditioning.
Reinforcement	In operant conditioning, reinforcement is any change in an environment that (a) occurs after the behavior, (b) seems to make that behavior re-occur more often in the future and (c) that reoccurence of behavior must be the result of the change.
Punishment	Punishment is the addtion of a stimulus that reduces the frequency of a response, or the removal of a stimulus that results in a reduction of the response.
Conditioning	Conditioning describes the process by which behaviors can be learned or modified through interaction with the environment.
Positive reinforcement	In positive reinforcement, a stimulus is added and the rate of responding increases.
Negative Reinforcement	During negative reinforcement, a stimulus is removed and the frequency of the behavior or response increases.
Baseline	Measure of a particular behavior or process taken before the introduction of the independent variable or treatment is called the baseline.
Behavior modification	Behavior Modification is a technique of altering an individual's reactions to stimuli through positive reinforcement and the extinction of maladaptive behavior.
Behavior therapy	Behavior therapy refers to the systematic application of the principles of learning to direct modification of a client's problem behaviors.
Eating disorders	Psychological disorders characterized by distortion of the body image and gross disturbances in eating patterns are called eating disorders.
Autism	Autism is a neurodevelopmental disorder that manifests itself in markedly abnormal social interaction, communication ability, patterns of interests, and patterns of behavior.
Social learning	Social learning is learning that occurs as a function of observing, retaining and replicating behavior observed in others. Although social learning can occur at any stage in life, it is thought to be particularly important during childhood, particularly as authority becomes important.
Bandura	Bandura is best known for his work on social learning theory or Social Cognitivism. His famous Bobo doll experiment illustrated that people learn from observing others.
Applied Behavior Analysis	Applied Behavior Analysis is the application of behavioral science to the analysis of behavior. It is widely regarded as the most researched intervention in addressing the social, linguistic, and mental differences in autistics.
Social cognitive theory	Social cognitive theory defines human behavior as a triadic, dynamic, and reciprocal interaction of personal factors, behavior, and the environment. Response consequences of a behavior are used to form expectations of behavioral outcomes. It is the ability to form these expectations that give humans the capability to predict the outcomes of their behavior, before the behavior is performed.
Perception	Perception is the process of acquiring, interpreting, selecting, and organizing sensory

	information.
Evolution	Commonly used to refer to gradual change, evolution is the change in the frequency of alleles within a population from one generation to the next. This change may be caused by different mechanisms, including natural selection, genetic drift, or changes in population (gene flow).
Feedback	Feedback refers to information returned to a person about the effects a response has had.
Information-processing approach	Information-processing approach emphasizes that individuals act on information, monitor it, and strategize about it--contrary to strict behaviorists. Central to information processing are the processes of memory and thinking. The computer serves as a metaphor whereby the brain is the hardware and behavior is the software.
Brain	The brain controls and coordinates most movement, behavior and homeostatic body functions such as heartbeat, blood pressure, fluid balance and body temperature. Functions of the brain are responsible for cognition, emotion, memory, motor learning and other sorts of learning. The brain is primarily made up of two types of cells: glia and neurons.
Cognitive revolution	The cognitive revolution is a name for an intellectual movement in the 1950s that combined new thinking in psychology, anthropology and linguistics with the nascent fields of computer science and neuroscience. In psychology, the movement was a response to behaviorism.
Mental processes	The thoughts, feelings, and motives that each of us experiences privately but that cannot be observed directly are called mental processes.
Cognitive development	The process by which a child's understanding of the world changes as a function of age and experience is called cognitive development.
Clinical method	Studying psychological problems and therapies in clinical settings is referred to as the clinical method. It usually involves case histories, pathology, or non-experimentally controlled environments.
Scheme	According to Piaget, a hypothetical mental structure that permits the classification and organization of new information is called a scheme.
Cognitive structure	According to Piaget, the number of schemata available to an organism at any given time constitutes that organism's cognitive structure. How the organism interacts with its environment depends on the current cognitive structure available. As the cognitive structure develops, new assimilations can occur.
Assimilation	According to Piaget, assimilation is the process of the organism interacting with the environment given the organism's cognitive structure. Assimilation is reuse of schemas to fit new information.
Accommodation	Piaget's developmental process of accommodation is the modification of currently held schemes or new schemes so that new information inconsistent with the existing schemes can be integrated and understood.
Equilibration	Equilibration is a mechanism in Piaget's theory that explains how children or adolescents shift from one state of thought to the next. The shift occurs as they experience cognitive conflict or disequilibrium in trying to understand the world. It is an innate drive to organize experiences to ensure maximal adaptation.
Problem solving	An attempt to find an appropriate way of attaining a goal when the goal is not readily available is called problem solving.
Wisdom	Wisdom is the ability to make correct judgments and decisions. It is an intangible quality gained through experience. Whether or not something is wise is determined in a pragmatic sense by its popularity, how long it has been around, and its ability to predict against future events.

Neo-Piagetians	Developmentalists who have elaborated on Piaget's theory, believing that children's cognitive development is even more specific in many respects than Piaget himself, are neo-Piagetians.
Individual differences	Individual differences psychology studies the ways in which individual people differ in their behavior. This is distinguished from other aspects of psychology in that although psychology is ostensibly a study of individuals, modern psychologists invariably study groups.
Neuroscience	A field that combines the work of psychologists, biologists, biochemists, medical researchers, and others in the study of the structure and function of the nervous system is neuroscience.
Obsessive-compulsive disorder	Obsessive-compulsive disorder is an anxiety disorder manifested in a variety of forms, but is most commonly characterized by a subject's obsessive drive to perform a particular task or set of tasks, compulsions commonly termed rituals.
Phobia	A persistent, irrational fear of an object, situation, or activity that the person feels compelled to avoid is referred to as a phobia.
Darwin	Darwin achieved lasting fame as originator of the theory of evolution through natural selection. His book Expression of Emotions in Man and Animals is generally considered the first text on comparative psychology.
Natural selection	Natural selection is a process by which biological populations are altered over time, as a result of the propagation of heritable traits that affect the capacity of individual organisms to survive and reproduce.
Species	Species refers to a reproductively isolated breeding population.
Extinction	In operant extinction, if no reinforcement is delivered after the response, gradually the behavior will no longer occur in the presence of the stimulus. The process is more rapid following continuous reinforcement rather than after partial reinforcement. In Classical Conditioning, repeated presentations of the CS without being followed by the US results in the extinction of the CS.
Adaptive behavior	An adaptive behavior increases the probability of the individual or organism to survive or exist within its environment.
Innate	Innate behavior is not learned or influenced by the environment, rather, it is present or predisposed at birth.
Instinct	Instinct is the word used to describe inherent dispositions towards particular actions. They are generally an inherited pattern of responses or reactions to certain kinds of situations.
Lorenz	Lorenz demonstrated how incubator-hatched geese would imprint on the first suitable moving stimulus they saw within what he called a "critical period" of about 36 hours shortly after hatching. Most famously, the goslings would imprint on Lorenz himself .
Comparative research	Comparative research is a research methodology that aims to make comparisons across different countries or cultures. A major problem is that the data sets in different countries may not use the same categories, or define categories differently.
Bowlby	Bowlby, a developmental psychologist of the psychoanalytic tradition, was responsible for much of the early research conducted on attachment in humans. He identified three stages of separation: protest, despair, and detachment.
Altruism	Altruism is being helpful to other people with little or no interest in being rewarded for one's efforts. This is distinct from merely helping others.
Evolutionary psychology	Evolutionary psychology proposes that cognition and behavior can be better understood in light of evolutionary history.

Ethology	Where comparative psychology sees the study of animal behavior in the context of what is known about human psychology, ethology sees the study of animal behavior in the context of what is known about animal anatomy and physiology.
Genetics	Genetics is the science of genes, heredity, and the variation of organisms.
Ecology	Ecology refers to the branch of biology that deals with the relationships between living organisms and their environment.
Contextual perspective	The contextual perspective of development sees the individual as inseparable from the social context.
Bronfenbrenner	Bronfenbrenner was a co-founder of the U.S. national Head Start program and founder of the Ecological Theory of Development.
Cultural values	The importance and desirability of various objects and activities as defined by people in a given culture are referred to as cultural values.
Evolutionary theory	Evolutionary theory is concerned with heritable variability rather than behavioral variations. Natural selection requirements: (1) natural variability within a species must exist, (2) only some individual differences are heritable, and (3) natural selection only takes place when there is an interaction between the inborn attributes of organisms and the environment in which they live.
Plasticity	The capacity for modification and change is referred to as plasticity.
Pretend play	According to Piaget and Smilansky, pretend play is the third cognitive level of play. It involves imaginary people or situations.
Social role	Social role refers to expected behavior patterns associated with particular social positions.
Mesosystem	Relationships between microsystems or connections between contexts, such as the connection between family experience and the school experience are referred to as a mesosystem.
Exosystem	The level at which experiences in another social setting, in which the individual does not have an active role, influence what the individual experiences in an immediate context is referred to as the exosystem.
Control group	A group that does not receive the treatment effect in an experiment is referred to as the control group or sometimes as the comparison group.
Subculture	As understood in sociology, anthropology and cultural studies, a subculture is a set of people with a distinct set of behavior and beliefs that differentiate them from a larger culture of which they are a part.
Temperament	Temperament refers to a basic, innate disposition to change behavior. The activity level is an important dimension of temperament.
Sociocultural theory	Vygotsky's theory of how contextual factors affect children's development is called sociocultural theory.
Vygotsky	The Vygotsky model of human development has been termed as a sociocultural approach. The individual's development is a result of his or her culture.
Proximal	Students can set both long-term (distal) and short-term (proximal) goals .
Metaphor	A metaphor is a rhetorical trope where a comparison is made between two seemingly unrelated subjects
Bruner	Bruner has had an enormous impact on educational psychology with his contributions to cognitive learning theory. His ideas are based on categorization, maintaining that people interpret the world in terms of its similarities and differences.

Task analysis	The procedure of identifying the component elements of a behavior chain is called task analysis.
Quantitative	A quantitative property is one that exists in a range of magnitudes, and can therefore be measured. Measurements of any particular quantitative property are expressed as as a specific quantity, referred to as a unit, multiplied by a number.
Physiological changes	Alterations in heart rate, blood pressure, perspiration, and other involuntary responses are physiological changes.
Quantitative research	Quantitative research is based on the numerical representation of observations for the purpose of describing and explaining the phenomena. Quantitative research begins with the collection of data, followed by the application of various descriptive and inferential statistical methods.
Standardized test	An oral or written assessment for which an individual receives a score indicating how the individual reponded relative to a previously tested large sample of others is referred to as a standardized test.
Subjective experience	Subjective experience refers to reality as it is perceived and interpreted, not as it exists objectively.
Qualitative research	Qualitative research is a broad term that describes research that focuses on how individuals and groups view and understand the world and construct meaning out of their experiences.
Emotion	An emotion is a mental states that arise spontaneously, rather than through conscious effort. They are often accompanied by physiological changes.
Scientific method	Psychologists gather data in order to describe, understand, predict, and control behavior. Scientific method refers to an approach that can be used to discover accurate information. It includes these steps: understand the problem, collect data, draw conclusions, and revise research conclusions.
Hypothesis	A specific statement about behavior or mental processes that is testable through research is a hypothesis.
Attitude	An enduring mental representation of a person, place, or thing that evokes an emotional response and related behavior is called attitude.
Laboratory setting	Research setting in which the behavior of interest does not naturally occur is called a laboratory setting.
Random selection	Choosing a sample so that each member of the population has an equal chance of being included in the sample is called random selection.
Random sample	A sample drawn so that each member of a population has an equal chance of being selected to participate is referred to as a random sample.
Post-traumatic stress disorder	Post-traumatic stress disorder is a term for the psychological consequences of exposure to or confrontation with stressful experiences, which involve actual or threatened death, serious physical injury or a threat to physical integrity and which the person found highly traumatic.
Depression	In everyday language depression refers to any downturn in mood, which may be relatively transitory and perhaps due to something trivial. This is differentiated from Clinical depression which is marked by symptoms that last two weeks or more and are so severe that they interfere with daily living.
Research design	A research design tests a hypothesis. The basic typess are: descriptive, correlational, and experimental.

Questionnaire | A self-report method of data collection or clinical assessment method in which the individual being studied checks off items on a printed list, answers multiple-choice questions, or writes out answers to essay questions aimed at producing a selfdescription is called questionnaire.

Naturalistic observation | Naturalistic observation is a method of observation that involves observing subjects in their natural habitats. Researchers take great care in avoiding making interferences with the behavior they are observing by using unobtrusive methods.

Observer bias | Observer bias is an error introduced into measurement when observers overemphasize behavior they expect to find and fail to notice behavior they do not expect. Observer bias can also be introduced because researchers see a behavior and interpret it according to what it means to them, whereas it may mean something else to the person showing the behavior.

Survey | A method of scientific investigation in which a large sample of people answer questions about their attitudes or behavior is referred to as a survey.

Habit | A habit is a response that has become completely separated from its eliciting stimulus. Early learning theorists used the term to describe S-R associations, however not all S-R associations become a habit, rather many are extinguished after reinforcement is withdrawn.

Intelligence test | An intelligence test is a standardized means of assessing a person's current mental ability, for example, the Stanford-Binet test and the Wechsler Adult Intelligence Scale.

Research method | The scope of the research method is to produce some new knowledge. This, in principle, can take three main forms: Exploratory research; Constructive research; and Empirical research.

Negative relationship | An inverse relationship, often called a negative relationship, occurs when increases in one variable are matched by decreases in another variable.

Variable | A variable refers to a measurable factor, characteristic, or attribute of an individual or a system.

Independent variable | A condition in a scientific study that is manipulated (assigned different values by a researcher) so that the effects of the manipulation may be observed is called an independent variable.

Dependent variable | A measure of an assumed effect of an independent variable is called the dependent variable.

Participant observation | Participant observation is a major research strategy which aims to gain a close and intimate familiarity with a given group of individuals (such as a religious, occupational, or deviant group) and their practices through an intensive involvement with people in their natural environment.

Ethnographic study | Ethnographic study is an in-depth study of a culture, which uses a combination of methods including participant observation.

Correlational study | A correlational study observes or measures two or more variables to find relationships between them. Such studies can identify lawful relationships but cannot determine whether change in one variable is the cause of change in another.

Correlation | A statistical technique for determining the degree of association between two or more variables is referred to as correlation.

Negative correlation | A negative correlation refers to a relationship between two variables in which one variable increases as the other decreases.

Dementia | Dementia is progressive decline in cognitive function due to damage or disease in the brain beyond what might be expected from normal aging.

Positive correlation	A relationship between two variables in which both vary in the same direction is called a positive correlation.
Causation	Causation concerns the time order relationship between two or more objects such that if a specific antecendent condition occurs the same consequent must always follow.
Experimental manipulation	The change that an experimenter deliberately produces in a situation under study is called the experimental manipulation.
Experimental group	Experimental group refers to any group receiving a treatment effect in an experiment.
Random assignment	Assignment of participants to experimental and control groups by chance is called random assignment. Random assigment reduces the likelihood that the results are due to preexisiting systematic differences between the groups.
Socioeconomic Status	A family's socioeconomic status is based on family income, parental education level, parental occupation, and social status in the community. Those with high status often have more success in preparing their children for school because they have access to a wide range of resources.
Validity	The extent to which a test measures what it is intended to measure is called validity.
Field experiment	A field experiment applies the scientific method to experimentally examine an intervention in the real world rather than in the laboratory. Field experiments generally randomize subjects into treatment and control groups and compare outcomes between these groups.
Microgenetic	A design that allows researchers to directly observe change by repeated testing over a relatively short time period is called a microgenetic study. The idea is to study change as change is occurring.
Longitudinal study	Longitudinal study is a type of developmental study in which the same group of participants is followed and measured for an extended period of time, often years.
Cross-sectional study	A type of developmental study in which researchers compare groups of participants of different ages on certain characteristics to determine age related differences is called a cross-sectional study.
Early adulthood	The developmental period beginning in the late teens or early twenties and lasting into the thirties is called early adulthood; characterized by an increasing self-awareness.
Cohort	A cohort is a group of individuals defined by their date of birth.
Cross-sectional research	A research method in which people of different ages are compared at the same point in time is called cross-sectional research.
Cohort effect	Similarities in behavior among a group of peers that stem from the fact that group members are approximately of the same age are referred to as the cohort effect.
Sequential design	A combination of the cross-sectional and longitudinal research methods that involves a repeated study of different cohorts over an extended period of time is a sequential design.
American Psychological Association	The American Psychological Association is a professional organization representing psychology in the US. The mission statement is to "advance psychology as a science and profession and as a means of promoting health, education , and human welfare".
Child development	Scientific study of the processes of change from conception through adolescence is called child development.
Informed consent	The term used by psychologists to indicate that a person has agreed to participate in research after receiving information about the purposes of the study and the nature of the treatments is informed consent. Even with informed consent, subjects may withdraw from any

experiment at any time.

Observational learning
The acquisition of knowledge and skills through the observation of others rather than by means of direct experience is observational learning. Four major processes are thought to influence the observational learning: attentional, retentional, behavioral production, and motivational.

Generalizability
The ability to extend a set of findings observed in one piece of research to other situations and groups is called generalizability.

Operational definition
An operational definition is the definition of a concept or action in terms of the observable and repeatable process, procedures, and appartaus that illustrates the concept or action.

Case study
A carefully drawn biography that may be obtained through interviews, questionnaires, and psychological tests is called a case study.

Direct observation
Direct observation refers to assessing behavior through direct surveillance.

Central nervous system
The vertebrate central nervous system consists of the brain and spinal cord.

Acquisition
Acquisition is the process of adapting to the environment, learning or becoming conditioned. In classical conditoning terms, it is the initial learning of the stimulus response link, which involves a neutral stimulus being associated with a unconditioned stimulus and becoming a conditioned stimulus.

Autonomy
Autonomy is the condition of something that does not depend on anything else.

Senses
The senses are systems that consist of a sensory cell type that respond to a specific kind of physical energy, and that correspond to a defined region within the brain where the signals are received and interpreted.

Fetus
A fetus develops from the end of the 8th week of pregnancy (when the major structures have formed), until birth.

Fetal alcohol syndrome
A cluster of abnormalities that appears in the offspring of mothers who drink alcohol heavily during pregnancy is called fetal alcohol syndrome.

Mental retardation
Mental retardation refers to having significantly below-average intellectual functioning and limitations in at least two areas of adaptive functioning. Many categorize retardation as mild, moderate, severe, or profound.

Syndrome
The term syndrome is the association of several clinically recognizable features, signs, symptoms, phenomena or characteristics which often occur together, so that the presence of one feature indicates the presence of the others.

Primary color
A primary color cannot be created by mixing other colors in the gamut of a given color space.

Genetic counseling
Genetic counseling generally refers to prenatal counseling done when a genetic condition is suspected in a pregnancy. Genetic counseling is the process by which patients or relatives at risk of an inherited disorder are advised of the consequences and nature of the disorder, the probability of developing or transmitting it, and the options open to them in management and family planning in order to prevent, avoid or ameliorate it.

Prenatal
Prenatal period refers to the time from conception to birth.

Nurture
Nurture refers to the environmental influences on behavior due to nutrition, culture, socioeconomic status, and learning.

Genetic testing
Genetic testing allows the genetic diagnosis of vulnerabilities to inherited diseases, and can also be used to determine a person's ancestry. Every person carries two copies of every

gene, one inherited from their mother, one inherited from their father.

Suicide

Suicide behavior is rare in childhood but escalates in adolescence. The suicide rate increases in a linear fashion from adolescence through late adulthood.

Embryo	A developed zygote that has a rudimentary heart, brain, and other organs is referred to as an embryo.
Clone	A clone is a genetic, not behavioral, copy of an organism.
Ovum	Ovum is a female sex cell or gamete.
Zygote	A zygote is a cell that is the result of fertilization. That is, two haploid cells—usually (but not always) a sperm cell from a male and an ovum from a female—merge into a single diploid cell called the zygote.
Menopause	Menopause is a stage of the human female reproductive cycle that occurs as the ovaries stop producing estrogen, causing the reproductive system to gradually shut down.
Ovulation	Ovulation is the process in the menstrual cycle by which a mature ovarian follicle ruptures and discharges an ovum (also known as an oocyte, female gamete, or casually, an egg) that participates in reproduction.
Ovary	The female reproductive organ is the ovary. It performs two major functions: producing eggs and secreting hormones.
Fallopian tube	A tube through which the eggs travel from the ovaries to the uterus is a fallopian tube.
Hair cells	Hair cells are the sensory cells of both the auditory system and the vestibular system. The auditory hair cells are located within the organ of Corti on a thin basilar membrane in the cochlea of the inner ear.
Uterus	The uterus or womb is the major female reproductive organ. The main function of the uterus is to accept a fertilized ovum which becomes implanted into the endometrium, and derives nourishment from blood vessels which develop exclusively for this purpose.
Testes	Testes are the male reproductive glands or gonads; this is where sperm develop and are stored.
Gland	A gland is an organ in an animal's body that synthesizes a substance for release such as hormones, often into the bloodstream or into cavities inside the body or its outer surface.
Semen	Semen is a fluid that contains spermatozoa. It is secreted by the gonads of males for the fertilization of female ova.
Dizygotic	Fraternal twins (commonly known as "non-identical twins") usually occur when two fertilized eggs are implanted in the uterine wall at the same time. The two eggs form two zygotes, and these twins are therefore also known as dizygotic.
Fraternal twins	Fraternal twins usually occur when two fertilized eggs are implanted in the uterine wall at the same time. The two eggs form two zygotes, and these twins are therefore also known as dizygotic. Dizygotic twins are no more similar genetically than any siblings.
Identical twins	Identical twins occur when a single egg is fertilized to form one zygote (monozygotic) but the zygote then divides into two separate embryos. The two embryos develop into foetuses sharing the same womb. Monozygotic twins are genetically identical unless there has been a mutation in development, and they are almost always the same gender.
Monozygotic	Identical twins occur when a single egg is fertilized to form one zygote, calld monozygotic, but the zygote then divides into two separate embryos. The two embryos develop into foetuses sharing the same womb. Monozygotic twins are genetically identical unless there has been a mutation in development, and they are almost always the same gender.
Postnatal	Postnatal is the period beginning immediately after the birth of a child and extending for about six weeks. The period is also known as postpartum and, less commonly, puerperium.
Prenatal	Prenatal period refers to the time from conception to birth.

Cervix	The cervix is the lower end of the uterus that joins with the top portion of the vaginia.
Urethra	The urethra is the tube that urine drains from as it leaves the body.
Vas deferens	The vas deferens are two muscular tubes that carry sperm from the testes to the urethra.
Prostate	The prostate is a gland that supplies most of the fluid that makes up semen, it is located at the base of the uninary bladder.
Scrotum	The scrotum is an external sack of skin that holds the testes.
Penis	The penis is the external male copulatory organ and the external male organ of urination. In humans, the penis is homologous to the female clitoris, as it develops from the same embryonic structure. It is capable of erection for use in copulation.
Ethnic group	An ethnic group is a culture or subculture whose members are readily distinguishable by outsiders based on traits originating from a common racial, national, linguistic, or religious source. Members of an ethnic group are often presumed to be culturally or biologically similar, although this is not in fact necessarily the case.
In vitro fertilization	In vitro fertilization is a technique in which egg cells are fertilized outside the woman's body. It is a major treatment in infertility where other methods of achieving conception have failed.
Personality	Personality refers to the pattern of enduring characteristics that differentiates a person, the patterns of behaviors that make each individual unique.
Deoxyribonuc-eic acid	Deoxyribonucleic acid contains the genetic instructions specifying the biological development of all cellular forms of life. It is often referred to as the molecule of heredity, as it is responsible for the genetic propagation of most inherited traits.
Genetic code	The genetic code is a set of rules, which maps DNA sequences to proteins in the living cell, and is employed in the process of protein synthesis. Nearly all living things use the same genetic code, called the standard genetic code, although a few organisms use minor variations of the standard code.
Heredity	Heredity is the transfer of characteristics from parent to offspring through their genes.
Protein	A protein is a complex, high-molecular-weight organic compound that consists of amino acids joined by peptide bonds. It is essential to the structure and function of all living cells and viruses. Many are enzymes or subunits of enzymes.
Chromosome	The DNA which carries genetic information in biological cells is normally packaged in the form of one or more large macromolecules called a chromosome. Humans normally have 46.
Nucleus	In neuroanatomy, a cluster of cell bodies of neurons within the central nervous system is a nucleus.
Gene	A gene is an ultramicroscopic area of the chromosome. It is the smallest physical unit of the DNA molecule that carries a piece of hereditary information.
Human genome	The complete sequence or mapping of genes in the human body and their locations is the human genome. It is made up of 23 chromosome pairs with a total of about 3 billion DNA base pairs.
Meiosis	The process of cell doubling and separation of chromosomes in which each pair of chromosomes in a cell separates, with one member of each pair going into each gamete is called meiosis.
Temperament	Temperament refers to a basic, innate disposition to change behavior. The activity level is an important dimension of temperament.
Autosome	An autosome is a non-sex chromosome. It is an ordinary paired chromosome that is the same in both sexes of a species.

Sex chromosomes	The sex chromosomes are the 23rd pair of chromosomes. They determine whether the child will be male or female. A pair with two X-shaped chromosomes produces a female. A pair with an X chromosome and a Y chromosome produces a male.
Gametes	Gametes are the specialized cells that come together during fertilization (conception) in organisms that reproduce sexually. In those species that produce two morphologically distinct types of gametes, and in which a particular individual produces only one type, "females" of the species produce the larger gamete called an ovum (or egg) and "males" produce the smaller gamete termed (in animals) a spermatozoon (or sperm).
Brain	The brain controls and coordinates most movement, behavior and homeostatic body functions such as heartbeat, blood pressure, fluid balance and body temperature. Functions of the brain are responsible for cognition, emotion, memory, motor learning and other sorts of learning. The brain is primarily made up of two types of cells: glia and neurons.
X chromosome	The sex chromosomes are one of the 23 pairs of human chromosomes. Each person normally has one pair of sex chromosomes in each cell. Females have two X chromosomes, while males have one X and one Y chromosome. The X chromosome carries hundreds of genes but few, if any, of these have anything to do directly with sex determination.
Y chromosome	The Y chromosome is one of the two sex chromosomes in humans and most other mammals. The sex chromosomes are one of the 23 pairs of human chromosomes. The Y chromosome contains the fewest genes of any of the chromosomes. It contains the genes that cause testis development, thus determining maleness. It is usually contributed by the father.
Testosterone	Testosterone is a steroid hormone from the androgen group. It is the principal male sex hormone and the "original" anabolic steroid.
Hormone	A hormone is a chemical messenger from one cell (or group of cells) to another. The best known are those produced by endocrine glands, but they are produced by nearly every organ system. The function of hormones is to serve as a signal to the target cells; the action of the hormone is determined by the pattern of secretion and the signal transduction of the receiving tissue.
Mendel	Mendel is often called the "father of genetics" for his study of the inheritance of traits in pea plants. Mendel showed that there was particulate inheritance of traits according to his laws of inheritance.
Trait	An enduring personality characteristic that tends to lead to certain behaviors is called a trait. The term trait also means a genetically inherited feature of an organism.
Dominant inheritance	Pattern of inheritance when a child receives contradictory alleles, only the dominant one is expressed, is called dominant inheritance.
Allele	An allele is any one of a number of alternative forms of the same gene (sometimes the term refers to a non-gene sequence) occupying a given locus (position) on a chromosome.
Affect	A subjective feeling or emotional tone often accompanied by bodily expressions noticeable to others is called affect.
Homozygous	When an organism is referred to as being homozygous for a specific gene, it means that it carries two identical copies of that gene for a given trait on the two corresponding chromosomes (e.g., the genotype is AA or aa). Such a cell or an organism is called a homozygote.
Dominant allele	The dominant allele, of two alleles for the same trait, is the one that is expressed in a heterozygote. Many traits are determined by pairs of complementary genes, each inherited from a single parent. Often when these are paired and compared, one gene will be found to effectively shut out the instructions from the other gene.

Heterozygous	Heterozygous refers to the condition in which a pair of genes occupying the same locus on a pair of chromosomes are different from one another.
Recessive allele	Recessive allele refers to an unexpressed allele in a heterozygote, but is phenotypically expressed when homozygous (an organism that has two copies of the same allele).. Thus, both parents have to be carriers of a recessive trait in order for a child to express that trait.
Phenotype	The phenotype of an individual organism is either its total physical appearance and constitution, or a specific manifestation of a trait, such as size or eye color, that varies between individuals. Phenotype is determined to some extent by genotype, or by the identity of the alleles that an individual carries at one or more positions on the chromosomes.
Genotype	The genotype is the specific genetic makeup of an individual, usually in the form of DNA. It codes for the phenotype of that individual. Any given gene will usually cause an observable change in an organism, known as the phenotype.
Effect size	An effect size is the strength or magnitude of the difference between two sets of data or, in outcome studies, between two time points for the same population. (The degree to which the null hypothesis is false).
Personality trait	According to the Diagnostic and Statistical Manual of the American Psychiatric Association, a personality trait is a "prominent aspect of personality that is exhibited in a wide range of important social and personal contexts. ...".
Adolescence	The period of life bounded by puberty and the assumption of adult responsibilities is adolescence.
Mental retardation	Mental retardation refers to having significantly below-average intellectual functioning and limitations in at least two areas of adaptive functioning. Many categorize retardation as mild, moderate, severe, or profound.
Arthritis	Arthritis is a group of conditions that affect the health of the bone joints in the body. Arthritis can be caused from strains and injuries caused by repetitive motion, sports, overexertion, and falls. Unlike the autoimmune diseases, it largely affects older people and results from the degeneration of joint cartilage.
Hypertension	Hypertension is a medical condition where the blood pressure in the arteries is chronically elevated. Persistent hypertension is one of the risk factors for strokes, heart attacks, heart failure and arterial aneurysm, and is a leading cause of chronic renal failure.
Chronic	Chronic refers to a relatively long duration, usually more than a few months.
Stroke	A stroke occurs when the blood supply to a part of the brain is suddenly interrupted by occlusion, by hemorrhage, or other causes
Nerve	A nerve is an enclosed, cable-like bundle of nerve fibers or axons, which includes the glia that ensheath the axons in myelin. Neurons are sometimes called nerve cells, though this term is technically imprecise since many neurons do not form nerves.
Physical therapy	Physical therapy is a health profession concerned with the assessment, diagnosis, and treatment of disease and disability through physical means. It is based upon principles of medical science, and is generally held to be within the sphere of conventional medicine.
Enzyme	An enzyme is a protein that catalyzes, or speeds up, a chemical reaction. Enzymes are essential to sustain life because most chemical reactions in biological cells would occur too slowly, or would lead to different products, without enzymes.
Mutation	Mutation is a permanent, sometimes transmissible (if the change is to a germ cell) change to the genetic material (usually DNA or RNA) of a cell. They can be caused by copying errors in the genetic material during cell division and by exposure to radiation, chemicals, or

viruses, or can occur deliberately under cellular control during the processes such as meiosis or hypermutation.

Species Species refers to a reproductively isolated breeding population.

Predisposition Predisposition refers to an inclination or diathesis to respond in a certain way, either inborn or acquired. In abnormal psychology, it is a factor that lowers the ability to withstand stress and inclines the individual toward pathology.

Hyperactivity Hyperactivity can be described as a state in which a individual is abnormally easily excitable and exuberant. Strong emotional reactions and a very short span of attention is also typical for the individual.

Spina bifida Spina bifida are birth defects caused by an incomplete closure of one or more vertebral arches of the spine, resulting in malformations of the spinal cord. Spina bifida results in varying degrees of paralysis, absence of skin sensation, incontinence, and spine and limb problems depending on the severity and location of the lesion damage on the spine.

Cleft palate Cleft palate is a condition in which the two plates of the skull that form the hard palate (roof of the mouth) are not completely joined. The soft palate is in these cases cleft as well. In most cases, cleft lip is also present.

Attention Attention is the cognitive process of selectively concentrating on one thing while ignoring other things. Psychologists have labeled three types of attention: sustained attention, selective attention, and divided attention.

Central nervous system The vertebrate central nervous system consists of the brain and spinal cord.

Sickle-cell anemia Sickle-cell anemia is a genetic disorder in which red blood cells may change shape under certain circumstances. This causes the cells to become stuck in capillaries which deprives the downstream tissues of oxygen . The disease usually occurs in periodic painful attacks, eventually leading to damage of internal organs, stroke, or anemia, and usually resulting in decreased lifespan.

Tay-Sachs disease Tay-Sachs disease is a fatal genetic disorder, inherited in an autosomal recessive pattern, in which harmful quantities of a fatty substance called ganglioside GM2 accumulate in the nerve cells in the brain.

Cystic fibrosis Cystic fibrosis is an autosomal recessive hereditary disease of the exocrine glands. It affects the lungs, sweat glands and the digestive system. It causes chronic respiratory and digestive problems.

Nervous system The body's electrochemical communication circuitry, made up of billions of neurons is a nervous system.

Glaucoma Glaucoma is a group of diseases of the optic nerve involving loss of retinal ganglion cells. Untreated glaucoma leads to permanent damage of the optic nerve and resultant visual field loss, which can progress to blindness.

Lungs The lungs are the essential organs of respiration. Its principal function is to transport oxygen from the atmosphere into the bloodstream, and excrete carbon dioxide from the bloodstream into the atmosphere.

Recessive gene Recessive gene refers to an allele that causes a phenotype (visible or detectable characteristic) that is only seen in a homozygous genotype (an organism that has two copies of the same allele). Thus, both parents have to be carriers of a recessive trait in order for a child to express that trait.

Color blindness Color blindness in humans is the inability to perceive differences between some or all colors

	that other people can distinguish. It is most often of genetic nature, but may also occur because of eye, nerve, or brain damage, or due to exposure to certain chemicals.
Hemophilia	Hemophilia is the name of any of several hereditary genetic illnesses that impair the body's ability to control bleeding. Genetic deficiencies cause lowered plasma clotting factor activity so as to compromise blood-clotting; when a blood vessel is injured, a scab will not form and the vessel can continue to bleed excessively for a very long period of time.
Dominant gene	In genetics, the term dominant gene refers to the allele that causes a phenotype that is seen in a heterozygous genotype.
Imprinting	Imprinting describes any kind of critical period sensitive learning (learning occurring at a particular age or a particular life stage) that is rapid and apparently independent of the consequences of behavior.
Diabetes	Diabetes is a medical disorder characterized by varying or persistent elevated blood sugar levels, especially after eating. All types of diabetes share similar symptoms and complications at advanced stages: dehydration and ketoacidosis, cardiovascular disease, chronic renal failure, retinal damage which can lead to blindness, nerve damage which can lead to erectile dysfunction, gangrene with risk of amputation of toes, feet, and even legs.
Asthma	Asthma is a complex disease characterized by bronchial hyperresponsiveness (BHR), inflammation, mucus production and intermittent airway obstruction.
Cognitive skills	Cognitive skills such as reasoning, attention, and memory can be advanced and sustained through practice and training.
Down syndrome	Down syndrome encompasses a number of genetic disorders, of which trisomy 21 (a nondisjunction, the so-called extrachromosone) is the most representative, causing highly variable degrees of learning difficulties as well as physical disabilities. Incidence of Down syndrome is estimated at 1 per 660 births, making it the most common chromosomal abnormality.
Learning disorder	A disorder characterized by a discrepancy between one's academic achievement and one's intellectual ability is referred to as a learning disorder.
Secondary sex characteristics	Secondary sex characteristics are traits that distinguish the two sexes of a species, but that are not directly part of the reproductive system.
Infertility	Infertility is the inability to naturally conceive a child or the inability to carry a pregnancy to term.
Prognosis	A forecast about the probable course of an illess is referred to as prognosis.
Genetic counseling	Genetic counseling generally refers to prenatal counseling done when a genetic condition is suspected in a pregnancy. Genetic counseling is the process by which patients or relatives at risk of an inherited disorder are advised of the consequences and nature of the disorder, the probability of developing or transmitting it, and the options open to them in management and family planning in order to prevent, avoid or ameliorate it.
Counselor	A counselor is a mental health professional who specializes in helping people with problems not involving serious mental disorders.
Karyotype	A karyotype is the complete set of all chromosomes of a cell of any living organism. The chromosomes are arranged and displayed in a standard format: in pairs, ordered by size. Karyotypes are examined in searches for chromosomal aberrations, and may be used to determine other macroscopically visible aspects of an individual's genotype.
Quantitative	A quantitative property is one that exists in a range of magnitudes, and can therefore be measured. Measurements of any particular quantitative property are expressed as as a specific quantity, referred to as a unit, multiplied by a number.

Individual differences	Individual differences psychology studies the ways in which individual people differ in their behavior. This is distinguished from other aspects of psychology in that although psychology is ostensibly a study of individuals, modern psychologists invariably study groups.
Heritability	Heritability It is that proportion of the observed variation in a particular phenotype within a particular population, that can be attributed to the contribution of genotype. In other words: it measures the extent to which differences between individuals in a population are due their being different genetically.
Population	Population refers to all members of a well-defined group of organisms, events, or things.
Genetic disorder	A genetic disorder is a disease caused by abnormal expression of one or more genes in a person causing a clinical phenotype.
Phenylketonuria	Phenylketonuria is a genetic disorder in which an individual cannot properly metabolize amino acids. The disorder is now easily detected but, if left untreated, results in mental retardation and hyperactivity.
Genetics	Genetics is the science of genes, heredity, and the variation of organisms.
Informed consent	The term used by psychologists to indicate that a person has agreed to participate in research after receiving information about the purposes of the study and the nature of the treatments is informed consent. Even with informed consent, subjects may withdraw from any experiment at any time.
Genetic testing	Genetic testing allows the genetic diagnosis of vulnerabilities to inherited diseases, and can also be used to determine a person's ancestry. Every person carries two copies of every gene, one inherited from their mother, one inherited from their father.
Liver	The liver plays a major role in metabolism and has a number of functions in the body including detoxification, glycogen storage and plasma protein synthesis. It also produces bile, which is important for digestion. The liver converts most carbohydrates, proteing, and fats into glucose.
Genetic determinism	Genetic determinism is the idea that genes determine a physical or behavioral phenotype. The term may be applied to the mapping of a single gene to a single phenotype or to the idea that all phenotypes are determined by genes.
Discrimination	In Learning theory, discrimination refers the ability to distinguish between a conditioned stimulus and other stimuli. It can be brought about by extensive training or differential reinforcement. In social terms, it is the denial of privileges to a person or a group on the basis of prejudice.
False negative	A false negative, also called a Type II error or miss, exists when a test incorrectly reports that a result was not detected, when it was really present.
False positive	A false positive, also called a Type I error, exists when a test incorrectly reports that it has found a result where none really exists.
Anxiety	Anxiety is a complex combination of the feeling of fear, apprehension and worry often accompanied by physical sensations such as palpitations, chest pain and/or shortness of breath.
Fetus	A fetus develops from the end of the 8th week of pregnancy (when the major structures have formed), until birth.
Society	The social sciences use the term society to mean a group of people that form a semi-closed (or semi-open) social system, in which most interactions are with other individuals belonging to the group.
Correlation	A statistical technique for determining the degree of association between two or more

	variables is referred to as correlation.
Adoption studies	Research studies that assess hereditary influence by examining the resemblance between adopted children and both their biological and their adoptive parents are referred to as adoption studies. The studies have been inconclusive about the relative importance of heredity in intelligence.
Obesity	The state of being more than 20 percent above the average weight for a person of one's height is called obesity.
Concordance	Concordance as used in genetics means the presence of the same trait in both members of a pair of twins, or in sets of individuals. A twin study examines the concordance rates of twins having the same trait, especially a disease, which can help determine how much the disease is affected by genetics versus environment.
Infancy	The developmental period that extends from birth to 18 or 24 months is called infancy.
Behavioral genetics	Behavioral genetics is the field of biology that studies the role of genetics in behavior.
Control group	A group that does not receive the treatment effect in an experiment is referred to as the control group or sometimes as the comparison group.
Chorion	The amniotic sac is a tough but thin transparent pair of membranes, which hold a developing embryo (and later fetus) until shortly before birth. The inner membrane, the amnion, contains the amniotic fluid and the fetus. The outer membrane, the chorion, contains the amnion and is part of the placenta.
Family studies	Scientific studies in which researchers assess hereditary influence by examining blood relatives to see how much they resemble each other on a specific trait are called family studies.
Cholesterol	Cholesterol is a steroid, a lipid, and an alcohol, found in the cell membranes of all body tissues, and transported in the blood plasma of all animals. Cholesterol is an important component of the membranes of cells, providing stability; it makes the membrane's fluidity stable over a bigger temperature interval.
Neuroscience	A field that combines the work of psychologists, biologists, biochemists, medical researchers, and others in the study of the structure and function of the nervous system is neuroscience.
Canalization	Canalization refers to the process by which characteristics take a narrow path over a developmental course.
Metaphor	A metaphor is a rhetorical trope where a comparison is made between two seemingly unrelated subjects
Genotype-environment	Genotype-environment correlation refers to tendency of certain genetic and environmental influences to reinforce each other; may be passive, reactive, or active.
Variance	The degree to which scores differ among individuals in a distribution of scores is the variance.
Maturation	The orderly unfolding of traits, as regulated by the genetic code is called maturation.
Cognition	The intellectual processes through which information is obtained, transformed, stored, retrieved, and otherwise used is cognition.
Nonshared environment	A home environment that is unique to an individual, not shared by a sibling, for instance is a called a nonshared environment.
Early childhood	Early childhood refers to the developmental period extending from the end of infancy to about

	5 or 6 years of age; sometimes called the preschool years.
Niche-picking	Tendency of a person, especially after early childhood, to seek out environments compatible with his or her phenotype is referred to as niche-picking.
Nature-nurture	Nature-nurture is a shorthand expression for debates about the relative importance of an individual's "nature" versus personal experiences ("nurture") in determining or causing physical and behavioral traits.
Life span	Life span refers to the upper boundary of life, the maximum number of years an individual can live. The maximum life span of human beings is about 120 years of age. Females live an average of 6 years longer than males.
Epilepsy	Epilepsy is a chronic neurological condition characterized by recurrent unprovoked neural discharges. It is commonly controlled with medication, although surgical methods are used as well.
Genetic mapping	Genetic mapping refers to the process of determining the location and chemical sequence of specific genes on specific chromosomes.
Genetic marker	A genetic marker is an inherited characteristic for which the chromosomal location of the responsible gene is known.
Innate	Innate behavior is not learned or influenced by the environment, rather, it is present or predisposed at birth.
Openness to Experience	Openness to Experience, one of the big-five traits, describes a dimension of cognitive style that distinguishes imaginative, creative people from down-to-earth, conventional people.
Conscientiou-ness	Conscientiousness is one of the dimensions of the five-factor model of personality and individual differences involving being organized, thorough, and reliable as opposed to careless, negligent, and unreliable.
Agreeableness	Agreeableness, one of the big-five personality traits, reflects individual differences in concern with cooperation and social harmony. It is the degree individuals value getting along with others.
Extraversion	Extraversion, one of the big-five personailty traits, is marked by pronounced engagement with the external world. They are people who enjoy being with people, are full of energy, and often experience positive emotions.
Neuroticism	Eysenck's use of the term neuroticism (or Emotional Stability) was proposed as the dimension describing individual differences in the predisposition towards neurotic disorder.
Depression	In everyday language depression refers to any downturn in mood, which may be relatively transitory and perhaps due to something trivial. This is differentiated from Clinical depression which is marked by symptoms that last two weeks or more and are so severe that they interfere with daily living.
Shyness	A tendency to avoid others plus uneasiness and strain when socializing is called shyness.
Psychopathology	Psychopathology refers to the field concerned with the nature and development of mental disorders.
Schizophrenia	Schizophrenia is characterized by persistent defects in the perception or expression of reality. A person suffering from untreated schizophrenia typically demonstrates grossly disorganized thinking, and may also experience delusions or auditory hallucinations
Alcoholism	A disorder that involves long-term, repeated, uncontrolled, compulsive, and excessive use of alcoholic beverages and that impairs the drinker's health and work and social relationships is called alcoholism.

Autism	Autism is a neurodevelopmental disorder that manifests itself in markedly abnormal social interaction, communication ability, patterns of interests, and patterns of behavior.
Brain imaging	Brain imaging is a fairly recent discipline within medicine and neuroscience. Brain imaging falls into two broad categories -- structural imaging and functional imaging.
Pervasive developmental disorder	The diagnostic category pervasive developmental disorder refers to a group of disorders characterized by delays in the development of multiple basic functions including socialization and communication.
Autistic spectrum	The autistic spectrum is the idea that autism is a developmental and behavioral syndrome that results from certain combinations of traits. At the severe end of the spectrum is low-functioning autism, which can cause severe-profound impairments in many areas, to a milder form of autism known as Asperger's syndrome and finally a shading into typicality and perhaps then hypersocialization.
Behavior therapy	Behavior therapy refers to the systematic application of the principles of learning to direct modification of a client's problem behaviors.
Social skills	Social skills are skills used to interact and communicate with others to assist status in the social structure and other motivations.
Syndrome	The term syndrome is the association of several clinically recognizable features, signs, symptoms, phenomena or characteristics which often occur together, so that the presence of one feature indicates the presence of the others.
Stages	Stages represent relatively discrete periods of time in which functioning is qualitatively different from functioning at other periods.
Cephalocaudal	The sequence in which the greatest growth occurs at the top, the head, with physical growth in size, weight, and feature differentiation gradually working from top to bottom is referred to as a cephalocaudal pattern.
Proximodistal	Development originating from the center of the body towards the extremities is referred to as proximodistal development. The human embroyo normally develops in this fashion and averages 5-10 pounds in brith-weight and between 18 to 22 inches in length.
Germinal stage	The germinal stage refers to the period of prenatal development that takes place in the first 2 weeks after conception. It includes the creation of the zygote, continued cell division, and the attachment of the zygote to the uterine wall.
Mitosis	Mitosis is the process by which a cell separates its duplicated genome into two identical halves.
Blastocyst	The Blastocyst si an inner layer of cells that develops during the germinal period. These cells later develop into the embryo.
Cell differentiation	Cell differentiation is a concept from developmental biology describing the process by which cells acquire a "type". The morphology of a cell may change dramatically during differentiation, but the genetic material remains the same, with few exceptions.
Fisher	Fisher was a eugenicist, evolutionary biologist, geneticist and statistician. He has been described as "The greatest of Darwin's successors", and a genius who almost single-handedly created the foundations for modern statistical science inventing the techniques of maximum likelihood and analysis of variance.
Umbilical cord	The umbilical cord is a tube that connects a developing embryo or fetus to its placenta. It contains major arteries and veins for the exchange of nutrient- and oxygen-rich blood between the embryo and placenta.
Tactile	Pertaining to the sense of touch is referred to as tactile.

Amniotic fluid	Amniotic fluid refers to fluid within the amniotic sac that suspends and protects the fetus.
Reflex	A simple, involuntary response to a stimulus is referred to as reflex. Reflex actions originate at the spinal cord rather than the brain.
Lanugo	Lanugo are hairs that grow on the body to attempt to insulate it because of lack of fat. It is normal in gestating fetuses. Lanugo hair is usually shed and replaced by vellus hair at 36-40 weeks gestation. The presence of lanugo in newborns is a sign of premature birth.
Embryonic disk	The plate-like inner part of the blastocyst that differentiates into the ectoderm, mesoderm, and endoderm of the embryo is called the embryonic disk.
Spinal cord	The spinal cord is a part of the vertebrate nervous system that is enclosed in and protected by the vertebral column (it passes through the spinal canal). It consists of nerve cells. The spinal cord carries sensory signals and motor innervation to most of the skeletal muscles in the body.
Ectoderm	Ectoderm refers to the outermost cell layer of the newly formed embryo, from which the skin and nervous systems develop.
Pancreas	The pancreas is a retroperitoneal organ that serves two functions: it produces juice containing digestive enzymes; and it produces several important hormones including insulin, glucagon, and several other hormones.
Endoderm	The endoderm is one of the three germ layers of the developing embryo, the other two being the ectoderm and the mesoderm. The endoderm gives rise to various tissues including the gastrointestinal tract, respiratory tract, and endocrine glands.
Mesoderm	The mesoderm is one of the three germ layers in the early developing embryo. The mesoderm gives rise to tissues including connective tissue, muscles and the circulatory system.
Placenta	A membrane that permits the exchange of nutrients and waste products between the mother and her developing child but does not allow the maternal and fetal bloodstreams to mix is the placenta.
Amniotic sac	The amniotic sac is a tough but thin transparent pair of membranes, which hold a developing embryo (and later fetus) until shortly before birth. The inner membrane, the amnion, contains the amniotic fluid and the fetus.
Trophoblast	The trophoblast is the outer layer of cells that develops in the germinal period. These cells provide nutrition and support for the embryo.
Embryonic stage	The embryonic stage lasts from the third through the eighth week following conception. During this stage the major organ systems undergo rapid differentiation.
Spontaneous abortion	Spontaneous abortion is the natural or accidental termination of a pregnancy at a stage where the embryo or the fetus is incapable of surviving, generally defined at a gestation less than 20 weeks.
Critical period	A period of time when an innate response can be elicited by a particular stimulus is referred to as the critical period.
Fetal stage	The fetal stage occurs from the third month following conception through childbirth, during which time there is maturation of organ systems and dramatic gains in length and weight.
Ultrasound	Ultrasound is sound with a frequency greater than the upper limit of human hearing, approximately 20 kilohertz. Medical use can visualise muscle and soft tissue, making them useful for scanning the organs, and obstetric ultrasonography is commonly used during pregnancy.
Senses	The senses are systems that consist of a sensory cell type that respond to a specific kind of

	physical energy, and that correspond to a defined region within the brain where the signals are received and interpreted.
Olfactory system	The olfactory system is the sensory system used for the sense of smell. The olfactory system is often spoken of along with the gustatory system as the chemosensory senses because both transduce chemical signals into perception
Spence	Spence attributed improvement in performance to motivational factors rather than habit factors. His Discrimination Learning Theory argued that reinforcement combined with frustration or inhibitors facilitates finding a correct stimulus among a cluster which includes incorrect ones.
Teratogen	Teratogen refers to from the Greek word tera, meaning 'monster.' It is any agent that causes a birth defect.
Early adulthood	The developmental period beginning in the late teens or early twenties and lasting into the thirties is called early adulthood; characterized by an increasing self-awareness.
Cretinism	Cretinism is a condition of severely stunted physical and mental growth due to untreated congenital deficiency of thyroid hormones (hypothyroidism).
Thyroid	In anatomy, the thyroid is the largest endocrine gland in the body. The primary function of the thyroid is production of hormones.
Neural tube	The neural tube is the embryonal structure that gives rise to the brain and spinal cord.
Marijuana	Marijuana is the dried vegetable matter of the Cannabis sativa plant. It contains large concentrations of compounds that have medicinal and psychoactive effects when consumed, usually by smoking or eating.
Nicotine	Nicotine is an organic compound, an alkaloid found naturally throughout the tobacco plant, with a high concentration in the leaves. It is a potent nerve poison and is included in many insecticides. In lower concentrations, the substance is a stimulant and is one of the main factors leading to the pleasure and habit-forming qualities of tobacco smoking.
Cocaine	Cocaine is a crystalline tropane alkaloid that is obtained from the leaves of the coca plant. It is a stimulant of the central nervous system and an appetite suppressant, creating what has been described as a euphoric sense of happiness and increased energy.
Opiates	A group of narcotics derived from the opium poppy that provide a euphoric rush and depress the nervous system are referred to as opiates.
Rubella	An infectious disease that, if contracted by the mother during the first three months of pregnancy, has a high risk of causing mental retardation and physical deformity in the child is called rubella.
Barbiturate	A barbiturate is a drug that acts as a central nervous system (CNS) depressant, and by virtue of this produces a wide spectrum of effects, from mild sedation to anesthesia.
Teratogenic	Capacity for causing birth defects is referred to as teratogenic.
Depressant	A depressant is a chemical agent that diminishes a body function or activity. The term is used in particular with regard to the central nervous system where these chemicals are known as neurotransmitters. They tend to act on the CNS by increasing the activity of a particular neurotransmitter known as gamma-aminobutyric acid (GABA).
Androgen	Androgen is the generic term for any natural or synthetic compound, usually a steroid hormone, that stimulates or controls the development and maintenance of masculine characteristics in vertebrates by binding to androgen receptors.
Tranquilizer	A sedative, or tranquilizer, is a drug that depresses the central nervous system (CNS), which

	causes calmness, relaxation, reduction of anxiety, sleepiness, slowed breathing, slurred speech, staggering gait, poor judgment, and slow, uncertain reflexes.
Thalidomide	Thalidomide is a drug which was sold during the 1950s and 1960s as a sleeping aid and to pregnant women as an antiemetic to combat morning sickness and other symptoms. It was later (1960–61) found to be teratogenic in fetal development, most visibly as a cause of amelia or phocomelia.
Tumor	A tumor is an abnormal growth that when located in the brain can either be malignant and directly destroy brain tissue, or be benign and disrupt functioning by increasing intracranial pressure.
Withdrawal symptoms	Withdrawal symptoms are physiological changes that occur when the use of a drug is stopped or dosage decreased.
Antipsychotic	The term antipsychotic is applied to a group of drugs used to treat psychosis.
Fetal alcohol syndrome	A cluster of abnormalities that appears in the offspring of mothers who drink alcohol heavily during pregnancy is called fetal alcohol syndrome.
Information processing	Information processing is an approach to the goal of understanding human thinking. The essence of the approach is to see cognition as being essentially computational in nature, with mind being the software and the brain being the hardware.
Learning	Learning is a relatively permanent change in behavior that results from experience. Thus, to attribute a behavioral change to learning, the change must be relatively permanent and must result from experience.
Corpus callosum	The corpus callosum is the largest white matter structure in the brain. It consists of mostly of contralateral axon projections. The corpus callosum connects the left and right cerebral hemispheres. Most communication between regions in different halves of the brain are carried over the corpus callosum.
Longitudinal study	Longitudinal study is a type of developmental study in which the same group of participants is followed and measured for an extended period of time, often years.
Substance abuse	Substance abuse refers to the overindulgence in and dependence on a stimulant, depressant, or other chemical substance, leading to effects that are detrimental to the individual's physical or mental health, or the welfare of others.
Tremor	Tremor is the rhythmic, oscillating shaking movement of the whole body or just a certain part of it, caused by problems of the neurons responsible from muscle action.
Lewin	Lewin ranks as one of the pioneers of social psychology, as one of the founders of group dynamics and as one of the most eminent representatives of Gestalt psychology.
Morphine	Morphine, the principal active agent in opium, is a powerful opioid analgesic drug. According to recent research, it may also be produced naturally by the human brain. Morphine is usually highly addictive, and tolerance and physical and psychological dependence develop quickly.
Codeine	Codeine is an opioid used for its analgesic, antitussive and antidiarrheal properties
Heroin	Heroin is widely and illegally used as a powerful and addictive drug producing intense euphoria, which often disappears with increasing tolerance. Heroin is a semi-synthetic opioid. It is the 3,6-diacetyl derivative of morphine and is synthesised from it by acetylation.
Genital herpes	Genital herpes refers to a sexually transmitted disease caused by a large family of viruses of different strains. These strains also produce other, nonsexually transmitted diseases such as chicken pox and mononucleosis.

Gonorrhea	Gonorrhea is among the most common curable sexually transmitted diseases in the world. In men, epididymitis, prostatitis and urethral stricture can result from untreated gonorrhoea.In women, Bartholinitis and abscess formation, pelvic inflammatory disease and Fitz-Hugh-Curtis syndrome can occur.
Perinatal	Perinatal is the period occurring around the time of birth (5 months before and 1 month after).
Syphilis	Syphilis is a sexually transmitted disease that is caused by a spirochaete bacterium, Treponema pallidum. If not treated, syphilis can cause serious effects such as damage to the nervous system, heart, or brain. Untreated syphilis can be ultimately fatal.
Hull	Hull is best known for the Drive Reduction Theory which postulated that behavior occurs in response to primary drives such as hunger, thirst, sexual interest, etc. When the goal of the drive is attained the drive is reduced. This reduction of drive serves as a reinforcer for learning.
Measles	Measles, also known as rubeola, is a common disease caused by a virus of the genus Morbillivirus. Complications with measles are relatively common, ranging from relatively common and less serious diarrhea, to pneumonia and encephalitis. Complications are usually more severe amongst infants and adults who catch the virus.
Seizure	A seizure is a temporary alteration in brain function expressed as a changed mental state, tonic or clonic movements and various other symptoms. They are due to temporary abnormal electrical activity of a group of brain cells.
Preterm	Born at or prior to completion of 37 weeks of gestation is referred to as preterm.
IQ test	An IQ test is a standardized test developed to measure a person's cognitive abilities ("intelligence") in relation to their age group.
Amniocentesis	Amniocentesis is a medical procedure used for prenatal diagnosis, in which from the amnion around a developing fetus a small amount of amniotic fluid is extracted. It is usually offered when there may be an increased risk for genetic conditions in the pregnancy.
Projection	Attributing one's own undesirable thoughts, impulses, traits, or behaviors to others is referred to as projection.
Polygenic inheritance	Polygenic inheritance refers to pattern of inheritance in which multiple genes affect a complex trait.
Nonshared environmental	Nonshared environmental experiences refer to the child's own unique experiences, both within the family and outside the family, that are not shared by another sibling. Thus, experiences occurring within the family can be also be a part.
Chorionic villus sampling	Chorionic villus sampling is a form of prenatal diagnosis to determine genetic abnormalities in the fetus. It entails getting a sample of the placental tissue and testing it.
Doula	A doula is a non-medical assistant in prenatal care, childbirth and during the postpartum period.

Uterus	The uterus or womb is the major female reproductive organ. The main function of the uterus is to accept a fertilized ovum which becomes implanted into the endometrium, and derives nourishment from blood vessels which develop exclusively for this purpose.
Fetus	A fetus develops from the end of the 8th week of pregnancy (when the major structures have formed), until birth.
Progesterone	A female sex hormone that promotes growth of the sex organs and helps maintain pregnancy is called progesterone.
Parturition	Process of uterine, cervical, and other changes, usually lasting about two weeks, preceding childbirth are referred to as parturition.
Estrogen	Estrogen is a group of steroid compounds that function as the primary female sex hormone. They are produced primarily by developing follicles in the ovaries, the corpus luteum and the placenta.
Stages	Stages represent relatively discrete periods of time in which functioning is qualitatively different from functioning at other periods.
Cervix	The cervix is the lower end of the uterus that joins with the top portion of the vaginia.
Maturation	The orderly unfolding of traits, as regulated by the genetic code is called maturation.
Placenta	A membrane that permits the exchange of nutrients and waste products between the mother and her developing child but does not allow the maternal and fetal bloodstreams to mix is the placenta.
Hormone	A hormone is a chemical messenger from one cell (or group of cells) to another. The best known are those produced by endocrine glands, but they are produced by nearly every organ system. The function of hormones is to serve as a signal to the target cells; the action of the hormone is determined by the pattern of secretion and the signal transduction of the receiving tissue.
Protein	A protein is a complex, high-molecular-weight organic compound that consists of amino acids joined by peptide bonds. It is essential to the structure and function of all living cells and viruses. Many are enzymes or subunits of enzymes.
Lungs	The lungs are the essential organs of respiration. Its principal function is to transport oxygen from the atmosphere into the bloodstream, and excrete carbon dioxide from the bloodstream into the atmosphere.
Umbilical cord	The umbilical cord is a tube that connects a developing embryo or fetus to its placenta. It contains major arteries and veins for the exchange of nutrient- and oxygen-rich blood between the embryo and placenta.
Brain	The brain controls and coordinates most movement, behavior and homeostatic body functions such as heartbeat, blood pressure, fluid balance and body temperature. Functions of the brain are responsible for cognition, emotion, memory, motor learning and other sorts of learning. The brain is primarily made up of two types of cells: glia and neurons.
False positive	A false positive, also called a Type I error, exists when a test incorrectly reports that it has found a result where none really exists.
Midwife	A Midwife is a blanket term used to describe a number of different types of health practitioners, other than physicians, who provide prenatal care to expecting mothers, attend the birth of the infant and provide postnatal care to the mother and infant.
Breech position	The baby's position in the uterus that causes the buttocks to be the first part to emerge from the vagina is a breech position.

Prepared childbirth	Developed by French obstetrician Ferdinand Lamaze, this childbirth strategy is similar to natural childbirth but includes a special breathing technique to control pushing in the final stages of labor is called prepared childbirth.
Social support	Social Support is the physical and emotional comfort given by family, friends, co-workers and others. Research has identified three main types of social support: emotional, practical, sharing points of view.
Anesthesia	Anesthesia is the process of blocking the perception of pain and other sensations. This allows patients to undergo surgery and other procedures without the distress and pain they would otherwise experience.
General anesthesia	General anesthesia refers to the process of eliminating pain by putting the person to sleep.
Sensation	Sensation is the first stage in the chain of biochemical and neurologic events that begins with the impinging of a stimulus upon the receptor cells of a sensory organ, which then leads to perception, the mental state that is reflected in statements like "I see a uniformly blue wall."
Nerve	A nerve is an enclosed, cable-like bundle of nerve fibers or axons, which includes the glia that ensheath the axons in myelin. Neurons are sometimes called nerve cells, though this term is technically imprecise since many neurons do not form nerves.
Natural childbirth	The natural childbirth technique attempts to minimize medical intervention, particularly anaesthetics, during childbirth.
Physiology	The study of the functions and activities of living cells, tissues, and organs and of the physical and chemical phenomena involved is referred to as physiology.
Lamaze	Modern Lamaze childbirth classes teach expectant mothers breathing techniques and often other ways to work with the labor process to reduce the pain often associated with childbirth.
Narcotic	The term narcotic originally referred to a variety of substances that induced sleep (such state is narcosis). In legal context, narcotic refers to opium, opium derivatives, and their semisynthetic or totally synthetic substitutes.
Neonatal period	The first 4 weeks of life, a time of transition from intrauterine dependency to independent existence is called the neonatal period.
Distinctive features	The characteristics of an object that differentiate it from other objects are distinctive features.
Prenatal	Prenatal period refers to the time from conception to birth.
Lanugo	Lanugo are hairs that grow on the body to attempt to insulate it because of lack of fat. It is normal in gestating fetuses. Lanugo hair is usually shed and replaced by vellus hair at 36-40 weeks gestation. The presence of lanugo in newborns is a sign of premature birth.
Anoxia	Asphyxia is a condition of severely deficient supply of oxygen to the body. In the absence of remedial action it will very rapidly lead to unconsciousness and death. Anoxia means the pathological state in which tissues do not get (enough of) oxygen. Problems during childbirth can lead to the newborn experiencing asphyxia.
Meconium	Meconium is the first stool of an infant, composed of materials ingested during the time the infant spends in the uterus: intestinal epithelial cells, lanugo, mucus, amniotic fluid, bile, and water. Meconium can be tested for drugs the baby was exposed to in utero.
Neonatal jaundice	Neonatal jaundice occurs in many newborn babies. It is caused by immaturity of the liver and is evidenced by yellowish appearance. Though usually harmless it can cause brain damage if not treated promptly.

Liver
The liver plays a major role in metabolism and has a number of functions in the body including detoxification, glycogen storage and plasma protein synthesis. It also produces bile, which is important for digestion. The liver converts most carbohydrates, proteing, and fats into glucose.

Metabolism
Metabolism is the biochemical modification of chemical compounds in living organisms and cells.

Gland
A gland is an organ in an animal's body that synthesizes a substance for release such as hormones, often into the bloodstream or into cavities inside the body or its outer surface.

Rapid Eye Movement
Rapid eye movement is the stage of sleep during which the most vivid (though not all) dreams occur. During this stage, the eyes move rapidly, and the activity of the brain's neurons is quite similar to that during waking hours. It is the lightest form of sleep in that people awakened during REM usually feel alert and refreshed.

Consciousness
The awareness of the sensations, thoughts, and feelings being experienced at a given moment is called consciousness.

Toddler
A toddler is a child between the ages of one and three years old. During this period, the child learns a great deal about social roles and develops motor skills; to toddle is to walk unsteadily.

Attitude
An enduring mental representation of a person, place, or thing that evokes an emotional response and related behavior is called attitude.

Behavioral assessment
Direct measures of an individual's behavior used to describe characteristics indicative of personality are called behavioral assessment.

Apgar score
The Apgar score was devised in 1952 by Virginia Apgar as a simple and repeatable method to quickly and summarily assess the health of newborn children immediately after childbirth.

Brazelton
Brazelton Neonatal Behavioral Assessment Scale is a test given several days after birth to assess newborns' neurological development, reflexes, and reactions to people.

Affect
A subjective feeling or emotional tone often accompanied by bodily expressions noticeable to others is called affect.

Birth trauma
Birth trauma refers to injury or disturbing experiences sustained at the time of birth.

Deprivation
Deprivation, is the loss or withholding of normal stimulation, nutrition, comfort, love, and so forth; a condition of lacking. The level of stimulation is less than what is required.

Mental retardation
Mental retardation refers to having significantly below-average intellectual functioning and limitations in at least two areas of adaptive functioning. Many categorize retardation as mild, moderate, severe, or profound.

Preterm
Born at or prior to completion of 37 weeks of gestation is referred to as preterm.

Ultrasound
Ultrasound is sound with a frequency greater than the upper limit of human hearing, approximately 20 kilohertz. Medical use can visualise muscle and soft tissue, making them useful for scanning the organs, and obstetric ultrasonography is commonly used during pregnancy.

Amniotic fluid
Amniotic fluid refers to fluid within the amniotic sac that suspends and protects the fetus.

Infancy
The developmental period that extends from birth to 18 or 24 months is called infancy.

Socioeconomic
Socioeconomic pertains to the study of the social and economic impacts of any product or service offering, market intervention or other activity on an economy as a whole and on the companies, organization and individuals who are its main economic actors.

Hypertension | Hypertension is a medical condition where the blood pressure in the arteries is chronically elevated. Persistent hypertension is one of the risk factors for strokes, heart attacks, heart failure and arterial aneurysm, and is a leading cause of chronic renal failure.

Chronic | Chronic refers to a relatively long duration, usually more than a few months.

Respiratory distress syndrome | Infant respiratory distress syndrome is a syndrome caused by developmental lack of surfactant and structural immaturity in the lungs of premature infants. The syndrome is more frequent in infants of diabetic mothers and in the second born of premature twins.

Sudden infant death syndrome | Sudden Infant Death Syndrome is the term for the sudden and unexplained death of an apparently healthy infant aged one month to one year.

Immune system | The most important function of the human immune system occurs at the cellular level of the blood and tissues. The lymphatic and blood circulation systems are highways for specialized white blood cells. These cells include B cells, T cells, natural killer cells, and macrophages. All function with the primary objective of recognizing, attacking and destroying bacteria, viruses, cancer cells, and all substances seen as foreign.

Nervous system | The body's electrochemical communication circuitry, made up of billions of neurons is a nervous system.

Preterm infant | An infant born before completing the thirty-seventh week of gestation is a preterm infant.

Cerebral palsy | Cerebral palsy is a group of permanent disorders associated with developmental brain injuries that occur during fetal development, birth, or shortly after birth. It is characterized by a disruption of motor skills, with symptoms such as spasticity, paralysis, or seizures.

Longitudinal study | Longitudinal study is a type of developmental study in which the same group of participants is followed and measured for an extended period of time, often years.

Sullivan | Sullivan developed the Self System, a configuration of the personality traits developed in childhood and reinforced by positive affirmation and the security operations developed in childhood to avoid anxiety and threats to self-esteem.

Control group | A group that does not receive the treatment effect in an experiment is referred to as the control group or sometimes as the comparison group.

Achievement test | A test designed to determine a person's level of knowledge in a given subject area is referred to as an achievement test.

Early childhood | Early childhood refers to the developmental period extending from the end of infancy to about 5 or 6 years of age; sometimes called the preschool years.

Attention | Attention is the cognitive process of selectively concentrating on one thing while ignoring other things. Psychologists have labeled three types of attention: sustained attention, selective attention, and divided attention.

Learning | Learning is a relatively permanent change in behavior that results from experience. Thus, to attribute a behavioral change to learning, the change must be relatively permanent and must result from experience.

Child development | Scientific study of the processes of change from conception through adolescence is called child development.

Population | Population refers to all members of a well-defined group of organisms, events, or things.

Infant mortality | Infant mortality is the death of infants in the first year of life. The leading causes of infant mortality are dehydration and disease. Major causes of infant mortality in more developed countries include congenital malformation, infection and SIDS. Infant mortality rate is the number of newborns dying under a year of age divided by the number of live births

during the year.

UNICEF UNICEF, the United Nations International Children's Emergency Fund, was established by the United Nations General Assembly on December 11, 1946. UNICEF provides long-term humanitarian and developmental assistance to children and mothers in developing countries.

Critical period A period of time when an innate response can be elicited by a particular stimulus is referred to as the critical period.

Brain stem The brain stem is the stalk of the brain below the cerebral hemispheres. It is the major route for communication between the forebrain and the spinal cord and peripheral nerves. It also controls various functions including respiration, regulation of heart rhythms, and primary aspects of sound localization.

Receptor A sensory receptor is a structure that recognizes a stimulus in the internal or external environment of an organism. In response to stimuli the sensory receptor initiates sensory transduction by creating graded potentials or action potentials in the same cell or in an adjacent one.

Enzyme An enzyme is a protein that catalyzes, or speeds up, a chemical reaction. Enzymes are essential to sustain life because most chemical reactions in biological cells would occur too slowly, or would lead to different products, without enzymes.

Gene A gene is an ultramicroscopic area of the chromosome. It is the smallest physical unit of the DNA molecule that carries a piece of hereditary information.

Measles Measles, also known as rubeola, is a common disease caused by a virus of the genus Morbillivirus. Complications with measles are relatively common, ranging from relatively common and less serious diarrhea, to pneumonia and encephalitis. Complications are usually more severe amongst infants and adults who catch the virus.

Cephalocaudal The sequence in which the greatest growth occurs at the top, the head, with physical growth in size, weight, and feature differentiation gradually working from top to bottom is referred to as a cephalocaudal pattern.

Proximodistal Development originating from the center of the body towards the extremities is referred to as proximodistal development. The human embroyo normally develops in this fashion and averages 5-10 pounds in brith-weight and between 18 to 22 inches in length.

Breastfeeding Extensive research, especially in recent years, documents diverse and compelling advantages to infants, mothers, families, and society from breastfeeding and the use of human milk for infant feeding. These include health, nutritional, immunologic, developmental, psychological, social, economic, and environmental benefits.

Otitis media Otitis media refers to infection of the middle ear, an extremely common childhood problem; the attendant temporary or chronic hearing loss may lead to language development delays.

Middle ear The middle ear consists of the eardrum, hammer, anvil, and stirrup.

Obesity The state of being more than 20 percent above the average weight for a person of one's height is called obesity.

Cholesterol Cholesterol is a steroid, a lipid, and an alcohol, found in the cell membranes of all body tissues, and transported in the blood plasma of all animals. Cholesterol is an important component of the membranes of cells, providing stability; it makes the membrane's fluidity stable over a bigger temperature interval.

Atherosclerosis Process by which a fatty substance or plaque builds up inside arteries to form obstructions is called atherosclerosis.

Positron Positron Emission Tomography measures emissions from radioactively labeled chemicals that

emission tomography	have been injected into the bloodstream. The greatest benefit is that different compounds can show blood flow and oxygen and glucose metabolism in the tissues of the working brain.
Brain-imaging	Brain-imaging is a fairly recent discipline within medicine and neuroscience. Brain imaging falls into two broad categories -- structural imaging and functional imaging.
Cerebellum	The cerebellum is located in the inferior posterior portion of the head (the hindbrain), directly dorsal to the brainstem and pons, inferior to the occipital lobe. The cerebellum is a region of the brain that plays an important role in the integration of sensory perception and fine motor output.
Cerebrum	The cerebrum (the portion of the brain that performs motor and sensory functions and a variety of mental activities) is divided into four lobes - the frontal, temporal, parietal and occipital lobes.
Corpus callosum	The corpus callosum is the largest white matter structure in the brain. It consists of mostly of contralateral axon projections. The corpus callosum connects the left and right cerebral hemispheres. Most communication between regions in different halves of the brain are carried over the corpus callosum.
Lateralization	Lateralization refers to the dominance of one hemisphere of the brain for specific functions.
Problem solving	An attempt to find an appropriate way of attaining a goal when the goal is not readily available is called problem solving.
Reflex	A simple, involuntary response to a stimulus is referred to as reflex. Reflex actions originate at the spinal cord rather than the brain.
Cerebral cortex	The cerebral cortex is the outermost layer of the cerebrum and has a grey color. It is made up of four lobes and it is involved in many complex brain functions including memory, perceptual awareness, "thinking", language and consciousness. The cerebral cortex receives sensory information from many different sensory organs eg: eyes, ears, etc. and processes the information.
Frontal lobe	The frontal lobe comprises four major folds of cortical tissue: the precentral gyrus, superior gyrus and the middle gyrus of the frontal gyri, the inferior frontal gyrus. It has been found to play a part in impulse control, judgement, language, memory, motor function, problem solving, sexual behavior, socialization and spontaneity.
Neuron	The neuron is the primary cell of the nervous system. They are found in the brain, the spinal cord, in the nerves and ganglia of the peripheral nervous system. It is a specialized cell that conducts impulses through the nervous system and contains three major parts: cell body, dendrites, and an axon. It can have many dendrites but only one axon.
Glial	Glial cells are non-neuronal cells that provide support and nutrition, maintain homeostasis, form myelin, and participate in signal transmission in the nervous system.
Mitosis	Mitosis is the process by which a cell separates its duplicated genome into two identical halves.
Deoxyribonuc-eic acid	Deoxyribonucleic acid contains the genetic instructions specifying the biological development of all cellular forms of life. It is often referred to as the molecule of heredity, as it is responsible for the genetic propagation of most inherited traits.
Nucleus	In neuroanatomy, a cluster of cell bodies of neurons within the central nervous system is a nucleus.
Dendrite	A dendrite is a slender, typically branched projection of a nerve cell, or "neuron," which conducts the electrical stimulation received from other cells to the body or soma of the cell from which it projects. This stimulation arrives through synapses, which typically are

	located near the tips of the dendrites and away from the soma.
Axon	An axon, or "nerve fiber," is a long slender projection of a nerve cell, or "neuron," which conducts electrical impulses away from the neuron's cell body or soma.
Synapse	A synapse is specialized junction through which cells of the nervous system signal to one another and to non-neuronal cells such as muscles or glands.
Neurotransmitter	A neurotransmitter is a chemical that is used to relay, amplify and modulate electrical signals between a neurons and another cell.
Prefrontal cortex	The prefrontal cortex is the anterior part of the frontal lobes of the brain, lying in front of the motor and associative areas. It has been implicated in planning complex cognitive behaviors, personality expression and moderating correct social behavior. The prefrontal cortex continues to develop until around age 6.
Hippocampus	The hippocampus is a part of the brain located inside the temporal lobe. It forms a part of the limbic system and plays a part in memory and navigation.
Spinal cord	The spinal cord is a part of the vertebrate nervous system that is enclosed in and protected by the vertebral column (it passes through the spinal canal). It consists of nerve cells. The spinal cord carries sensory signals and motor innervation to most of the skeletal muscles in the body.
Emotion	An emotion is a mental states that arise spontaneously, rather than through conscious effort. They are often accompanied by physiological changes.
Occipital lobe	The occipital lobe is the smallest of four true lobes in the human brain. Located in the rearmost portion of the skull, the occipital lobe is part of the forebrain structure. It is the visual processing center.
Lobes	The four major sections of the cerebral cortex: frontal, parietal, temporal, and occipital are called lobes.
Temporal lobe	The temporal lobe is part of the cerebrum. It lies at the side of the brain, beneath the lateral or Sylvian fissure. Adjacent areas in the superior, posterior and lateral parts of the temporal lobe are involved in high-level auditory processing.
Parietal lobe	The parietal lobe is positioned above (superior to) the occipital lobe and behind (posterior to) the frontal lobe. It plays important roles in integrating sensory information from various senses, and in the manipulation of objects.
Reasoning	Reasoning is the act of using reason to derive a conclusion from certain premises. There are two main methods to reach a conclusion,deductive reasoning and inductive reasoning.
Gray matter	Gray matter is a category of nervous tissue with many nerve cell bodies and few myelinated axons. Generally, gray matter can be understood as the parts of the brain responsible for information processing; whereas, white matter is responsible for information transmission. In addition, gray matter does not have a myelin sheath and does not regenerate after injury unlike white matter.
Cingulate cortex	The part of the limbic system that is believed to process cognitive information in emotion is the cingulate cortex. The cingulate cortex is part of the brain and situated roughly in the middle of the cortex.
Basal ganglia	The basal ganglia are a group of nuclei in the brain associated with motor and learning functions.
Sensorimotor	The first of Piaget's stages is the Sensorimotor stage. This stage typically ranges from birth to 2 years. In this stage, children experience the world through their senses. During this stage, object permanence and stranger anxiety develop.

Thalamus	An area near the center of the brain involved in the relay of sensory information to the cortex and in the functions of sleep and attention is the thalamus.
Central nervous system	The vertebrate central nervous system consists of the brain and spinal cord.
Sensory receptor	A sensory receptor is a structure that recognizes a stimulus in the environment of an organism. In response to stimuli the sensory receptor initiates sensory transduction by creating graded potentials or action potentials in the same cell or in an adjacent one.
Adolescence	The period of life bounded by puberty and the assumption of adult responsibilities is adolescence.
Myelination	The process in which the nerve cells are covered and insulated with a layer of fat cells, which increases the speed at which information travels through the nervous system is referred to as myelination.
Embryo	A developed zygote that has a rudimentary heart, brain, and other organs is referred to as an embryo.
Innate	Innate behavior is not learned or influenced by the environment, rather, it is present or predisposed at birth.
Pupil	In the eye, the pupil is the opening in the middle of the iris. It appears black because most of the light entering it is absorbed by the tissues inside the eye. The size of the pupil is controlled by involuntary contraction and dilation of the iris, in order to regulate the intensity of light entering the eye. This is known as the pupillary reflex.
Babbling	Babbling is a stage in child language acquisition, during which an infant appears to be experimenting with making the sounds of language, but not yet producing any recognizable words.
Visual cortex	The visual cortex is the general term applied to both the primary visual cortex and the visual association area. Anatomically, the visual cortex occupies the entire occipital lobe, the inferior temporal lobe (IT), posterior parts of the parietal lobe, and a few small regions in the frontal lobe.
Babinski reflex	A reflex in which infants fan their toes when the undersides of their feet are stroked is called the Babinski reflex.
Enrichment	Deliberately making an environment more novel, complex, and perceptually or intellectually stimulating is referred to as enrichment.
Psychosocial development	Erikson's psychosocial development describe eight developmental stages through which a healthily developing human should pass from infancy to late adulthood. In each stage the person confronts, and hopefully masters, new challenges.
Social skills	Social skills are skills used to interact and communicate with others to assist status in the social structure and other motivations.
Senses	The senses are systems that consist of a sensory cell type that respond to a specific kind of physical energy, and that correspond to a defined region within the brain where the signals are received and interpreted.
Society	The social sciences use the term society to mean a group of people that form a semi-closed (or semi-open) social system, in which most interactions are with other individuals belonging to the group.
Taste bud	The taste bud (or lingual papillae) is a small structure on the upper surface of the tongue that provides information about the taste of food being eaten. It is known that there are five taste sensations: Sweet, Bitter, Umami, Salty and Sour.

Discrimination	In Learning theory, discrimination refers the ability to distinguish between a conditioned stimulus and other stimuli. It can be brought about by extensive training or differential reinforcement. In social terms, it is the denial of privileges to a person or a group on the basis of prejudice.
Optic nerve	The optic nerve is the nerve that transmits visual information from the retina to the brain. The optic nerve is composed of retinal ganglion cell axons and support cells.
Perception	Perception is the process of acquiring, interpreting, selecting, and organizing sensory information.
Denver Developmental Screening Test	The Denver Developmental Screening Test is given to children 1 month to 6 years old to determine whether they are developing normally.
Gross motor skills	Gross motor skills refer to motor skills that involve large muscle activities, such as walking.
Grasping reflex	The grasping reflex is a neonatal reflex that occurs when something touches the infant's palms. The infant responds by grasping tightly.
Pincer grasp	The use of the opposing thumb to grasp objects between the thumb and other fingers is referred to as the pincer grasp.
Cognitive development	The process by which a child's understanding of the world changes as a function of age and experience is called cognitive development.
Self-esteem	Self-esteem refers to a person's subjective appraisal of himself or herself as intrinsically positive or negative to some degree.
Species	Species refers to a reproductively isolated breeding population.
Fisher	Fisher was a eugenicist, evolutionary biologist, geneticist and statistician. He has been described as "The greatest of Darwin's successors", and a genius who almost single-handedly created the foundations for modern statistical science inventing the techniques of maximum likelihood and analysis of variance.
Motivation	In psychology, motivation is the driving force (desire) behind all actions of an organism.
Hypothesis	A specific statement about behavior or mental processes that is testable through research is a hypothesis.
Retina	The retina is a thin layer of cells at the back of the eyeball. It is the part of the eye which converts light into nervous signals. The retina contains photoreceptor cells which receive the light; the resulting neural signals then undergo complex processing by other neurons of the retina, and are transformed into action potentials in retinal ganglion cells whose axons form the optic nerve.
Haptic perception	Haptic perception is the ability to acquire information about properties of objects, such as size, weight, and texture, through handling them.
Relative size	Relative size is a monocular cue where an an automobile that is close to us seems larger than one that is far away. The visual system exploits the relative size of similar (or familiar) objects to judge distance.
Ecological theory of perception	The ecological theory of perception was developed by Eleanor and James Gibson. It describes developing motor and perceptual abilities as interdependent parts of a single function. It is a form of direct realism as proposed by Reid.
Ecological Theory	Bronfenbrenner's Ecological theory is an environmental system view of development, involving five systems: microsystem, mesosystem, exosystem, macrosystem, and chronosystem. These

emphasize the role of social contexts in development.

James Gibson — James Gibson is considered one of the most important 20th century psychologists in the field of visual perception. In his classic work The Perception of the Visual World (1950) he rejected the behaviorism then fashionable for a view based on his own experimental work, which pioneered the idea that animals 'sampled' information from the 'ambient' outside world.

Affordance — An affordance is a property of an object, or a feature of the immediate environment, that indicates how that object or feature can be interfaced with. The empty space within an open doorway, for instance, affords movement across that threshold.

Perceptual learning — Perceptual learning refers to changes in perception that can be attributed to experience.

Electronic fetal monitoring — The cardiotocograph is more commonly known as Electronic Fetal Monitoring. A cardiotocograph measures the heart rate and the frequency of uterine contractions. When introduced, it was thought that this practice would reduce the incidence of fetal demise in labor and make for a reduction in cerebral palsy (CP). Its use became almost universal in the US.

Doula — A doula is a non-medical assistant in prenatal care, childbirth and during the postpartum period.

Fontanel — A fontanel is one of two "soft spots" on a newborn human's skull. The skull of a newborn consists of five main bones: two frontal bones, two parietal bones, and one occipital bone. These are joined by fibrous "sutures" which allow movement that facilitates childbirth and brain growth.

Vernix — An oily, white substance that coats the skin of the neonate, especially preterm babies is referred to as vernix.

Sucking reflex — The sucking reflex is a newborn's built-in reaction of automatically sucking an object placed in its mouth. The sucking reflex enables the infant to get nourishment before it has associated a nipple with food.

Temperament — Temperament refers to a basic, innate disposition to change behavior. The activity level is an important dimension of temperament.

Hypothyroidism — Hypothyroidism refers to slower metabolism and sluggishness caused by an underactive thyroid gland.

Congenital — A condition existing at birth is referred to as congenital.

Protective factors — Protective factors are influences that reduce the impact of early stress and tend to lead to positive outcomes.

Postnatal — Postnatal is the period beginning immediately after the birth of a child and extending for about six weeks. The period is also known as postpartum and, less commonly, puerperium.

Sleep patterns — The order and timing of daily sleep and waking periods are called sleep patterns.

Peripheral vision — Peripheral vision is that part of vision that occurs outside the very center of gaze. Peripheral vision is weak in humans, especially at distinguishing color and shape. This is because the density of receptor cells on the retina is greatest at the center and lowest at the edges

Binocular vision — Binocular vision is vision in which both eyes are used synchronously to produce a single image. It confers two advantages over monocular vision: binocular summation in which the ability to detect faint objects is enhanced, and stereopsis in which parallax provided by the two eye's different positions on the head give precise depth perception.

Darwin — Darwin achieved lasting fame as originator of the theory of evolution through natural

selection. His book Expression of Emotions in Man and Animals is generally considered the first text on comparative psychology.

Origin of Species

The Origin of Species by Charles Darwin makes the argument that groups of organisms gradually evolve through the process of natural selection. Characteristics that favor survival and reproduction are passed on to the next generation, those that do not, are gradually lost.

Evolution

Commonly used to refer to gradual change, evolution is the change in the frequency of alleles within a population from one generation to the next. This change may be caused by different mechanisms, including natural selection, genetic drift, or changes in population (gene flow).

Cognitive skills

Cognitive skills such as reasoning, attention, and memory can be advanced and sustained through practice and training.

Information-processing approach

Information-processing approach emphasizes that individuals act on information, monitor it, and strategize about it--contrary to strict behaviorists. Central to information processing are the processes of memory and thinking. The computer serves as a metaphor whereby the brain is the hardware and behavior is the software.

Cognitive structure

According to Piaget, the number of schemata available to an organism at any given time constitutes that organism's cognitive structure. How the organism interacts with its environment depends on the current cognitive structure available. As the cognitive structure develops, new assimilations can occur.

Piagetian approach

A Piagetian approach is the study of cognitive development where there are a distinct sequence of qualitative critical stages that are met biologically, experientially, and cognitively.

Nature-nurture

Nature-nurture is a shorthand expression for debates about the relative importance of an individual's "nature" versus personal experiences ("nurture") in determining or causing physical and behavioral traits.

Psychometric

Psychometric study is concerned with the theory and technique of psychological measurement, which includes the measurement of knowledge, abilities, attitudes, and personality traits. The field is primarily concerned with the study of differences between individuals

Neuroscience

A field that combines the work of psychologists, biologists, biochemists, medical researchers, and others in the study of the structure and function of the nervous system is neuroscience.

Acquisition

Acquisition is the process of adapting to the environment, learning or becoming conditioned. In classical conditoning terms, it is the initial learning of the stimulus response link, which involves a neutral stimulus being associated with a unconditioned stimulus and becoming a conditioned stimulus.

Theories

Theories are logically self-consistent models or frameworks describing the behavior of a certain natural or social phenomenon. They are broad explanations and predictions concerning phenomena of interest.

Reflection

Reflection is the process of rephrasing or repeating thoughts and feelings expressed, making the person more aware of what they are saying or thinking.

Cognitive development	The process by which a child's understanding of the world changes as a function of age and experience is called cognitive development.
Learning	Learning is a relatively permanent change in behavior that results from experience. Thus, to attribute a behavioral change to learning, the change must be relatively permanent and must result from experience.
Psychometric	Psychometric study is concerned with the theory and technique of psychological measurement, which includes the measurement of knowledge, abilities, attitudes, and personality traits. The field is primarily concerned with the study of differences between individuals
Quantitative	A quantitative property is one that exists in a range of magnitudes, and can therefore be measured. Measurements of any particular quantitative property are expressed as as a specific quantity, referred to as a unit, multiplied by a number.
Piagetian approach	A Piagetian approach is the study of cognitive development where there are a distinct sequence of qualitative critical stages that are met biologically, experientially, and cognitively.
Stages	Stages represent relatively discrete periods of time in which functioning is qualitatively different from functioning at other periods.
Cognitive approach	A cognitive approach focuses on the mental processes involved in knowing: how we direct our attention, perceive, remember, think, and solve problems.
Neuroscience	A field that combines the work of psychologists, biologists, biochemists, medical researchers, and others in the study of the structure and function of the nervous system is neuroscience.
Operant Conditioning	A simple form of learning in which an organism learns to engage in behavior because it is reinforced is referred to as operant conditioning. The consequences of a behavior produce changes in the probability of the behavior's occurence.
Little Albert	The Little Albert experiment was an experiment showing empirical evidence of classical conditioning in children. The actual experiment with Little Albert on conditioned fear involved exposing the child to a loud sound while being presented with a white rat.
Classical conditioning	Classical conditioning is a simple form of learning in which an organism comes to associate or anticipate events. A neutral stimulus comes to evoke the response usually evoked by a natural or unconditioned stimulus by being paired repeatedly with the unconditioned stimulus.
Stimulus	A change in an environmental condition that elicits a response is a stimulus.
Reflex	A simple, involuntary response to a stimulus is referred to as reflex. Reflex actions originate at the spinal cord rather than the brain.
Reinforcement	In operant conditioning, reinforcement is any change in an environment that (a) occurs after the behavior, (b) seems to make that behavior re-occur more often in the future and (c) that reoccurence of behavior must be the result of the change.
Punishment	Punishment is the addtion of a stimulus that reduces the frequency of a response, or the removal of a stimulus that results in a reduction of the response.
Attention	Attention is the cognitive process of selectively concentrating on one thing while ignoring other things. Psychologists have labeled three types of attention: sustained attention, selective attention, and divided attention.
Piaget	Piaget argued that young children's answers were qualitatively different than older children rather than quantitative. There are two major aspects to his theory: the process of coming to know and the stages we move through as we gradually acquire this ability.

Brain The brain controls and coordinates most movement, behavior and homeostatic body functions such as heartbeat, blood pressure, fluid balance and body temperature. Functions of the brain are responsible for cognition, emotion, memory, motor learning and other sorts of learning. The brain is primarily made up of two types of cells: glia and neurons.

Conditioned response A conditioned response is the response to a stimulus that occurs when an animal has learned to associate the stimulus with a certain positive or negative effect.

Affect A subjective feeling or emotional tone often accompanied by bodily expressions noticeable to others is called affect.

Infancy The developmental period that extends from birth to 18 or 24 months is called infancy.

Darwin Darwin achieved lasting fame as originator of the theory of evolution through natural selection. His book Expression of Emotions in Man and Animals is generally considered the first text on comparative psychology.

Discrimination In Learning theory, discrimination refers the ability to distinguish between a conditioned stimulus and other stimuli. It can be brought about by extensive training or differential reinforcement. In social terms, it is the denial of privileges to a person or a group on the basis of prejudice.

Reaction time The amount of time required to respond to a stimulus is referred to as reaction time.

Rote Rote learning, is a learning technique which avoids grasping the inner complexities and inferences of the subject that is being learned and instead focuses on memorizing the material so that it can be recalled by the learner exactly the way it was read or heard.

Theodore Simon Theodore Simon co-created the Stanford-Binet Intelligence Scale test with Alfred Binet.

Intelligence quotient An intelligence quotient is a score derived from a set of standardized tests that were developed with the purpose of measuring a person's cognitive abilities ("intelligence") in relation to their age group.

Stanford-Binet Terman released the "Stanford Revision of the Binet-Simon Scale" or the Stanford-Binet for short. Using validation experiments, he removed several of the Binet-Simon test items and added new ones. In 1985 it was revised to analyze an individual's responses in four content areas: verbal reasoning, quantitative reasoning, abstract reasoning, and short-term memory.

Reasoning Reasoning is the act of using reason to derive a conclusion from certain premises. There are two main methods to reach a conclusion,deductive reasoning and inductive reasoning.

Intelligence test An intelligence test is a standardized means of assessing a person's current mental ability, for example, the Stanford-Binet test and the Wechsler Adult Intelligence Scale.

Toddler A toddler is a child between the ages of one and three years old. During this period, the child learns a great deal about social roles and develops motor skills; to toddle is to walk unsteadily.

Norms In testing, standards of test performance that permit the comparison of one person's score on the test to the scores of others who have taken the same test are referred to as norms.

Standardized test An oral or written assessment for which an individual receives a score indicating how the individual reponded relative to a previously tested large sample of others is referred to as a standardized test.

Sensorimotor The first of Piaget's stages is the Sensorimotor stage. This stage typically ranges from birth to 2 years. In this stage, children experience the world through their senses. During this stage, object permanence and stranger anxiety develop.

Developmental An overall developmental score that combines subscores in motor, language, adaptive, and

quotient	personal-social domains in the Gesell assessment of infants is a developmental quotient.
Parental responsiveness	Parental responsiveness is the degree of caregiving that is based on sensitivity to a child's feelings, needs, rhythms, and signals.
Longitudinal study	Longitudinal study is a type of developmental study in which the same group of participants is followed and measured for an extended period of time, often years.
Gene	A gene is an ultramicroscopic area of the chromosome. It is the smallest physical unit of the DNA molecule that carries a piece of hereditary information.
IQ test	An IQ test is a standardized test developed to measure a person's cognitive abilities ("intelligence") in relation to their age group.
Priming	A phenomenon in which exposure to a word or concept later makes it easier to recall related information, even when one has no conscious memory of the word or concept is called priming.
Mentoring	Mentoring refers to a developmental relationship between a more experienced individual and a less experienced partner sometimes referred to as a protégé. In well-designed formal mentoring programs, there are program goals, schedules, and training.
Early Intervention	Early intervention is a process used to recognize warning signs for mental health problems and to take early action against factors that put individuals at risk.
Child development	Scientific study of the processes of change from conception through adolescence is called child development.
Social skills	Social skills are skills used to interact and communicate with others to assist status in the social structure and other motivations.
Control group	A group that does not receive the treatment effect in an experiment is referred to as the control group or sometimes as the comparison group.
Population	Population refers to all members of a well-defined group of organisms, events, or things.
Alfred Binet	Alfred Binet published the first modern intelligence test, the Binet-Simon intelligence scale, in 1905. Binet stressed that the core of intelligence consists of complex cognitive processes, such as memory, imagery, comprehension, and judgment; and, that these developed over time in the individual.
Cognition	The intellectual processes through which information is obtained, transformed, stored, retrieved, and otherwise used is cognition.
Senses	The senses are systems that consist of a sensory cell type that respond to a specific kind of physical energy, and that correspond to a defined region within the brain where the signals are received and interpreted.
Adaptation	Adaptation is a lowering of sensitivity to a stimulus following prolonged exposure to that stimulus. Behavioral adaptations are special ways a particular organism behaves to survive in its natural habitat.
Trial and error	Trial and error is an approach to problem solving in which one solution after another is tried in no particular order until an answer is found.
Circular reaction	A Circular reaction is Piaget's term for processes by which an infant learns to reproduce desired occurrences originally discovered by chance.
Sensation	Sensation is the first stage in the chain of biochemical and neurologic events that begins with the impinging of a stimulus upon the receptor cells of a sensory organ, which then leads to perception, the mental state that is reflected in statements like "I see a uniformly blue wall."

Primary circular reaction	A primary circular reaction is a scheme based on the attempt to reproduce an event that initially occurred by chance.
Secondary Circular Reactions	The third stage of Piaget's sensorimotor substages, Secondary Circular Reactions, occurs from four to nine months. The critical requirement for the infant to progress into this substage is hand-eye coordination. Three novelties occur at this stage: intentional grasping for a desired object, repetition of an action involving an external object, and differentiations between ends and means.
Preoperational stage	The Preoperational stage is the second stage of development in Piaget's theory. By observing sequences of play, Piaget was able to demonstrate that towards the end of the second year a qualitatively quite new kind of functioning occurs. Operation in Piagetian theory is any procedure for mentally acting on objects.
Mental combinations	In Piaget's theory, the final substage of sensorimotor development is a transition between the action-oriented world of the infant and the symbol-oriented world of the child. The stage is characterized by mental combinations.
Early childhood	Early childhood refers to the developmental period extending from the end of infancy to about 5 or 6 years of age; sometimes called the preschool years.
Representational ability	The child's representational ability in Piaget's theory is the capacity to store mental images or symbols of objects and events.
Object permanence	Object permanence is the term used to describe the awareness that objects continue to exist even when they are no longer visible. According to Piaget, object permance for the infant develops once the sensorimotor stage is complete.
Deferred imitation	Imitation that occurs after a time delay of hours or days is referred to as deferred imitation.
Psychoanalyst	A psychoanalyst is a specially trained therapist who attempts to treat the individual by uncovering and revealing to the individual otherwise subconscious factors that are contributing to some undesirable behavor.
Anxiety	Anxiety is a complex combination of the feeling of fear, apprehension and worry often accompanied by physical sensations such as palpitations, chest pain and/or shortness of breath.
Play therapy	Play therapy is often used to help the diagnostician to try to determine the cause of disturbed behavior in a child. Treatment therapists then used a type of systematic desensitization or relearning therapy to change the disturbing behavior, either systematically or in less formal social settings.
Egocentrism	The inability to distinguish between one's own perspective and someone else's is referred to as egocentrism.
Mental Representation	Stage six of the sensorimotor substages, Mental representation, 18 months to 2 years, marks the beginnings of insight, or true creativity. This marks the passage into unique thought in Piaget's later three areas of development.
Perception	Perception is the process of acquiring, interpreting, selecting, and organizing sensory information.
Inference	Inference is the act or process of drawing a conclusion based solely on what one already knows.
Information-processing	Information-processing approach emphasizes that individuals act on information, monitor it, and strategize about it--contrary to strict behaviorists. Central to information processing

approach	are the processes of memory and thinking. The computer serves as a metaphor whereby the brain is the hardware and behavior is the software.
Problem solving	An attempt to find an appropriate way of attaining a goal when the goal is not readily available is called problem solving.
Individual differences	Individual differences psychology studies the ways in which individual people differ in their behavior. This is distinguished from other aspects of psychology in that although psychology is ostensibly a study of individuals, modern psychologists invariably study groups.
Mental processes	The thoughts, feelings, and motives that each of us experiences privately but that cannot be observed directly are called mental processes.
Habituation	In habituation there is a progressive reduction in the response probability with continued repetition of a stimulus.
Information processing	Information processing is an approach to the goal of understanding human thinking. The essence of the approach is to see cognition as being essentially computational in nature, with mind being the software and the brain being the hardware.
Dishabituation	A renewed interest in a stimulus is referred to as dishabituation.
McClelland	McClelland asserts that human motivation comprises three dominant needs: the need for achievement (N-Ach), the need for power (N-Pow) and the need for affiliation (N-Affil). The subjective importance of each need varies from individual to individual and depends also on an individual's cultural background.
Cognitive structure	According to Piaget, the number of schemata available to an organism at any given time constitutes that organism's cognitive structure. How the organism interacts with its environment depends on the current cognitive structure available. As the cognitive structure develops, new assimilations can occur.
Maturation	The orderly unfolding of traits, as regulated by the genetic code is called maturation.
Long-term memory	Long-term memory is memory that lasts from over 30 seconds to years.
Explicit memory	Intentional or conscious recollection of information is referred to as explicit memory. Children under age three are usually poorest at explicit memory which may be due to the immaturity of the prefrontal lobes of the brain, which are believed to play an important role in memory for events.
Implicit memory	Implicit memory is the long-term memory of skills and procedures, or "how to" knowledge. It is often not easily verbalized, but can be used without consciously thinking about it.
Habit	A habit is a response that has become completely separated from its eliciting stimulus. Early learning theorists used the term to describe S-R associations, however not all S-R associations become a habit, rather many are extinguished after reinforcement is withdrawn.
Procedural memory	Procedural memory is the long-term memory of skills and procedures, or "how to" knowledge.
Cerebellum	The cerebellum is located in the inferior posterior portion of the head (the hindbrain), directly dorsal to the brainstem and pons, inferior to the occipital lobe. The cerebellum is a region of the brain that plays an important role in the integration of sensory perception and fine motor output.
Brain stem	The brain stem is the stalk of the brain below the cerebral hemispheres. It is the major route for communication between the forebrain and the spinal cord and peripheral nerves. It also controls various functions including respiration, regulation of heart rhythms, and primary aspects of sound localization.

Temporal lobe	The temporal lobe is part of the cerebrum. It lies at the side of the brain, beneath the lateral or Sylvian fissure. Adjacent areas in the superior, posterior and lateral parts of the temporal lobe are involved in high-level auditory processing.
Episodic memory	Episodic memory is the explicit memory of events. It includes time, place, and associated emotions (which affect the quality of the memorization).
Hippocampus	The hippocampus is a part of the brain located inside the temporal lobe. It forms a part of the limbic system and plays a part in memory and navigation.
Prefrontal cortex	The prefrontal cortex is the anterior part of the frontal lobes of the brain, lying in front of the motor and associative areas. It has been implicated in planning complex cognitive behaviors, personality expression and moderating correct social behavior. The prefrontal cortex continues to develop until around age 6.
Frontal lobe	The frontal lobe comprises four major folds of cortical tissue: the precentral gyrus, superior gyrus and the middle gyrus of the frontal gyri, the inferior frontal gyrus. It has been found to play a part in impulse control, judgement, language, memory, motor function, problem solving, sexual behavior, socialization and spontaneity.
Working Memory	Working memory is the collection of structures and processes in the brain used for temporarily storing and manipulating information. Working memory consists of both memory for items that are currently being processed, and components governing attention and directing the processing itself.
Memory structure	Patterns of associations among bits of information stored in memory is a memory structure.
Guided participation	Guided participation refers to adult-child interactions, not only during explicit instruction but also during the more routine activities and communication of everyday life. It is the process and system of involvement of individuals with others as they communicate and engage in shared activities.
Proximal	Students can set both long-term (distal) and short-term (proximal) goals .
Vygotsky	The Vygotsky model of human development has been termed as a sociocultural approach. The individual's development is a result of his or her culture.
Syntax	Syntax can be described as the study of the rules, or "patterned relations" that govern the way the words in a sentence come together.
Babbling	Babbling is a stage in child language acquisition, during which an infant appears to be experimenting with making the sounds of language, but not yet producing any recognizable words.
Cooing	Cooing is the spontaneous repetition of vowel sounds by infants.
Pitch	Pitch is the psychological interpretation of a sound or musical tone corresponding to its physical frequency
Linguistic speech	Verbal expression designed to convey meaning is referred to as linguistic speech.
Fetus	A fetus develops from the end of the 8th week of pregnancy (when the major structures have formed), until birth.
Intonation	The use of pitches of varying levels to help communicate meaning is called intonation.
Holophrase	A holophrase is a single word expressing a complex idea. Children go through a stage early in life where they are only able to communicate complex ideas using single words. Sometimes the single words can seem to communicate as much as a full sentence would.
Single-word	Single-word stage in language development describes the period during which a child first

stage	begins to use single word sentences.
Chronological age	Chronological age refers to the number of years that have elapsed since a person's birth.
Telegraphic speech	Telegraphic speech refers to the use of short and precise words to communicate. Young children's two- and three-word utterances characteristically are telegraphic.
Feedback	Feedback refers to information returned to a person about the effects a response has had.
Acquisition	Acquisition is the process of adapting to the environment, learning or becoming conditioned. In classical conditoning terms, it is the initial learning of the stimulus response link, which involves a neutral stimulus being associated with a unconditioned stimulus and becoming a conditioned stimulus.
Chomsky	Chomsky has greatly influenced the field of theoretical linguistics with his work on the theory of generative grammar. Accordingly, humans are biologically prewired to learn language at a certain time and in a certain way.
Skinner	Skinner conducted research on shaping behavior through positive and negative reinforcement, and demonstrated operant conditioning, a technique which he developed in contrast with classical conditioning.
Nativism	Nativism is the view that certain skills or abilities are innate or hard wired into the brain at birth. This is in contrast to the 'blank slate' or tabula rasa view which states that the brain has little innate ability and almost everything is learnt through interaction with the environment.
Innate	Innate behavior is not learned or influenced by the environment, rather, it is present or predisposed at birth.
Nativist	A nativist believes that certain skills or abilities are native or hard wired into the brain at birth.
Nurture	Nurture refers to the environmental influences on behavior due to nutrition, culture, socioeconomic status, and learning.
Motor cortex	Motor cortex refers to the section of cortex that lies in the frontal lobe, just across the central fissure from the sensory cortex. Neural impulses in the motor cortex are linked to muscular responses throughout the body.
Larynx	The larynx, or voicebox, is an organ in the neck of mammals involved in protection of the trachea and sound production. The larynx houses the vocal cords, and is situated at the point where the upper tract splits into the trachea and the esophagus.
Pons	The pons is a knob on the brain stem. It is part of the autonomic nervous system, and relays sensory information between the cerebellum and cerebrum. Some theories posit that it has a role in dreaming.
Right hemisphere	The brain is divided into left and right cerebral hemispheres. The right hemisphere of the cortex controls the left side of the body.
Left hemisphere	The left hemisphere of the cortex controls the right side of the body, coordinates complex movements, and, in 95% of people, controls the production of speech and written language.
Sensitive period	A sensitive period is a developmental window in which a predisposed behavior is most likely to develop given appropriate stimulation. In linguistic theory, the period from about 18 months to puberty is when the brain is thought to be primed for learning language because of plasticity of the brain.
Lateralization	Lateralization refers to the dominance of one hemisphere of the brain for specific functions.

Code mixing	Code mixing is the use of elements of two or more languages, sometimes in the same utterance, by young children in households where multiple languages are spoken.
Naturalistic observation	Naturalistic observation is a method of observation that involves observing subjects in their natural habitats. Researchers take great care in avoiding making interferences with the behavior they are observing by using unobtrusive methods.
Child-directed speech	Baby talk, motherese, parentese, caretaker, or child-directed speech is a nonstandard form of speech used by adults, particularly mothers, in talking to children.
Code switching	Code switching is a term in linguistics referring to alternation between two or more languages, dialects, or language registers in the course of discourse between people who have more than one language in common. Sometimes the switch lasts only for a few sentences, or even for a single phrase.
Reading comprehension	Reading comprehension can be defined as the level of understanding of a passage or text. For normal reading rates (around 200-220 words per minute) an acceptable level of comprehension is above 75%.
Psychosocial development	Erikson's psychosocial development describe eight developmental stages through which a healthily developing human should pass from infancy to late adulthood. In each stage the person confronts, and hopefully masters, new challenges.
Bayley Scales	The Bayley Scales of Infant Development are widely used in assessing infant development for infants 1-42 months of age. The current version has three parts: a Mental Scale, a Motor Scale, and the Infant Behavior Profile. Among the uses are the diagnosis of developmental delays and the planning of intervention strategies.
Socioeconomic Status	A family's socioeconomic status is based on family income, parental education level, parental occupation, and social status in the community. Those with high status often have more success in preparing their children for school because they have access to a wide range of resources.
Scheme	According to Piaget, a hypothetical mental structure that permits the classification and organization of new information is called a scheme.
Egocentric thought	A way of thinking in which the child views the world entirely from his or her own perspective is referred to as egocentric thought.
Temperament	Temperament refers to a basic, innate disposition to change behavior. The activity level is an important dimension of temperament.
Attachment	Attachment is the tendency to seek closeness to another person and feel secure when that person is present.
Bateson	Bateson is most famous for developing the "Double Bind" theory of schizophrenia together with Paul Watzlawick.
Emotion	An emotion is a mental states that arise spontaneously, rather than through conscious effort. They are often accompanied by physiological changes.
Separation anxiety	Separation anxiety is a psychological condition in which an individual has excessive anxiety regarding separation from home, or from those with whom the individual has a strong attachment.
Autonomy	Autonomy is the condition of something that does not depend on anything else.
Internalization	The developmental change from behavior that is externally controlled to behavior that is controlled by internal standards and principles is referred to as internalization.
Erik Erikson	Erik Erikson conceived eight stages of development, each confronting the individual with its

own psychosocial demands, that continued into old age. Personality development, according to Erikson, takes place through a series of crises that must be overcome and internalized by the individual in preparation for the next developmental stage. Such crisis are not catastrophes but vulnerabilities.

Mutual regulation

Mutual regulation is the process by which infant and caregiver communicate emotional states to each other and respond appropriately.

Depression

In everyday language depression refers to any downturn in mood, which may be relatively transitory and perhaps due to something trivial. This is differentiated from Clinical depression which is marked by symptoms that last two weeks or more and are so severe that they interfere with daily living.

Emotion	An emotion is a mental states that arise spontaneously, rather than through conscious effort. They are often accompanied by physiological changes.
Self-assertion	Self-assertion refers to a direct, honest expression of feelings and desires.
Self-esteem	Self-esteem refers to a person's subjective appraisal of himself or herself as intrinsically positive or negative to some degree.
Ambivalence	The simultaneous holding of strong positive and negative emotional attitudes toward the same situation or person is called ambivalence.
Conditioning	Conditioning describes the process by which behaviors can be learned or modified through interaction with the environment.
Learning	Learning is a relatively permanent change in behavior that results from experience. Thus, to attribute a behavioral change to learning, the change must be relatively permanent and must result from experience.
Personality	Personality refers to the pattern of enduring characteristics that differentiates a person, the patterns of behaviors that make each individual unique.
Infancy	The developmental period that extends from birth to 18 or 24 months is called infancy.
Stranger anxiety	Stranger anxiety refers to an infant's fear and wariness of strangers; it typically appears in the second half of the first year of life.
Toddler	A toddler is a child between the ages of one and three years old. During this period, the child learns a great deal about social roles and develops motor skills; to toddle is to walk unsteadily.
Coronary heart disease	Coronary heart disease is the end result of the accumulation of atheromatous plaques within the walls of the arteries that supply the myocardium (the muscle of the heart).
Syndrome	The term syndrome is the association of several clinically recognizable features, signs, symptoms, phenomena or characteristics which often occur together, so that the presence of one feature indicates the presence of the others.
Anxiety	Anxiety is a complex combination of the feeling of fear, apprehension and worry often accompanied by physical sensations such as palpitations, chest pain and/or shortness of breath.
Guthrie	The theory of learning proposed by Guthrie was based on one principle, Contiguity : A combination of stimuli which has accompanied a movement will on its recurrence tend to be followed by that movement. Prediction of behavior will always be probabilistic.
Asthma	Asthma is a complex disease characterized by bronchial hyperresponsiveness (BHR), inflammation, mucus production and intermittent airway obstruction.
Guilt	Guilt describes many concepts related to a negative emotion or condition caused by actions which are believed to be, morally wrong. According to Freud, the avoidance of guilt is the basis for moral behavior.
Cooing	Cooing is the spontaneous repetition of vowel sounds by infants.
Bateson	Bateson is most famous for developing the "Double Bind" theory of schizophrenia together with Paul Watzlawick.
Nervous system	The body's electrochemical communication circuitry, made up of billions of neurons is a nervous system.
Sensation	Sensation is the first stage in the chain of biochemical and neurologic events that begins with the impinging of a stimulus upon the receptor cells of a sensory organ, which then leads

	to perception, the mental state that is reflected in statements like "I see a uniformly blue wall."
Attention	Attention is the cognitive process of selectively concentrating on one thing while ignoring other things. Psychologists have labeled three types of attention: sustained attention, selective attention, and divided attention.
Physiological changes	Alterations in heart rate, blood pressure, perspiration, and other involuntary responses are physiological changes.
Self-conscious emotions	The self-conscious emotions include feelings of guilt, shame, embarrassment, and pride, which are linked to thoughts about the self or one's own actions.
Self-awareness	Realization that one's existence and functioning are separate from those of other people and things is called self-awareness.
Consciousness	The awareness of the sensations, thoughts, and feelings being experienced at a given moment is called consciousness.
Basic emotions	Basic emotions are those found in all cultures, as evidinced by the same facial expressions. They include: fear, anger, disgust, surprise, happiness, and distress.
Attitude	An enduring mental representation of a person, place, or thing that evokes an emotional response and related behavior is called attitude.
Innate	Innate behavior is not learned or influenced by the environment, rather, it is present or predisposed at birth.
Empathy	Empathy is the recognition and understanding of the states of mind, including beliefs, desires and particularly emotions of others without injecting your own.
Mental Representation	Stage six of the sensorimotor substages, Mental representation, 18 months to 2 years, marks the beginnings of insight, or true creativity. This marks the passage into unique thought in Piaget's later three areas of development.
Piaget	Piaget argued that young children's answers were qualitatively different than older children rather than quantitative. There are two major aspects to his theory: the process of coming to know and the stages we move through as we gradually acquire this ability.
Society	The social sciences use the term society to mean a group of people that form a semi-closed (or semi-open) social system, in which most interactions are with other individuals belonging to the group.
Self-worth	In psychology, self-esteem or self-worth refers to a person's subjective appraisal of himself or herself as intrinsically positive or negative to some degree.
Social cognition	Social cognition is the name for both a branch of psychology that studies the cognitive processes involved in social interaction, and an umbrella term for the processes themselves. It uses the tools and assumptions of cognitive psychology to study how people understand themselves and others in society and social situations.
Egocentrism	The inability to distinguish between one's own perspective and someone else's is referred to as egocentrism.
Central nervous system	The vertebrate central nervous system consists of the brain and spinal cord.
Hypothalamus	The hypothalamus is a region of the brain located below the thalamus, forming the major portion of the ventral region of the diencephalon and functioning to regulate certain metabolic processes and other autonomic activities.
Temperament	Temperament refers to a basic, innate disposition to change behavior. The activity level is

	an important dimension of temperament.
Individual differences	Individual differences psychology studies the ways in which individual people differ in their behavior. This is distinguished from other aspects of psychology in that although psychology is ostensibly a study of individuals, modern psychologists invariably study groups.
Longitudinal study	Longitudinal study is a type of developmental study in which the same group of participants is followed and measured for an extended period of time, often years.
Habit	A habit is a response that has become completely separated from its eliciting stimulus. Early learning theorists used the term to describe S-R associations, however not all S-R associations become a habit, rather many are extinguished after reinforcement is withdrawn.
Biological rhythm	A biological rhythm is a hypothetical cyclic pattern of alterations in physiology, emotions, and/or intellect
Goodness of Fit	With respect to care giving, the degree to which parents and children have compatible temperaments is called goodness of fit.
Questionnaire	A self-report method of data collection or clinical assessment method in which the individual being studied checks off items on a printed list, answers multiple-choice questions, or writes out answers to essay questions aimed at producing a selfdescription is called questionnaire.
Self-Regulatory	Bandura proposes that self-regulatory systems mediate external influences and provide a basis for purposeful action, allowing people to have personal control over their own thoughts, feelings, motivations, and actions.
Longitudinal research	Research that studies the same subjects over an extended period of time, usually several years or more, is called longitudinal research.
Shyness	A tendency to avoid others plus uneasiness and strain when socializing is called shyness.
Kagan	The work of Kagan supports the concept of an inborn, biologically based temperamental predisposition to severe anxiety.
Variable	A variable refers to a measurable factor, characteristic, or attribute of an individual or a system.
Pupil	In the eye, the pupil is the opening in the middle of the iris. It appears black because most of the light entering it is absorbed by the tissues inside the eye. The size of the pupil is controlled by involuntary contraction and dilation of the iris, in order to regulate the intensity of light entering the eye. This is known as the pupillary reflex.
Adolescence	The period of life bounded by puberty and the assumption of adult responsibilities is adolescence.
Infant mortality	Infant mortality is the death of infants in the first year of life. The leading causes of infant mortality are dehydration and disease. Major causes of infant mortality in more developed countries include congenital malformation, infection and SIDS. Infant mortality rate is the number of newborns dying under a year of age divided by the number of live births during the year.
Harlow	Harlow and his famous wire and cloth surrogate mother monkey studies demonstrated that the need for affection created a stronger bond between mother and infant than did physical needs. He also found that the more discrimination problems the monkeys solved, the better they became at solving them.
Surrogate mother	A surrogate mother is a woman who carries a child for a couple or single person with the intention of giving that child up once it is born.

Nurture	Nurture refers to the environmental influences on behavior due to nutrition, culture, socioeconomic status, and learning.
Psychosocial development	Erikson's psychosocial development describe eight developmental stages through which a healthily developing human should pass from infancy to late adulthood. In each stage the person confronts, and hopefully masters, new challenges.
Primary caregiver	Primary caregiver refers to a person primarily responsible for the care of an infant, usually the infant's mother or father.
Gender role	A cluster of behaviors that characterizes traditional female or male behaviors within a cultural setting is a gender role.
Gender difference	A gender difference is a disparity between genders involving quality or quantity. Though some gender differences are controversial, they are not to be confused with sexist stereotypes.
Motivation	In psychology, motivation is the driving force (desire) behind all actions of an organism.
Affect	A subjective feeling or emotional tone often accompanied by bodily expressions noticeable to others is called affect.
Shaping	The concept of reinforcing successive, increasingly accurate approximations to a target behavior is called shaping. The target behavior is broken down into a hierarchy of elemental steps, each step more sophisticated then the last. By successively reinforcing each of the the elemental steps, a form of differential reinforcement, until that step is learned while extinguishing the step below, the target behavior is gradually achieved.
Gender-typing	The process by which people acquire a sense of being female or male and acquire the traits considered typical of females or males within a cultural setting is referred to as gender-typing.
Socialization	Social rules and social relations are created, communicated, and changed in verbal and nonverbal ways creating social complexity useful in identifying outsiders and intelligent breeding partners. The process of learning these skills is called socialization.
Reliability	Reliability means the extent to which a test produces a consistent , reproducible score .
Attachment	Attachment is the tendency to seek closeness to another person and feel secure when that person is present.
Ethological theory	Ethological theory is a developmental theory based on biological and evolutionary determinants characterized by critical periods for development to occur normally.
Bowlby	Bowlby, a developmental psychologist of the psychoanalytic tradition, was responsible for much of the early research conducted on attachment in humans. He identified three stages of separation: protest, despair, and detachment.
Psychoanalytic	Freud's theory that unconscious forces act as determinants of personality is called psychoanalytic theory. The theory is a developmental theory characterized by critical stages of development.
Strange situation	An observational measure of infant attachment that requires the infant to move through a series of introductions, separations, and reunions with the caregiver and an adult stranger in a prescribed order is called Ainsworth's strange situation.
Basic trust versus basic mistrust	Erikson's first stage, when infants develop trust or mistrust based on the quality of care, love, and affection provided is called the basic trust versus basic mistrust stage.
Secure attachment	With secure attachment, the infant uses a caregiver as a secure base from which to explore the environment. Ainsworth believes that secure attachment in the first year of life provides

	an important foundation for psychological development later in life.
Avoidant attachment	A type of insecure attachment characterized by apparent indifference to the leave-takings of, and reunions with, an attachment figure is referred to as avoidant attachment.
Validity	The extent to which a test measures what it is intended to measure is called validity.
Disorganized-disoriented attachment	Disorganized-disoriented attachment is insecure attachment characterized by dazed and contradictory behaviors toward an attachment figure.
Q-sort technique	The Q-sort technique is a standardized procedure forassessing the self-concept. It entails making ranked comparative judgments of statements about one's self.
Population	Population refers to all members of a well-defined group of organisms, events, or things.
Insecure attachment	Insecure attachment occurs when infants either avoid the caregiver or show considerable resistance or ambivalence toward the caregiver.
Sexual abuse	Sexual abuse is a term used to describe non- consentual sexual relations between two or more parties which are considered criminally and/or morally offensive.
Perception	Perception is the process of acquiring, interpreting, selecting, and organizing sensory information.
Attachment theory	Attachment theory is a theory about the psychological tendency to seek closeness to another person and feel secure when that person is present. A criticism of the theory is that it ignores the diversity of socializing agents and contexts that exists.
Continuity of development	The gradual, cumulative change from conception to death is called the continuity of development.
Friendship	The essentials of friendship are reciprocity and commitment between individuals who see themselves more or less as equals. Interaction between friends rests on a more equal power base than the interaction between children and adults.
Self-image	A person's self-image is the mental picture, generally of a kind that is quite resistant to change, that depicts not only details that are potentially available to objective investigation by others, but also items that have been learned by that person about himself or herself.
Mutual regulation	Mutual regulation is the process by which infant and caregiver communicate emotional states to each other and respond appropriately.
Research method	The scope of the research method is to produce some new knowledge. This, in principle, can take three main forms: Exploratory research; Constructive research; and Empirical research.
Brazelton	Brazelton Neonatal Behavioral Assessment Scale is a test given several days after birth to assess newborns' neurological development, reflexes, and reactions to people.
Paradigm	Paradigm refers to the set of practices that defines a scientific discipline during a particular period of time. It provides a framework from which to conduct research, it ensures that a certain range of phenomena, those on which the paradigm focuses, are explored thoroughly. Itmay also blind scientists to other, perhaps more fruitful, ways of dealing with their subject matter.
Postpartum depression	After giving birth, about 70-80% of women experience an episode of baby blues, feelings of depression, anger, anxiety and guilt lasting for several days. About 10% of new mothers develop the more severe postpartum depression, a form of major depression for which treatment is widely recommended.
Depression	In everyday language depression refers to any downturn in mood, which may be relatively

	transitory and perhaps due to something trivial. This is differentiated from Clinical depression which is marked by symptoms that last two weeks or more and are so severe that they interfere with daily living.
Chronic	Chronic refers to a relatively long duration, usually more than a few months.
Brain	The brain controls and coordinates most movement, behavior and homeostatic body functions such as heartbeat, blood pressure, fluid balance and body temperature. Functions of the brain are responsible for cognition, emotion, memory, motor learning and other sorts of learning. The brain is primarily made up of two types of cells: glia and neurons.
Neurotransmitter	A neurotransmitter is a chemical that is used to relay, amplify and modulate electrical signals between a neurons and another cell.
Stress hormones	Group of hormones including cortico steroids, that are involved in the body's physiological stress response are referred to as stress hormones.
Norepinephrine	Norepinephrine is released from the adrenal glands as a hormone into the blood, but it is also a neurotransmitter in the nervous system. As a stress hormone, it affects parts of the human brain where attention and impulsivity are controlled. Along with epinephrine, this compound effects the fight-or-flight response, activating the sympathetic nervous system to directly increase heart rate, release energy from fat, and increase muscle readiness.
Dopamine	Dopamine is critical to the way the brain controls our movements and is a crucial part of the basal ganglia motor loop. It is commonly associated with the 'pleasure system' of the brain, providing feelings of enjoyment and reinforcement to motivate us to do, or continue doing, certain activities.
Cortisol	Cortisol is a corticosteroid hormone that is involved in the response to stress; it increases blood pressure and blood sugar levels and suppresses the immune system. Synthetic cortisol, also known as hydrocortisone, is used as a drug mainly to fight allergies and inflammation.
Prenatal	Prenatal period refers to the time from conception to birth.
Antidepressant	An antidepressant is a medication used primarily in the treatment of clinical depression. They are not thought to produce tolerance, although sudden withdrawal may produce adverse effects. They create little if any immediate change in mood and require between several days and several weeks to take effect.
Psychotherapy	Psychotherapy is a set of techniques based on psychological principles intended to improve mental health, emotional or behavioral issues.
Separation anxiety	Separation anxiety is a psychological condition in which an individual has excessive anxiety regarding separation from home, or from those with whom the individual has a strong attachment.
Cognitive development	The process by which a child's understanding of the world changes as a function of age and experience is called cognitive development.
Social referencing	Social referencing refers to the process by which infants use the nonverbal emotional expressions of a caregiver as cues to guide their behavior.
Internalization	The developmental change from behavior that is externally controlled to behavior that is controlled by internal standards and principles is referred to as internalization.
Autonomy	Autonomy is the condition of something that does not depend on anything else.
Self-concept	Self-concept refers to domain-specific evaluations of the self where a domain may be academics, athletics, etc.
Trait	An enduring personality characteristic that tends to lead to certain behaviors is called a

	trait. The term trait also means a genetically inherited feature of an organism.
Sensorimotor	The first of Piaget's stages is the Sensorimotor stage. This stage typically ranges from birth to 2 years. In this stage, children experience the world through their senses. During this stage, object permanence and stranger anxiety develop.
Self-efficacy	Self-efficacy is the belief that one has the capabilities to execute the courses of actions required to manage prospective situations.
Bandura	Bandura is best known for his work on social learning theory or Social Cognitivism. His famous Bobo doll experiment illustrated that people learn from observing others.
Connectedness	Connectedness, according to Cooper, consists of two dimensions: mutuality and permeability. Connectedness involves processes that link the self to others, as seen in acknowledgment of, respect for, and responsiveness to others.
Affective	Affective is the way people react emotionally, their ability to feel another living thing's pain or joy.
Discrimination	In Learning theory, discrimination refers the ability to distinguish between a conditioned stimulus and other stimuli. It can be brought about by extensive training or differential reinforcement. In social terms, it is the denial of privileges to a person or a group on the basis of prejudice.
Autonomy versus shame and doubt	In Erikson's second stage of development, autonomy versus shame and doubt, which occurs in late infancy and toddlerhood, infants begin to discover that their behavior is their own.
Stages	Stages represent relatively discrete periods of time in which functioning is qualitatively different from functioning at other periods.
Motives	Needs or desires that energize and direct behavior toward a goal are motives.
Punishment	Punishment is the addtion of a stimulus that reduces the frequency of a response, or the removal of a stimulus that results in a reduction of the response.
Moral development	Development regarding rules and conventions about what people should do in their interactions with other people is called moral development.
Superego	Frued's third psychic structure, which functions as a moral guardian and sets forth high standards for behavior is the superego.
Early childhood	Early childhood refers to the developmental period extending from the end of infancy to about 5 or 6 years of age; sometimes called the preschool years.
Mischel	Mischel is known for his cognitive social learning model of personality that focuses on the specific cognitive variables that mediate the manner in which new experiences affect the individual.
Obedience	Obedience is the willingness to follow the will of others. Humans have been shown to be surprisingly obedient in the presence of perceived legitimate authority figures, as demonstrated by the Milgram experiment in the 1960s.
Laboratory setting	Research setting in which the behavior of interest does not naturally occur is called a laboratory setting.
Situational compliance	Obedience of a parent's orders only in the presence of prompting or other signs of ongoing parental control is situational compliance.
Survey	A method of scientific investigation in which a large sample of people answer questions about their attitudes or behavior is referred to as a survey.
Sleep patterns	The order and timing of daily sleep and waking periods are called sleep patterns.

Child abuse	Child abuse is the physical or psychological maltreatment of a child.
Gross motor skills	Gross motor skills refer to motor skills that involve large muscle activities, such as walking.
Handedness	A preference for the right or left hand in most activities is referred to as handedness. Right-handedness is dominant in all cultures, and it appears before culture can influence the child.
Altruism	Altruism is being helpful to other people with little or no interest in being rewarded for one's efforts. This is distinct from merely helping others.
Stroke	A stroke occurs when the blood supply to a part of the brain is suddenly interrupted by occlusion, by hemorrhage, or other causes

Early childhood	Early childhood refers to the developmental period extending from the end of infancy to about 5 or 6 years of age; sometimes called the preschool years.
Toddler	A toddler is a child between the ages of one and three years old. During this period, the child learns a great deal about social roles and develops motor skills; to toddle is to walk unsteadily.
Protein	A protein is a complex, high-molecular-weight organic compound that consists of amino acids joined by peptide bonds. It is essential to the structure and function of all living cells and viruses. Many are enzymes or subunits of enzymes.
Body mass index	The body mass index is a calculated number, used to compare and analyse the health effects of body weight on human bodies of all heights. It is equal to the weight, divided by the square of the height.
Obesity	The state of being more than 20 percent above the average weight for a person of one's height is called obesity.
Nervous system	The body's electrochemical communication circuitry, made up of billions of neurons is a nervous system.
Brain	The brain controls and coordinates most movement, behavior and homeostatic body functions such as heartbeat, blood pressure, fluid balance and body temperature. Functions of the brain are responsible for cognition, emotion, memory, motor learning and other sorts of learning. The brain is primarily made up of two types of cells: glia and neurons.
Immune system	The most important function of the human immune system occurs at the cellular level of the blood and tissues. The lymphatic and blood circulation systems are highways for specialized white blood cells. These cells include B cells, T cells, natural killer cells, and macrophages. All function with the primary objective of recognizing, attacking and destroying bacteria, viruses, cancer cells, and all substances seen as foreign.
Habit	A habit is a response that has become completely separated from its eliciting stimulus. Early learning theorists used the term to describe S-R associations, however not all S-R associations become a habit, rather many are extinguished after reinforcement is withdrawn.
Sleep patterns	The order and timing of daily sleep and waking periods are called sleep patterns.
Separation anxiety	Separation anxiety is a psychological condition in which an individual has excessive anxiety regarding separation from home, or from those with whom the individual has a strong attachment.
Infancy	The developmental period that extends from birth to 18 or 24 months is called infancy.
Nightmare	Nightmare was the original term for the state later known as waking dream, and more currently as sleep paralysis, associated with rapid eye movement (REM) periods of sleep.
Sleep terror	A sleep terror is a parasomnia sleep disorder characterized by extreme terror and a temporary inability to regain full consciousness. The subject wakes abruptly from the fourth stage of sleep, with waking usually accompanied by gasping, moaning, or screaming. It is often impossible to fully awaken the person, and after the episode the subject normally settles back to sleep without waking. Sometimes the sleep terror can be recalled by the subject.
Deep sleep	Deep sleep refers to stage 4 sleep; the deepest form of normal sleep.
Sensation	Sensation is the first stage in the chain of biochemical and neurologic events that begins with the impinging of a stimulus upon the receptor cells of a sensory organ, which then leads to perception, the mental state that is reflected in statements like "I see a uniformly blue wall."
Behavioral	Behavioral control refers to the contingencies that determine the expression of a behavior

control	through manipulations of reinforcement and punishment.
Enuresis	Enuresis is involuntary urination while asleep. It is the normal state of affairs in infancy, but can be a source of embarrassment when it persists into school age or the teen years.
Gross motor skills	Gross motor skills refer to motor skills that involve large muscle activities, such as walking.
Cognitive development	The process by which a child's understanding of the world changes as a function of age and experience is called cognitive development.
Pictorial stage	A developmental stage in drawing attained between ages 4 and 5 in which designs begin to resemble recognizable objects is called the pictorial stage.
Creativity	Creativity is the ability to think about something in novel and unusual ways and come up with unique solutions to problems. It involves divergent thinking, having many solutions or views to a problem.
Handedness	A preference for the right or left hand in most activities is referred to as handedness. Right-handedness is dominant in all cultures, and it appears before culture can influence the child.
Representational ability	The child's representational ability in Piaget's theory is the capacity to store mental images or symbols of objects and events.
Left hemisphere	The left hemisphere of the cortex controls the right side of the body, coordinates complex movements, and, in 95% of people, controls the production of speech and written language.
Right hemisphere	The brain is divided into left and right cerebral hemispheres. The right hemisphere of the cortex controls the left side of the body.
Gene	A gene is an ultramicroscopic area of the chromosome. It is the smallest physical unit of the DNA molecule that carries a piece of hereditary information.
Population	Population refers to all members of a well-defined group of organisms, events, or things.
Monozygotic	Identical twins occur when a single egg is fertilized to form one zygote, calld monozygotic, but the zygote then divides into two separate embryos. The two embryos develop into foetuses sharing the same womb. Monozygotic twins are genetically identical unless there has been a mutation in development, and they are almost always the same gender.
Measles	Measles, also known as rubeola, is a common disease caused by a virus of the genus Morbillivirus. Complications with measles are relatively common, ranging from relatively common and less serious diarrhea, to pneumonia and encephalitis. Complications are usually more severe amongst infants and adults who catch the virus.
Statistics	Statistics is a type of data analysis which practice includes the planning, summarizing, and interpreting of observations of a system possibly followed by predicting or forecasting of future events based on a mathematical model of the system being observed.
Adolescence	The period of life bounded by puberty and the assumption of adult responsibilities is adolescence.
Attention	Attention is the cognitive process of selectively concentrating on one thing while ignoring other things. Psychologists have labeled three types of attention: sustained attention, selective attention, and divided attention.
Temperament	Temperament refers to a basic, innate disposition to change behavior. The activity level is an important dimension of temperament.
Bioecological theory	Urie Bronfenbrenner's theory, bioecological theory, suggests that human behavioral development is shaped by one's environment. The theory cites "spheres of influence" to show

	the relevance of social spheres on behavioral development. Key factors include culture, ethnicity, and gender.
Bronfenbrenner	Bronfenbrenner was a co-founder of the U.S. national Head Start program and founder of the Ecological Theory of Development.
Society	The social sciences use the term society to mean a group of people that form a semi-closed (or semi-open) social system, in which most interactions are with other individuals belonging to the group.
Secondhand smoke	Also referred to as sidestream smoke, the smoke from the burning end of a cigarette, which contains higher concentrations of ammonia, carbon monoxide, nicotine, and tar than does the smoke inhaled by the smoker is called secondhand smoke.
Substance abuse	Substance abuse refers to the overindulgence in and dependence on a stimulant, depressant, or other chemical substance, leading to effects that are detrimental to the individual's physical or mental health, or the welfare of others.
Otitis media	Otitis media refers to infection of the middle ear, an extremely common childhood problem; the attendant temporary or chronic hearing loss may lead to language development delays.
Middle ear	The middle ear consists of the eardrum, hammer, anvil, and stirrup.
Asthma	Asthma is a complex disease characterized by bronchial hyperresponsiveness (BHR), inflammation, mucus production and intermittent airway obstruction.
Prenatal	Prenatal period refers to the time from conception to birth.
Depression	In everyday language depression refers to any downturn in mood, which may be relatively transitory and perhaps due to something trivial. This is differentiated from Clinical depression which is marked by symptoms that last two weeks or more and are so severe that they interfere with daily living.
Learning	Learning is a relatively permanent change in behavior that results from experience. Thus, to attribute a behavioral change to learning, the change must be relatively permanent and must result from experience.
Anxiety	Anxiety is a complex combination of the feeling of fear, apprehension and worry often accompanied by physical sensations such as palpitations, chest pain and/or shortness of breath.
Piaget	Piaget argued that young children's answers were qualitatively different than older children rather than quantitative. There are two major aspects to his theory: the process of coming to know and the stages we move through as we gradually acquire this ability.
Mental Representation	Stage six of the sensorimotor substages, Mental representation, 18 months to 2 years, marks the beginnings of insight, or true creativity. This marks the passage into unique thought in Piaget's later three areas of development.
Symbolic function	The symbolic function in Piaget's theory is the underlying symbolic nature of cognition, occurring toward the end of the sensorimotor period and expressed via deferred imitation, language, symbolic play, and mental imagery.
Sensorimotor	The first of Piaget's stages is the Sensorimotor stage. This stage typically ranges from birth to 2 years. In this stage, children experience the world through their senses. During this stage, object permanence and stranger anxiety develop.
Cones	Cones are photoreceptors that transmit sensations of color, function in bright light, and used in visual acuity. Infants prior to months of age can only distinguish green and red indicating the cones are not fully developed; they can see all of the colors by 2 months of

Conservation	Conservation refers to the recognition that basic properties of substances such as weight and mass remain the same even when transformations merely alter their appearance.
Inductive reasoning	A form of reasoning in which we reason from individual cases or particular facts to a general conclusion is referred to as inductive reasoning. The conclusion can be said to follow with a probability rather than certainty.
Deferred imitation	Imitation that occurs after a time delay of hours or days is referred to as deferred imitation.
Pretend play	According to Piaget and Smilansky, pretend play is the third cognitive level of play. It involves imaginary people or situations.
Dual representation hypothesis	The dual representation hypothesis proposes that children under the age of 3 have difficulty grasping spatial relationships because of the need to keep more than one mental representation in mind at the same time.
Microgenetic	A design that allows researchers to directly observe change by repeated testing over a relatively short time period is called a microgenetic study. The idea is to study change as change is occurring.
Naturalistic observation	Naturalistic observation is a method of observation that involves observing subjects in their natural habitats. Researchers take great care in avoiding making interferences with the behavior they are observing by using unobtrusive methods.
Causation	Causation concerns the time order relationship between two or more objects such that if a specific antecendent condition occurs the same consequent must always follow.
Reasoning	Reasoning is the act of using reason to derive a conclusion from certain premises. There are two main methods to reach a conclusion,deductive reasoning and inductive reasoning.
Emotion	An emotion is a mental states that arise spontaneously, rather than through conscious effort. They are often accompanied by physiological changes.
Formal operations	Formal operations in Piaget's theory is the final stage of cognitive development, in which children are able to apply abstract logical rules. Not everyone reaches the formal operations stage of development.
Transduction	Transduction in the nervous system typically refers to synaptic events wherein an electrical signal, known as an action potential, is converted into a chemical one via the release of neurotransmitters. Conversely, in sensory transduction a chemical or physical stimulus is transduced by sensory receptors into an electrical signal.
Relative size	Relative size is a monocular cue where an an automobile that is close to us seems larger than one that is far away. The visual system exploits the relative size of similar (or familiar) objects to judge distance.
Parietal lobe	The parietal lobe is positioned above (superior to) the occipital lobe and behind (posterior to) the frontal lobe. It plays important roles in integrating sensory information from various senses, and in the manipulation of objects.
Concrete operations	In Piaget's theory, the third major stage of cognitive development, in which children can decenter their perception, are less egocentric, and can think logically about concrete objects is called concrete operations.
Egocentrism	The inability to distinguish between one's own perspective and someone else's is referred to as egocentrism.
Mental processes	The thoughts, feelings, and motives that each of us experiences privately but that cannot be observed directly are called mental processes.

Theory of mind A theory of mind considers the nature of mind, and its structure and processes

Social cognition Social cognition is the name for both a branch of psychology that studies the cognitive processes involved in social interaction, and an umbrella term for the processes themselves. It uses the tools and assumptions of cognitive psychology to study how people understand themselves and others in society and social situations.

Empathy Empathy is the recognition and understanding of the states of mind, including beliefs, desires and particularly emotions of others without injecting your own.

Sullivan Sullivan developed the Self System, a configuration of the personality traits developed in childhood and reinforced by positive affirmation and the security operations developed in childhood to avoid anxiety and threats to self-esteem.

Displacement An unconscious defense mechanism in which the individual directs aggressive or sexual feelings away from the primary object to someone or something safe is referred to as displacement. Displacement in linguistics is simply the ability to talk about things not present.

Magical thinking Magical thinking is a term used to describe non-scientific causal reasoning. Magical thinking depends on two laws: the law of similarity (an effect resembles its cause), and the law of contagion (things which were once in physical contact maintain a connection even after physical contact has been broken).

Syndrome The term syndrome is the association of several clinically recognizable features, signs, symptoms, phenomena or characteristics which often occur together, so that the presence of one feature indicates the presence of the others.

Frontal lobe The frontal lobe comprises four major folds of cortical tissue: the precentral gyrus, superior gyrus and the middle gyrus of the frontal gyri, the inferior frontal gyrus. It has been found to play a part in impulse control, judgement, language, memory, motor function, problem solving, sexual behavior, socialization and spontaneity.

Heritability Heritability It is that proportion of the observed variation in a particular phenotype within a particular population, that can be attributed to the contribution of genotype. In other words: it measures the extent to which differences between individuals in a population are due their being different genetically.

Affect A subjective feeling or emotional tone often accompanied by bodily expressions noticeable to others is called affect.

Social skills Social skills are skills used to interact and communicate with others to assist status in the social structure and other motivations.

Attitude An enduring mental representation of a person, place, or thing that evokes an emotional response and related behavior is called attitude.

Syntax Syntax can be described as the study of the rules, or "patterned relations" that govern the way the words in a sentence come together.

Fast mapping In cognitive psychology, fast mapping is a mental process whereby a new concept can be learned based only on a single exposure to a given unit of information. Fast mapping is particularly important during language acquisition in young children, and serves (at least in part) to explain the prodigious rate at which children gain vocabulary.

Hypothesis A specific statement about behavior or mental processes that is testable through research is a hypothesis.

Graham Graham has conducted a number of studies that reveal stronger socioeconomic-status influences rather than ethnic influences in achievement.

Private speech
Private speech refers to children's speech designed apparently for the self and not directed at others.

Preoperational stage
The Preoperational stage is the second stage of development in Piaget's theory. By observing sequences of play, Piaget was able to demonstrate that towards the end of the second year a qualitatively quite new kind of functioning occurs. Operation in Piagetian theory is any procedure for mentally acting on objects.

Maturation
The orderly unfolding of traits, as regulated by the genetic code is called maturation.

Pragmatics
Pragmatics is generally the study of natural language understanding, and specifically the study of how context influences the interpretation of meanings. It is a subfield of linguistics.

Inner speech
In Vvgotsky's theory, the covert language used to guide thought is referred to as inner speech.

Vygotsky
The Vygotsky model of human development has been termed as a sociocultural approach. The individual's development is a result of his or her culture.

Individual differences
Individual differences psychology studies the ways in which individual people differ in their behavior. This is distinguished from other aspects of psychology in that although psychology is ostensibly a study of individuals, modern psychologists invariably study groups.

Heredity
Heredity is the transfer of characteristics from parent to offspring through their genes.

Dizygotic
Fraternal twins (commonly known as "non-identical twins") usually occur when two fertilized eggs are implanted in the uterine wall at the same time. The two eggs form two zygotes, and these twins are therefore also known as dizygotic.

Self-image
A person's self-image is the mental picture, generally of a kind that is quite resistant to change, that depicts not only details that are potentially available to objective investigation by others, but also items that have been learned by that person about himself or herself.

Phonemic awareness
Phonemic Awareness is a subset of Phonological Awareness in which listeners are able to distinguish phonemes, the smallest units of sound.

Emergent literacy
Emergent literacy refers to the child's literacy development before receiving formal reading and writing instruction in school.

Phoneme
In oral language, a phoneme is the theoretical basic unit of sound that can be used to distinguish words or morphemes; in sign language, it is a similarly basic unit of hand shape, motion, position, or facial expression.

Longitudinal study
Longitudinal study is a type of developmental study in which the same group of participants is followed and measured for an extended period of time, often years.

Information-processing approach
Information-processing approach emphasizes that individuals act on information, monitor it, and strategize about it--contrary to strict behaviorists. Central to information processing are the processes of memory and thinking. The computer serves as a metaphor whereby the brain is the hardware and behavior is the software.

Retrieval
Retrieval is the location of stored information and its subsequent return to consciousness. It is the third stage of information processing.

Coding
In senation, coding is the process by which information about the quality and quantity of a stimulus is preserved in the pattern of action potentials sent through sensory neurons to the central nervous system.

Stimulus
A change in an environmental condition that elicits a response is a stimulus.

Explicit memory	Intentional or conscious recollection of information is referred to as explicit memory. Children under age three are usually poorest at explicit memory which may be due to the immaturity of the prefrontal lobes of the brain, which are believed to play an important role in memory for events.
Motivation	In psychology, motivation is the driving force (desire) behind all actions of an organism.
Lange	Lange along with William James, independently developed the James-Lange theory of emotion. Unlike James, Lange specifically stated that vasomotor changes are emotions. Lange also noted the psychotropic effects of lithium, although his work in this area was forgotten and independently rediscovered much later.
Script	A schema, or behavioral sequence, for an event is called a script. It is a form of schematic organization, with real-world events organized in terms of temporal and causal relations between component acts.
Episodic memory	Episodic memory is the explicit memory of events. It includes time, place, and associated emotions (which affect the quality of the memorization).
Long-term memory	Long-term memory is memory that lasts from over 30 seconds to years.
Child abuse	Child abuse is the physical or psychological maltreatment of a child.
Reliability	Reliability means the extent to which a test produces a consistent , reproducible score .
Autobiograph-cal memory	An Autobiographical Memory is a personal representation of general or specific events and personal facts.
Psychometric	Psychometric study is concerned with the theory and technique of psychological measurement, which includes the measurement of knowledge, abilities, attitudes, and personality traits. The field is primarily concerned with the study of differences between individuals
Intelligence test	An intelligence test is a standardized means of assessing a person's current mental ability, for example, the Stanford-Binet test and the Wechsler Adult Intelligence Scale.
Correlation	A statistical technique for determining the degree of association between two or more variables is referred to as correlation.
Wechsler Preschool and Primary Scale of Intelligence	The Wechsler Preschool and Primary Scale of intelligence is an IQ test for young children that measures a range of performance, verbal, and preverbal abilities for children from 3 to
Stanford-Binet	Terman released the "Stanford Revision of the Binet-Simon Scale" or the Stanford-Binet for short. Using validation experiments, he removed several of the Binet-Simon test items and added new ones. In 1985 it was revised to analyze an individual's responses in four content areas: verbal reasoning, quantitative reasoning, abstract reasoning, and short-term memory.
Spatial orientation	Spatial orientation refers to how people understand the placement of objects in space with themselves as the reference point.
Verbal intelligence	Verbal intelligence is measured by answering questions involving vocabulary , general information , arithmetic , and other languageor symbol-oriented tasks.
Wechsler Intelligence Scale for Children	The Wechsler Intelligence Scale for Children is an intelligence test that can be completed without reading or writing. It generates an IQ score. It also generates four composite scores; Verbal Comprehension, Perceptual Reasoning, Processing Speed and Working Memory.
Adoption studies	Research studies that assess hereditary influence by examining the resemblance between adopted children and both their biological and their adoptive parents are referred to as

	adoption studies. The studies have been inconclusive about the relative importance of heredity in intelligence.
Proximal	Students can set both long-term (distal) and short-term (proximal) goals .
Feedback	Feedback refers to information returned to a person about the effects a response has had.
Montessori	As an educational approach, the Montessori method's central focus is on the needs, talents, gifts, and special individuality of each child. Montessori practitioners believe children learn best in their own way at their own pace.
Theories	Theories are logically self-consistent models or frameworks describing the behavior of a certain natural or social phenomenon. They are broad explanations and predictions concerning phenomena of interest.
Individualism	Individualism refers to putting personal goals ahead of group goals and defining one's identity in terms of personal attributes rather than group memberships.
Field study	Field study refers to any scientific research study in which data are collected in a setting other than the laboratory.
Project head start	Project Head Start is a program of the US government's Department of Health and Human Services which focuses on assisting low-income children, through five years of age; so that they are prepared for school.
Cognitive skills	Cognitive skills such as reasoning, attention, and memory can be advanced and sustained through practice and training.
Self-worth	In psychology, self-esteem or self-worth refers to a person's subjective appraisal of himself or herself as intrinsically positive or negative to some degree.
Juvenile delinquent	An adolescent who breaks the law or engages in behavior that is considered illegal is referred to as a juvenile delinquent.
Control group	A group that does not receive the treatment effect in an experiment is referred to as the control group or sometimes as the comparison group.
Enrichment	Deliberately making an environment more novel, complex, and perceptually or intellectually stimulating is referred to as enrichment.
Punishment	Punishment is the addtion of a stimulus that reduces the frequency of a response, or the removal of a stimulus that results in a reduction of the response.
Protective factors	Protective factors are influences that reduce the impact of early stress and tend to lead to positive outcomes.
Design stage	A stage in drawing in which children begin to combine shapes is the design stage.
Shape stage	A stage in drawing, attained by age 3, in which children draw basic shapes such as circles, squares, triangles, crosses, and odd shapes is called the shape stage.
Stages	Stages represent relatively discrete periods of time in which functioning is qualitatively different from functioning at other periods.
Encoding	Encoding refers to interpreting; transforming; modifying information so that it can be placed in memory. It is the first stage of information processing.
Socioeconomic	Socioeconomic pertains to the study of the social and economic impacts of any product or service offering, market intervention or other activity on an economy as a whole and on the companies, organization and individuals who are its main economic actors.
Initiative versus guilt	Initiative versus guilt is Erikson's third stage of development, which occurs during the preschool years. As preschool children encounter a widening social world, they are challenged

	more than they were as infants.
Gender difference	A gender difference is a disparity between genders involving quality or quantity. Though some gender differences are controversial, they are not to be confused with sexist stereotypes.
Self-concept	Self-concept refers to domain-specific evaluations of the self where a domain may be academics, athletics, etc.
Self-esteem	Self-esteem refers to a person's subjective appraisal of himself or herself as intrinsically positive or negative to some degree.
Types of play	The most widely studied types of play include: sensorimotor and practice play, pretend and symbolic play, and games.
Altruism	Altruism is being helpful to other people with little or no interest in being rewarded for one's efforts. This is distinct from merely helping others.
Tics	Tics are a repeated, impulsive action, almost reflexive in nature, which the person feels powerless to control or avoid.

Trait	An enduring personality characteristic that tends to lead to certain behaviors is called a trait. The term trait also means a genetically inherited feature of an organism.
Self-image	A person's self-image is the mental picture, generally of a kind that is quite resistant to change, that depicts not only details that are potentially available to objective investigation by others, but also items that have been learned by that person about himself or herself.
Self-awareness	Realization that one's existence and functioning are separate from those of other people and things is called self-awareness.
Self-concept	Self-concept refers to domain-specific evaluations of the self where a domain may be academics, athletics, etc.
Adolescence	The period of life bounded by puberty and the assumption of adult responsibilities is adolescence.
Emotion	An emotion is a mental states that arise spontaneously, rather than through conscious effort. They are often accompanied by physiological changes.
Single representations	Single representations in neo-Piagetian terminology is the first stage in development of self-definition, in which children describe themselves in individual, unconnected characteristics and in all-or-nothing terms.
Representational mappings	In neo-Piagetian terminology, the second stage in development of self-definition, in which a child makes logical connections between aspects of the self but still sees these characteristics in all-or-nothing terms, is called representational mappings.
Attachment	Attachment is the tendency to seek closeness to another person and feel secure when that person is present.
Early childhood	Early childhood refers to the developmental period extending from the end of infancy to about 5 or 6 years of age; sometimes called the preschool years.
Guilt	Guilt describes many concepts related to a negative emotion or condition caused by actions which are believed to be, morally wrong. According to Freud, the avoidance of guilt is the basis for moral behavior.
Affect	A subjective feeling or emotional tone often accompanied by bodily expressions noticeable to others is called affect.
Individual differences	Individual differences psychology studies the ways in which individual people differ in their behavior. This is distinguished from other aspects of psychology in that although psychology is ostensibly a study of individuals, modern psychologists invariably study groups.
Psychosocial development	Erikson's psychosocial development describe eight developmental stages through which a healthily developing human should pass from infancy to late adulthood. In each stage the person confronts, and hopefully masters, new challenges.
Initiative versus guilt	Initiative versus guilt is Erikson's third stage of development, which occurs during the preschool years. As preschool children encounter a widening social world, they are challenged more than they were as infants.
Self-esteem	Self-esteem refers to a person's subjective appraisal of himself or herself as intrinsically positive or negative to some degree.
Punishment	Punishment is the addtion of a stimulus that reduces the frequency of a response, or the removal of a stimulus that results in a reduction of the response.
Self-worth	In psychology, self-esteem or self-worth refers to a person's subjective appraisal of himself or herself as intrinsically positive or negative to some degree.

Cowan	Cowan regards working memory not as a separate system, but as a part of long-term memory. Representations in working memory are a subset of the representations in long-term memory.
Perception	Perception is the process of acquiring, interpreting, selecting, and organizing sensory information.
Internalization	The developmental change from behavior that is externally controlled to behavior that is controlled by internal standards and principles is referred to as internalization.
All-or-none	All-or-none indicates a situation in which there are two possibilities (a binary choice set), one of which is 100% and one of which is 0%. It is a phrase commonly used to describe action potentials of neurons, which, if they fire at all, propagate from the beginning to the end of the axonal process.
Feedback	Feedback refers to information returned to a person about the effects a response has had.
Shaping	The concept of reinforcing successive, increasingly accurate approximations to a target behavior is called shaping. The target behavior is broken down into a hierarchy of elemental steps, each step more sophisticated then the last. By successively reinforcing each of the the elemental steps, a form of differential reinforcement, until that step is learned while extinguishing the step below, the target behavior is gradually achieved.
Personality	Personality refers to the pattern of enduring characteristics that differentiates a person, the patterns of behaviors that make each individual unique.
Gender identity	Gender identity describes the gender with which a person identifies, but can also be used to refer to the gender that other people attribute to the individual on the basis of what they know from gender role indications.
Society	The social sciences use the term society to mean a group of people that form a semi-closed (or semi-open) social system, in which most interactions are with other individuals belonging to the group.
Gender difference	A gender difference is a disparity between genders involving quality or quantity. Though some gender differences are controversial, they are not to be confused with sexist stereotypes.
Infancy	The developmental period that extends from birth to 18 or 24 months is called infancy.
Intelligence test	An intelligence test is a standardized means of assessing a person's current mental ability, for example, the Stanford-Binet test and the Wechsler Adult Intelligence Scale.
Overt aggression	Aggression that is openly directed at its target is referred to as overt aggression.
Scientific reasoning	A type of reasoning that involves the generation of hypotheses and the systematic testing of those hypotheses is scientific reasoning.
Gender stereotypes	Broad categories that reflect our impressions and beliefs about typical females and males are referred to as gender stereotypes.
Gender-typing	The process by which people acquire a sense of being female or male and acquire the traits considered typical of females or males within a cultural setting is referred to as gender-typing.
Gender role	A cluster of behaviors that characterizes traditional female or male behaviors within a cultural setting is a gender role.
Attitude	An enduring mental representation of a person, place, or thing that evokes an emotional response and related behavior is called attitude.
Generalization	In conditioning, the tendency for a conditioned response to be evoked by stimuli that are similar to the stimulus to which the response was conditioned is a generalization. The greater the similarity among the stimuli, the greater the probability of generalization.

Stereotype

A stereotype is considered to be a group concept, held by one social group about another.They are often used in a negative or prejudicial sense and are frequently used to justify certain discriminatory behaviors. This allows powerful social groups to legitimize and protect their dominant position

Nurture

Nurture refers to the environmental influences on behavior due to nutrition, culture, socioeconomic status, and learning.

Cerebral cortex

The cerebral cortex is the outermost layer of the cerebrum and has a grey color. It is made up of four lobes and it is involved in many complex brain functions including memory, perceptual awareness, "thinking", language and consciousness. The cerebral cortex receives sensory information from many different sensory organs eg: eyes, ears, etc. and processes the information.

Gray matter

Gray matter is a category of nervous tissue with many nerve cell bodies and few myelinated axons. Generally, gray matter can be understood as the parts of the brain responsible for information processing; whereas, white matter is responsible for information transmission. In addition, gray matter does not have a myelin sheath and does not regenerate after injury unlike white matter.

Brain

The brain controls and coordinates most movement, behavior and homeostatic body functions such as heartbeat, blood pressure, fluid balance and body temperature. Functions of the brain are responsible for cognition, emotion, memory, motor learning and other sorts of learning. The brain is primarily made up of two types of cells: glia and neurons.

Corpus callosum

The corpus callosum is the largest white matter structure in the brain. It consists of mostly of contralateral axon projections. The corpus callosum connects the left and right cerebral hemispheres. Most communication between regions in different halves of the brain are carried over the corpus callosum.

Hormone

A hormone is a chemical messenger from one cell (or group of cells) to another. The best known are those produced by endocrine glands, but they are produced by nearly every organ system. The function of hormones is to serve as a signal to the target cells; the action of the hormone is determined by the pattern of secretion and the signal transduction of the receiving tissue.

Psychoanalytic

Freud's theory that unconscious forces act as determinants of personality is called psychoanalytic theory. The theory is a developmental theory characterized by critical stages of development.

Cognitive approach

A cognitive approach focuses on the mental processes involved in knowing: how we direct our attention, perceive, remember, think, and solve problems.

Schema

Schema refers to a way of mentally representing the world, such as a belief or an expectation, that can influence perception of persons, objects, and situations.

Socialization

Social rules and social relations are created, communicated, and changed in verbal and nonverbal ways creating social complexity useful in identifying outsiders and intelligent breeding partners. The process of learning these skills is called socialization.

Congenital adrenal hyperplasia

Congenital adrenal hyperplasia refers to a group of inherited disorders relating to the adrenal glands, characterized by a deficiency in the hormones cortisol and aldosterone and an overproduction of androgen. Without these hormones, steroids are 'diverted' to becoming androgens, a form of male sex hormones. This causes early (or inappropriate) appearance of male characteristics.

Prenatal

Prenatal period refers to the time from conception to birth.

Androgen

Androgen is the generic term for any natural or synthetic compound, usually a steroid

hormone, that stimulates or controls the development and maintenance of masculine characteristics in vertebrates by binding to androgen receptors.

Estrogen — Estrogen is a group of steroid compounds that function as the primary female sex hormone. They are produced primarily by developing follicles in the ovaries, the corpus luteum and the placenta.

Puberty — Puberty refers to the process of physical changes by which a child's body becomes an adult body capable of reproduction.

Penis — The penis is the external male copulatory organ and the external male organ of urination. In humans, the penis is homologous to the female clitoris, as it develops from the same embryonic structure. It is capable of erection for use in copulation.

Acquisition — Acquisition is the process of adapting to the environment, learning or becoming conditioned. In classical conditoning terms, it is the initial learning of the stimulus response link, which involves a neutral stimulus being associated with a unconditioned stimulus and becoming a conditioned stimulus.

Social learning — Social learning is learning that occurs as a function of observing, retaining and replicating behavior observed in others. Although social learning can occur at any stage in life, it is thought to be particularly important during childhood, particularly as authority becomes important.

Developmental psychologist — A psychologist interested in human growth and development from conception until death is referred to as a developmental psychologist.

Kohlberg — Kohlberg believed that people progressed in their moral reasoning through a series of developmental stages.

Gender constancy — Gender constancy refers to the concept that gender remains the same despite changes in physical appearance, time, and behavior; includes gender identity, gender stability, and gender consistency.

Stages — Stages represent relatively discrete periods of time in which functioning is qualitatively different from functioning at other periods.

Genitals — Genitals refers to the internal and external reproductive organs.

Gender-schema theory — Gender-schema theory suggests that gender identity plus knowledge of behavior patterns of both feminine and masculine roles, motivate and guide the gender-typing of the child.

Gender schema — Gender schema refers to a cognitive structure that organizes the world in terms of maleness and femaleness.

Attention — Attention is the cognitive process of selectively concentrating on one thing while ignoring other things. Psychologists have labeled three types of attention: sustained attention, selective attention, and divided attention.

Learning — Learning is a relatively permanent change in behavior that results from experience. Thus, to attribute a behavioral change to learning, the change must be relatively permanent and must result from experience.

Bandura — Bandura is best known for his work on social learning theory or Social Cognitivism. His famous Bobo doll experiment illustrated that people learn from observing others.

Social cognitive theory — Social cognitive theory defines human behavior as a triadic, dynamic, and reciprocal interaction of personal factors, behavior, and the environment. Response consequences of a behavior are used to form expectations of behavioral outcomes. It is the ability to form these expectations that give humans the capability to predict the outcomes of their behavior, before the behavior is performed.

Vygotsky — The Vygotsky model of human development has been termed as a sociocultural approach. The individual's development is a result of his or her culture.

Friendship — The essentials of friendship are reciprocity and commitment between individuals who see themselves more or less as equals. Interaction between friends rests on a more equal power base than the interaction between children and adults.

Senses — The senses are systems that consist of a sensory cell type that respond to a specific kind of physical energy, and that correspond to a defined region within the brain where the signals are received and interpreted.

Types of play — The most widely studied types of play include: sensorimotor and practice play, pretend and symbolic play, and games.

Gross motor skills — Gross motor skills refer to motor skills that involve large muscle activities, such as walking.

Functional play — Piaget's and Smilansky's concept of functional play is the lowest cognitive level of play, involving repetitive muscular movements.

Pretend play — According to Piaget and Smilansky, pretend play is the third cognitive level of play. It involves imaginary people or situations.

Piaget — Piaget argued that young children's answers were qualitatively different than older children rather than quantitative. There are two major aspects to his theory: the process of coming to know and the stages we move through as we gradually acquire this ability.

Constructive play — Constructive play refers to play that combines sensorimotor repetitive activity with symbolic representation of ideas. Constructive play occurs when children engage in self-regulated creation or construction of a product or a problem solution.

Dramatic play — Dramatic play refers to play in which children enact social roles.

Parten — Parten grouped play into six categories and determined that children's play styles mirror their social development. These stages are identified as: Unoccupied, Onlooker, Parallel, Associative Play, and Cooperative Play.

Ion — An ion is an atom or group of atoms with a net electric charge. The energy required to detach an electron in its lowest energy state from an atom or molecule of a gas with less net electric charge is called the ionization potential, or ionization energy.

Social role — Social role refers to expected behavior patterns associated with particular social positions.

Rough-and-tumble play — Play-fighting and chasing is a form of rough-and-tumble play.

Cultural values — The importance and desirability of various objects and activities as defined by people in a given culture are referred to as cultural values.

Problem solving — An attempt to find an appropriate way of attaining a goal when the goal is not readily available is called problem solving.

Parallel play — Parallel play is playing with similar objects, clearly beside others but not with them. (Near but not with others.)

Social play — Play that involves social interactions with peers is called social play. It increases affiliation with peers, releases tension, advances cognitive development, and increases exploration.

Reflection — Reflection is the process of rephrasing or repeating thoughts and feelings expressed, making the person more aware of what they are saying or thinking.

Reinforcement	In operant conditioning, reinforcement is any change in an environment that (a) occurs after the behavior, (b) seems to make that behavior re-occur more often in the future and (c) that reoccurence of behavior must be the result of the change.
Corporal punishment	Corporal punishment is the use of physical force with the intention of causing pain, but not injury.
Withdrawal of love	Withdrawal of love is a disciplinary strategy that may involve ignoring, isolating, or showing dislike for a child.
Power assertion	A discipline technique in which a parent attempts to gain control over a child or a child's resources is called power assertion.
Inductive techniques	Inductive techniques in child development are disciplinary actions designed to create desirable behavior by appealing to a child's sense of reason and fairness.
Reasoning	Reasoning is the act of using reason to derive a conclusion from certain premises. There are two main methods to reach a conclusion,deductive reasoning and inductive reasoning.
Inductive reasoning	A form of reasoning in which we reason from individual cases or particular facts to a general conclusion is referred to as inductive reasoning. The conclusion can be said to follow with a probability rather than certainty.
Empathy	Empathy is the recognition and understanding of the states of mind, including beliefs, desires and particularly emotions of others without injecting your own.
Toddler	A toddler is a child between the ages of one and three years old. During this period, the child learns a great deal about social roles and develops motor skills; to toddle is to walk unsteadily.
Representative sample	Representative sample refers to a sample of participants selected from the larger population in such a way that important subgroups within the population are included in the sample in the same proportions as they are found in the larger population.
Cognitive development	The process by which a child's understanding of the world changes as a function of age and experience is called cognitive development.
Longitudinal study	Longitudinal study is a type of developmental study in which the same group of participants is followed and measured for an extended period of time, often years.
Positive reinforcement	In positive reinforcement, a stimulus is added and the rate of responding increases.
Time-out	Time-out is an operant conditioning punishment procedure in which, after unwanted behavior, the person is temporarily removed from a setting--in theory, a removal of stimuli resulting in an increase in the frequency of wanted behaviors; an example of negative reinforcement.
Temperament	Temperament refers to a basic, innate disposition to change behavior. The activity level is an important dimension of temperament.
Individuality	According to Cooper, individuality consists of two dimensions: self-assertion and separateness.
Authoritative parents	Authoritative parents are strict and warm. Authoritative parents demand mature behavior but use reason rather than force in discipline.
Authoritarian	The term authoritarian is used to describe a style that enforces strong and sometimes oppressive measures against those in its sphere of influence, generally without attempts at gaining their consent.
Authoritative parenting	Authoritative parenting encourages children to be independent but still places limits and controls on their actions. Extensive verbal give-and-take is allowed, and parents are warm

and nurturant toward the child.

Child development Scientific study of the processes of change from conception through adolescence is called child development.

Socioeconomic Socioeconomic pertains to the study of the social and economic impacts of any product or service offering, market intervention or other activity on an economy as a whole and on the companies, organization and individuals who are its main economic actors.

Obedience Obedience is the willingness to follow the will of others. Humans have been shown to be surprisingly obedient in the presence of perceived legitimate authority figures, as demonstrated by the Milgram experiment in the 1960s.

Altruism Altruism is being helpful to other people with little or no interest in being rewarded for one's efforts. This is distinct from merely helping others.

Early adulthood The developmental period beginning in the late teens or early twenties and lasting into the thirties is called early adulthood; characterized by an increasing self-awareness.

Sympathetic The sympathetic nervous system activates what is often termed the "fight or flight response". It is an automatic regulation system, that is, one that operates without the intervention of conscious thought.

Guthrie The theory of learning proposed by Guthrie was based on one principle, Contiguity : A combination of stimuli which has accompanied a movement will on its recurrence tend to be followed by that movement. Prediction of behavior will always be probabilistic.

Moral reasoning Moral reasoning involves concepts of justice, whereas social conventional judgments are concepts of social organization.

Motives Needs or desires that energize and direct behavior toward a goal are motives.

Relational aggression Relational Aggression usually stems from miscommunication and the unsynchronisation of feelings between the partners. The unspoken tension between partners in this kind of problematic relationship tends to manifest itself in aggression towards the partner in subtle, but potentially devastating mannerisms.

Insecure attachment Insecure attachment occurs when infants either avoid the caregiver or show considerable resistance or ambivalence toward the caregiver.

Experimental group Experimental group refers to any group receiving a treatment effect in an experiment.

Control group A group that does not receive the treatment effect in an experiment is referred to as the control group or sometimes as the comparison group.

Systematic desensitization Systematic desensitization refers to Wolpe's behavioral fear-reduction technique in which a hierarchy of fear-evoking stimuli are presented while the person remains relaxed. The fear-evoking stimuli thereby become associated with muscle relaxation.

Sexual abuse Sexual abuse is a term used to describe non- consentual sexual relations between two or more parties which are considered criminally and/or morally offensive.

Mental disorder Mental disorder refers to a disturbance in a person's emotions, drives, thought processes, or behavior that involves serious and relatively prolonged distress and/or impairment in ability to function, is not simply a normal response to some event or set of events in the person's environment.

Statistics Statistics is a type of data analysis which practice includes the planning, summarizing, and interpreting of observations of a system possibly followed by predicting or forecasting of future events based on a mathematical model of the system being observed.

Neglected children	Neglected children are infrequently nominated as a best friend but are not disliked by their peers.
Child abuse	Child abuse is the physical or psychological maltreatment of a child.
Ecological view	The view that perception and behavior functions to bring organisms in contact with the environment, to increase adaptation, is referred to as the ecological view.
Alcoholism	A disorder that involves long-term, repeated, uncontrolled, compulsive, and excessive use of alcoholic beverages and that impairs the drinker's health and work and social relationships is called alcoholism.
Reid	Reid was the founder of the Scottish School of Common Sense, and played an integral role in the Scottish Enlightenment. He advocated direct realism, or common sense realism, and argued strongly against the Theory of Ideas advocated by John Locke and René Descartes.
Social support	Social Support is the physical and emotional comfort given by family, friends, co-workers and others. Research has identified three main types of social support: emotional, practical, sharing points of view.
Disorganized-disoriented attachment	Disorganized-disoriented attachment is insecure attachment characterized by dazed and contradictory behaviors toward an attachment figure.
Learning disorder	A disorder characterized by a discrepancy between one's academic achievement and one's intellectual ability is referred to as a learning disorder.
Maladjustment	Maladjustment is the condition of being unable to adapt properly to your environment with resulting emotional instability.
Depression	In everyday language depression refers to any downturn in mood, which may be relatively transitory and perhaps due to something trivial. This is differentiated from Clinical depression which is marked by symptoms that last two weeks or more and are so severe that they interfere with daily living.
Suicide	Suicide behavior is rare in childhood but escalates in adolescence. The suicide rate increases in a linear fashion from adolescence through late adulthood.
Art therapy	Art therapy is a type of psychotherapy based upon the assumption that with an engagement in life-enhancing creative processes and the analyses of these processes, individuals will increase awareness and empathy with external reality and within one's self. They will improve skills to cope with symptoms, experiences and trauma, and enhance cognitive abilities.
Self-efficacy	Self-efficacy is the belief that one has the capabilities to execute the courses of actions required to manage prospective situations.
Hartup	According to Hartup, the single best childhood predictor of adult adaptation is not school grades, and not classroom behavior, but rather, the adequacy with which the child gets along with other children.
Propaganda	Propaganda is a specific type of message presentation directly aimed at influencing the opinions of people, rather than to impartially provide information.
Incentive	An incentive is what is expected once a behavior is performed. An incentive acts as a reinforcer.
Population	Population refers to all members of a well-defined group of organisms, events, or things.
Questionnaire	A self-report method of data collection or clinical assessment method in which the individual being studied checks off items on a printed list, answers multiple-choice questions, or writes out answers to essay questions aimed at producing a selfdescription is called

	questionnaire.
Anxiety	Anxiety is a complex combination of the feeling of fear, apprehension and worry often accompanied by physical sensations such as palpitations, chest pain and/or shortness of breath.
Direct observation	Direct observation refers to assessing behavior through direct surveillance.
Positive relationship	Statistically, a positive relationship refers to a mathematical relationship in which increases in one measure are matched by increases in the other.
Popular children	Children who are frequently nominated as a best friend and are rarely disliked by their peers are called popular children.
Neo-Piagetians	Developmentalists who have elaborated on Piaget's theory, believing that children's cognitive development is even more specific in many respects than Piaget himself, are neo-Piagetians.
Cognitive-developmental theory	The stage theory that holds that the child's abilities to mentally represent the world and solve problems unfold as a result of the interaction of experience and the maturation of neurological structures is called a cognitive-developmental theory.
Social development	The person's developing capacity for social relationships and the effects of those relationships on further development is referred to as social development.
Cognitive skills	Cognitive skills such as reasoning, attention, and memory can be advanced and sustained through practice and training.
Moral development	Development regarding rules and conventions about what people should do in their interactions with other people is called moral development.
Socioeconomic Status	A family's socioeconomic status is based on family income, parental education level, parental occupation, and social status in the community. Those with high status often have more success in preparing their children for school because they have access to a wide range of resources.
Moral judgment	Making decisions about which actions are right and which are wrong is a moral judgment.
Dyslexia	Dyslexia is a neurological disorder with biochemical and genetic markers. In its most common and apparent form, it is a disability in which a person's reading and/or writing ability is significantly lower than that which would be predicted by his or her general level of intelligence.
Concrete operations	In Piaget's theory, the third major stage of cognitive development, in which children can decenter their perception, are less egocentric, and can think logically about concrete objects is called concrete operations.

Moral reasoning Moral reasoning involves concepts of justice, whereas social conventional judgments are concepts of social organization.

Growth hormone Growth hormone is a polypeptide hormone synthesised and secreted by the anterior pituitary gland which stimulates growth and cell reproduction in humans and other vertebrate animals.

Hormone A hormone is a chemical messenger from one cell (or group of cells) to another. The best known are those produced by endocrine glands, but they are produced by nearly every organ system. The function of hormones is to serve as a signal to the target cells; the action of the hormone is determined by the pattern of secretion and the signal transduction of the receiving tissue.

Protein A protein is a complex, high-molecular-weight organic compound that consists of amino acids joined by peptide bonds. It is essential to the structure and function of all living cells and viruses. Many are enzymes or subunits of enzymes.

Malnutrition Malnutrition is a general term for the medical condition in a person or animal caused by an unbalanced diet—either too little or too much food, or a diet missing one or more important nutrients.

Deprivation Deprivation, is the loss or withholding of normal stimulation, nutrition, comfort, love, and so forth; a condition of lacking. The level of stimulation is less than what is required.

UNICEF UNICEF, the United Nations International Children's Emergency Fund, was established by the United Nations General Assembly on December 11, 1946. UNICEF provides long-term humanitarian and developmental assistance to children and mothers in developing countries.

Developmental level An individual's current state of physical, emotional, and intellectual development is called the developmental level.

Longitudinal study Longitudinal study is a type of developmental study in which the same group of participants is followed and measured for an extended period of time, often years.

Infancy The developmental period that extends from birth to 18 or 24 months is called infancy.

Experimental group Experimental group refers to any group receiving a treatment effect in an experiment.

Paraprofessional A paraprofessional is an individual lacking a doctoral degree but trained to perform certain functions usually reserved for clinicians.

Control group A group that does not receive the treatment effect in an experiment is referred to as the control group or sometimes as the comparison group.

Adolescence The period of life bounded by puberty and the assumption of adult responsibilities is adolescence.

Cognition The intellectual processes through which information is obtained, transformed, stored, retrieved, and otherwise used is cognition.

Body image A person's body image is their perception of their physical appearance. It is more than what a person thinks they will see in a mirror, it is inextricably tied to their self-esteem and acceptance by peers.

Obesity The state of being more than 20 percent above the average weight for a person of one's height is called obesity.

Leptin Leptin refers to a hormone produced by fat cells that acts in the brain to inhibit hunger and regulate body weight.

Brain The brain controls and coordinates most movement, behavior and homeostatic body functions such as heartbeat, blood pressure, fluid balance and body temperature. Functions of the brain

	are responsible for cognition, emotion, memory, motor learning and other sorts of learning. The brain is primarily made up of two types of cells: glia and neurons.
Habit	A habit is a response that has become completely separated from its eliciting stimulus. Early learning theorists used the term to describe S-R associations, however not all S-R associations become a habit, rather many are extinguished after reinforcement is withdrawn.
Gene	A gene is an ultramicroscopic area of the chromosome. It is the smallest physical unit of the DNA molecule that carries a piece of hereditary information.
Body mass index	The body mass index is a calculated number, used to compare and analyse the health effects of body weight on human bodies of all heights. It is equal to the weight, divided by the square of the height.
Diabetes	Diabetes is a medical disorder characterized by varying or persistent elevated blood sugar levels, especially after eating. All types of diabetes share similar symptoms and complications at advanced stages: dehydration and ketoacidosis, cardiovascular disease, chronic renal failure, retinal damage which can lead to blindness, nerve damage which can lead to erectile dysfunction, gangrene with risk of amputation of toes, feet, and even legs.
Rough-and-tumble play	Play-fighting and chasing is a form of rough-and-tumble play.
Socialization	Social rules and social relations are created, communicated, and changed in verbal and nonverbal ways creating social complexity useful in identifying outsiders and intelligent breeding partners. The process of learning these skills is called socialization.
Representative sample	Representative sample refers to a sample of participants selected from the larger population in such a way that important subgroups within the population are included in the sample in the same proportions as they are found in the larger population.
Anxiety	Anxiety is a complex combination of the feeling of fear, apprehension and worry often accompanied by physical sensations such as palpitations, chest pain and/or shortness of breath.
Life span	Life span refers to the upper boundary of life, the maximum number of years an individual can live. The maximum life span of human beings is about 120 years of age. Females live an average of 6 years longer than males.
Superstitious behavior	"When small amounts of food are repeatedly given, a 'superstitious ritual' may be set up. This is due not only to the fact that a reinforcing stimulus strengthens any behavior it may happen to follow, even though a contingency has not been explicitly arranged, but also to the fact that the change in behavior resulting from one accidental contingency makes similar accidents more probable."-- Skinner on superstitious behavior.
Theories	Theories are logically self-consistent models or frameworks describing the behavior of a certain natural or social phenomenon. They are broad explanations and predictions concerning phenomena of interest.
Piaget	Piaget argued that young children's answers were qualitatively different than older children rather than quantitative. There are two major aspects to his theory: the process of coming to know and the stages we move through as we gradually acquire this ability.
Acute	Acute means sudden, sharp, and abrupt. Usually short in duration.
Chronic	Chronic refers to a relatively long duration, usually more than a few months.
Puberty	Puberty refers to the process of physical changes by which a child's body becomes an adult body capable of reproduction.
Survey	A method of scientific investigation in which a large sample of people answer questions about

their attitudes or behavior is referred to as a survey.

Asthma Asthma is a complex disease characterized by bronchial hyperresponsiveness (BHR), inflammation, mucus production and intermittent airway obstruction.

Affect A subjective feeling or emotional tone often accompanied by bodily expressions noticeable to others is called affect.

Central nervous system The vertebrate central nervous system consists of the brain and spinal cord.

Early childhood Early childhood refers to the developmental period extending from the end of infancy to about 5 or 6 years of age; sometimes called the preschool years.

Consciousness The awareness of the sensations, thoughts, and feelings being experienced at a given moment is called consciousness.

Cognitive development The process by which a child's understanding of the world changes as a function of age and experience is called cognitive development.

Concrete operations In Piaget's theory, the third major stage of cognitive development, in which children can decenter their perception, are less egocentric, and can think logically about concrete objects is called concrete operations.

Conservation Conservation refers to the recognition that basic properties of substances such as weight and mass remain the same even when transformations merely alter their appearance.

Premise A premise is a statement presumed true within the context of a discourse, especially of a logical argument.

Transitive inference An understanding of the relationship between two objects that results by knowing the relationship of each to a third object is a transitive inference. Piaget provided evidence that most human children are able to exhibit transitive inference at or around age 13.

Seriation The concrete operation that involves ordering stimuli along a quantitative dimension is called seriation.

Inference Inference is the act or process of drawing a conclusion based solely on what one already knows.

Deductive reasoning Deductive reasoning refers to a form of reasoning about arguments in which conclusions are determined from the premises. The conclusions are true if the premises are true.

Inductive reasoning A form of reasoning in which we reason from individual cases or particular facts to a general conclusion is referred to as inductive reasoning. The conclusion can be said to follow with a probability rather than certainty.

Reasoning Reasoning is the act of using reason to derive a conclusion from certain premises. There are two main methods to reach a conclusion,deductive reasoning and inductive reasoning.

Horizontal decalage The sequential unfolding of the ability to master different kinds of cognitive tasks within the same stage is called horizontal decalage.

Maturation The orderly unfolding of traits, as regulated by the genetic code is called maturation.

Adaptation Adaptation is a lowering of sensitivity to a stimulus following prolonged exposure to that stimulus. Behavioral adaptations are special ways a particular organism behaves to survive in its natural habitat.

Learning Learning is a relatively permanent change in behavior that results from experience. Thus, to attribute a behavioral change to learning, the change must be relatively permanent and must result from experience.

Cross-cultural studies	Cross-cultural studies are comparisons of a culture with one or more other cultures, which provides information about the degree to which behavior is similar across cultures or the degree to which it is culture specific .
Stages	Stages represent relatively discrete periods of time in which functioning is qualitatively different from functioning at other periods.
Moral development	Development regarding rules and conventions about what people should do in their interactions with other people is called moral development.
Formal reasoning	The type of reasoning in which the form of an argument, not its semantic content, is crucial is referred to as formal reasoning.
Intelligence test	An intelligence test is a standardized means of assessing a person's current mental ability, for example, the Stanford-Binet test and the Wechsler Adult Intelligence Scale.
Psychometric	Psychometric study is concerned with the theory and technique of psychological measurement, which includes the measurement of knowledge, abilities, attitudes, and personality traits. The field is primarily concerned with the study of differences between individuals
Attention	Attention is the cognitive process of selectively concentrating on one thing while ignoring other things. Psychologists have labeled three types of attention: sustained attention, selective attention, and divided attention.
Long-term memory	Long-term memory is memory that lasts from over 30 seconds to years.
Sensory memory	Sensory memory is our ability to retain impressions of sensory information after the original stimulus has ceased.
Working Memory	Working memory is the collection of structures and processes in the brain used for temporarily storing and manipulating information. Working memory consists of both memory for items that are currently being processed, and components governing attention and directing the processing itself.
Mental Representation	Stage six of the sensorimotor substages, Mental representation, 18 months to 2 years, marks the beginnings of insight, or true creativity. This marks the passage into unique thought in Piaget's later three areas of development.
Prefrontal cortex	The prefrontal cortex is the anterior part of the frontal lobes of the brain, lying in front of the motor and associative areas. It has been implicated in planning complex cognitive behaviors, personality expression and moderating correct social behavior. The prefrontal cortex continues to develop until around age 6.
Brain imaging	Brain imaging is a fairly recent discipline within medicine and neuroscience. Brain imaging falls into two broad categories -- structural imaging and functional imaging.
Frontal lobe	The frontal lobe comprises four major folds of cortical tissue: the precentral gyrus, superior gyrus and the middle gyrus of the frontal gyri, the inferior frontal gyrus. It has been found to play a part in impulse control, judgement, language, memory, motor function, problem solving, sexual behavior, socialization and spontaneity.
Cowan	Cowan regards working memory not as a separate system, but as a part of long-term memory. Representations in working memory are a subset of the representations in long-term memory.
Central Executive	The central executive in working memory is, among other things, responsible for directing attention to relevant information, suppressing irrelevant information and inappropriate actions, and for coordinating cognitive processes when more than one task must be done at the same time.
Baddeley	Baddeley introduced a multicomponent model of working memory for the temporary maintenance and manipulation of information. It emphasizes the functional importance of such a system

	rather than its use as the unitary short-term store proposed by Atkinson and Shiffrin.
Metamemory	Metamemory refers to self-awareness of the ways in which memory functions, allowing the person to encode, store, and retrieve information effectively.
Mnemonic	A mnemonic is a memory aid. They are often verbal, are sometimes in verse form, and are often used to remember lists.
External memory aids	Mnemonic strategies using something outside the person are called external memory aids.
Elaboration	The extensiveness of processing at any given level of memory is called elaboration. The use of elaboration changes developmentally. Adolescents are more likely to use elaboration spontaneously than children.
Information processing	Information processing is an approach to the goal of understanding human thinking. The essence of the approach is to see cognition as being essentially computational in nature, with mind being the software and the brain being the hardware.
Short-term memory	Short-term memory is that part of memory which stores a limited amount of information for a limited amount of time (roughly 30-45 seconds). The second key concept associated with a short-term memory is that it has a finite capacity.
Scheme	According to Piaget, a hypothetical mental structure that permits the classification and organization of new information is called a scheme.
Cognitive structure	According to Piaget, the number of schemata available to an organism at any given time constitutes that organism's cognitive structure. How the organism interacts with its environment depends on the current cognitive structure available. As the cognitive structure develops, new assimilations can occur.
Achievement test	A test designed to determine a person's level of knowledge in a given subject area is referred to as an achievement test.
Theodore Simon	Theodore Simon co-created the Stanford-Binet Intelligence Scale test with Alfred Binet.
Alfred Binet	Alfred Binet published the first modern intelligence test, the Binet-Simon intelligence scale, in 1905. Binet stressed that the core of intelligence consists of complex cognitive processes, such as memory, imagery, comprehension, and judgment; and, that these developed over time in the individual.
IQ test	An IQ test is a standardized test developed to measure a person's cognitive abilities ("intelligence") in relation to their age group.
Otis-Lennon school ability test	Otis-Lennon school ability test is a measure of cognitive ability as related to school success for children in kindergarten through grade 12; there are seven levels of the test for the different grades, with clusters of 10-15 items in the five areas of verbal comprehension, verbal reasoning, pictorial reasoning, figural reasoning, and quantitative reasoning.
Quantitative	A quantitative property is one that exists in a range of magnitudes, and can therefore be measured. Measurements of any particular quantitative property are expressed as as a specific quantity, referred to as a unit, multiplied by a number.
Wechsler Intelligence Scale for Children	The Wechsler Intelligence Scale for Children is an intelligence test that can be completed without reading or writing. It generates an IQ score. It also generates four composite scores; Verbal Comprehension, Perceptual Reasoning, Processing Speed and Working Memory.
Identical twins	Identical twins occur when a single egg is fertilized to form one zygote (monozygotic) but the zygote then divides into two separate embryos. The two embryos develop into foetuses sharing the same womb. Monozygotic twins are genetically identical unless there has been a

	mutation in development, and they are almost always the same gender.
Bronfenbrenner	Bronfenbrenner was a co-founder of the U.S. national Head Start program and founder of the Ecological Theory of Development.
Ethnic group	An ethnic group is a culture or subculture whose members are readily distinguishable by outsiders based on traits originating from a common racial, national, linguistic, or religious source. Members of an ethnic group are often presumed to be culturally or biologically similar, although this is not in fact necessarily the case.
Ethnicity	Ethnicity refers to a characteristic based on cultural heritage, nationality characteristics, race, religion, and language.
Individual intelligence test	A test of intelligence designed to be given to a single individual by a trained specialist is an individual intelligence test. Background information supplements the test.
Individual differences	Individual differences psychology studies the ways in which individual people differ in their behavior. This is distinguished from other aspects of psychology in that although psychology is ostensibly a study of individuals, modern psychologists invariably study groups.
Self-esteem	Self-esteem refers to a person's subjective appraisal of himself or herself as intrinsically positive or negative to some degree.
Motivation	In psychology, motivation is the driving force (desire) behind all actions of an organism.
Herrnstein	Herrnstein was a prominent researcher in comparative psychology who did pioneering work on pigeon intelligence employing the Experimental Analysis of Behavior and formulated the "Matching Law" in the 1960s, a breakthrough in understanding how reinforcement and behavior are linked.
Kamin	Kamin argues that blocking is caused by lack of learning. In the compound stimulus training, there is lack of surprise about the outcome because one of the members of the compound stimulus already predicts the outcome. There is no surprise effect, therefore no learning.
Socioeconomic Status	A family's socioeconomic status is based on family income, parental education level, parental occupation, and social status in the community. Those with high status often have more success in preparing their children for school because they have access to a wide range of resources.
Cultural bias	Cultural bias is interpreting and judging phenomena in terms particular to one's own culture. This is a danger in any field of knowledge that claims objectivity and universality.
Howard Gardner	Howard Gardner is best known for his theory of multiple intelligences. He outlined seven dimensions of intelligence: Visual / Spatial Intelligence, Musical Intelligence, Verbal Intelligence, Logical/Mathematical Intelligence, Interpersonal Intelligence, Intrapersonal Intelligence, and Bodily / Kinesthetic Intelligence. Since the publication of Frames of Mind, he has additionally identified the 8th and 9th dimensions of intelligence: Naturalist Intelligence and Existentialist Intelligence.
Sternberg	Sternberg proposed the triarchic theory of intelligence: componential, experiential, and practical. His notion of general intelligence or the g-factor, is a composite of intelligence scores across multiple modalities.
Theory of multiple intelligences	Gardner's theory of multiple intelligences suggests several different kinds of "intelligence" exist in humans, each relating to a different sphere of human life and activity. .
Neuropsychol-gist	A psychologist concerned with the relationships among cognition, affect, behavior, and brain function is a neuropsychologist.

Self-understanding	Self-understanding is a child's cognitive representation of the self, the substance and content of the child's self-conceptions.
Intrapersonal	Intrapersonal is the ability to recognize, define, and pursue inner feelings and thoughts, as in poetry and self-knowledge.
Standardized test	An oral or written assessment for which an individual receives a score indicating how the individual reponded relative to a previously tested large sample of others is referred to as a standardized test.
Observer bias	Observer bias is an error introduced into measurement when observers overemphasize behavior they expect to find and fail to notice behavior they do not expect. Observer bias can also be introduced because researchers see a behavior and interpret it according to what it means to them, whereas it may mean something else to the person showing the behavior.
Sternberg Triarchic Abilities	Sternberg Triarchic Abilities is a test to measure componential, experiential, and contextual intelligence. The goal is to obtain a more complete assessment of intelligence than is possible with a conventional test.
Kaufman assessment battery for children	The Kaufman assessment battery for children is a nontraditional individual intelligence test designed to provide fair assessments of minority children and children with disabilities.
Triarchic Theory of Intelligence	The Triarchic Theory of Intelligence was formulated by Robert J. Sternberg. It proposes that intelligence consists of componential intelligence, experiential intelligence, and contextual intelligence.
Critical thinking	Critical thinking is a mental process of analyzing or evaluating information, particularly statements or propositions that are offered as true.
Problem solving	An attempt to find an appropriate way of attaining a goal when the goal is not readily available is called problem solving.
Correlation	A statistical technique for determining the degree of association between two or more variables is referred to as correlation.
Creativity	Creativity is the ability to think about something in novel and unusual ways and come up with unique solutions to problems. It involves divergent thinking, having many solutions or views to a problem.
Proximal	Students can set both long-term (distal) and short-term (proximal) goals .
Mental age	The mental age refers to the accumulated months of credit that a person earns on the Stanford-Binet Intelligence Scale.
Vygotsky	The Vygotsky model of human development has been termed as a sociocultural approach. The individual's development is a result of his or her culture.
Metaphor	A metaphor is a rhetorical trope where a comparison is made between two seemingly unrelated subjects
Chomsky	Chomsky has greatly influenced the field of theoretical linguistics with his work on the theory of generative grammar. Accordingly, humans are biologically prewired to learn language at a certain time and in a certain way.
Simile	A simile is a figure of speech in which the subject is compared to another subject.
Syntax	Syntax can be described as the study of the rules, or "patterned relations" that govern the way the words in a sentence come together.
Decoding	Process of phonetic analysis by which a printed word is converted to spoken form before

	retrieval from long-term memory is called decoding.
Whole-language approach	The whole-language approach argues that the teaching of reading skills should parallel the child's natural language learning.
Phonics	Phonics is the study of the way in which spellings represent the sounds that make up words.
Retrieval	Retrieval is the location of stored information and its subsequent return to consciousness. It is the third stage of information processing.
Phonetics	Phonetics is the study of sounds (voice). It is concerned with the actual properties of speech sounds (phones) as well as those of non-speech sounds, and their production, audition and perception.
Mental processes	The thoughts, feelings, and motives that each of us experiences privately but that cannot be observed directly are called mental processes.
Acquisition	Acquisition is the process of adapting to the environment, learning or becoming conditioned. In classical conditoning terms, it is the initial learning of the stimulus response link, which involves a neutral stimulus being associated with a unconditioned stimulus and becoming a conditioned stimulus.
Phoneme	In oral language, a phoneme is the theoretical basic unit of sound that can be used to distinguish words or morphemes; in sign language, it is a similarly basic unit of hand shape, motion, position, or facial expression.
Bioecological theory	Urie Bronfenbrenner's theory, bioecological theory, suggests that human behavioral development is shaped by one's environment. The theory cites "spheres of influence" to show the relevance of social spheres on behavioral development. Key factors include culture, ethnicity, and gender.
Learning disability	A learning disability exists when there is a significant discrepancy between one's ability and achievement.
Self-efficacy	Self-efficacy is the belief that one has the capabilities to execute the courses of actions required to manage prospective situations.
Authoritative parents	Authoritative parents are strict and warm. Authoritative parents demand mature behavior but use reason rather than force in discipline.
Authoritarian parents	Parents who are rigid in their rules and who demand obedience for the sake of obedience are called authoritarian parents.
Extrinsic motivation	Responding to external incentives such as rewards and punishments is form of extrinsic motivation. Traditionally, extrinsic motivation has been used to motivate employees: Payments, rewards, control, or punishments.
Intrinsic motivation	Intrinsic motivation causes people to engage in an activity for its own sake. They are subjective factors and include self-determination, curiosity, challenge, effort, and others.
Social capital	Family and community resources upon which a person or family can draw is called social capital.
Social promotion	Social promotion is the practice of promoting schoolchildren to the next grade, to keep them with their peers, regardless of whether they are capable of doing the grade-level work.
Social skills	Social skills are skills used to interact and communicate with others to assist status in the social structure and other motivations.
Attitude	An enduring mental representation of a person, place, or thing that evokes an emotional response and related behavior is called attitude.

Mental retardation	Mental retardation refers to having significantly below-average intellectual functioning and limitations in at least two areas of adaptive functioning. Many categorize retardation as mild, moderate, severe, or profound.
Adaptive behavior	An adaptive behavior increases the probability of the individual or organism to survive or exist within its environment.
Population	Population refers to all members of a well-defined group of organisms, events, or things.
Fetal alcohol syndrome	A cluster of abnormalities that appears in the offspring of mothers who drink alcohol heavily during pregnancy is called fetal alcohol syndrome.
Genetic counseling	Genetic counseling generally refers to prenatal counseling done when a genetic condition is suspected in a pregnancy. Genetic counseling is the process by which patients or relatives at risk of an inherited disorder are advised of the consequences and nature of the disorder, the probability of developing or transmitting it, and the options open to them in management and family planning in order to prevent, avoid or ameliorate it.
Tay-Sachs disease	Tay-Sachs disease is a fatal genetic disorder, inherited in an autosomal recessive pattern, in which harmful quantities of a fatty substance called ganglioside GM2 accumulate in the nerve cells in the brain.
Mental disorder	Mental disorder refers to a disturbance in a person's emotions, drives, thought processes, or behavior that involves serious and relatively prolonged distress and/or impairment in ability to function, is not simply a normal response to some event or set of events in the person's environment.
Amniocentesis	Amniocentesis is a medical procedure used for prenatal diagnosis, in which from the amnion around a developing fetus a small amount of amniotic fluid is extracted. It is usually offered when there may be an increased risk for genetic conditions in the pregnancy.
Birth trauma	Birth trauma refers to injury or disturbing experiences sustained at the time of birth.
Prenatal	Prenatal period refers to the time from conception to birth.
Autism	Autism is a neurodevelopmental disorder that manifests itself in markedly abnormal social interaction, communication ability, patterns of interests, and patterns of behavior.
Trauma	Trauma refers to a severe physical injury or wound to the body caused by an external force, or a psychological shock having a lasting effect on mental life.
Society	The social sciences use the term society to mean a group of people that form a semi-closed (or semi-open) social system, in which most interactions are with other individuals belonging to the group.
Dyslexia	Dyslexia is a neurological disorder with biochemical and genetic markers. In its most common and apparent form, it is a disability in which a person's reading and/or writing ability is significantly lower than that which would be predicted by his or her general level of intelligence.
Script	A schema, or behavioral sequence, for an event is called a script. It is a form of schematic organization, with real-world events organized in terms of temporal and causal relations between component acts.
Attention-deficit/hype-activity disorder	Attention-deficit/hyperactivity disorder refers to a disorder that begins in childhood and is characterized by a persistent pattern of lack of attention, with or without hyperactivity and impulsive behavior.
Hyperactivity	Hyperactivity can be described as a state in which a individual is abnormally easily excitable and exuberant. Strong emotional reactions and a very short span of attention is

	also typical for the individual.
Heritability	Heritability It is that proportion of the observed variation in a particular phenotype within a particular population, that can be attributed to the contribution of genotype. In other words: it measures the extent to which differences between individuals in a population are due their being different genetically.
Behavioral therapy	The treatment of a mental disorder through the application of basic principles of conditioning and learning is called behavioral therapy.
Substance abuse	Substance abuse refers to the overindulgence in and dependence on a stimulant, depressant, or other chemical substance, leading to effects that are detrimental to the individual's physical or mental health, or the welfare of others.
Depression	In everyday language depression refers to any downturn in mood, which may be relatively transitory and perhaps due to something trivial. This is differentiated from Clinical depression which is marked by symptoms that last two weeks or more and are so severe that they interfere with daily living.
Behavior modification	Behavior Modification is a technique of altering an individual's reactions to stimuli through positive reinforcement and the extinction of maladaptive behavior.
Methylphenidate	Methylphenidate is a central nervous system (CNS) stimulant. It has a "calming" effect on many children who have ADHD, reducing impulsive behavior and the tendency to "act out", and helps them concentrate on schoolwork and other tasks. Adults who have ADHD often find that it increases their ability to focus on tasks and organize their lives. Brand names include Ritalin, and Concerta.
Stimulant	A stimulant is a drug which increases the activity of the sympathetic nervous system and produces a sense of euphoria or awakeness.
Ritalin	Ritalin, a methylphenidate, is a central nervous system stimulant. It has a "calming" effect on many children who have ADHD, reducing impulsive behavior and the tendency to "act out", and helps them concentrate on schoolwork and other tasks.
Individuals with Disabilities Education Act	The Individuals with Disabilities Education Act is a United States law meant to ensure "a free appropriate public education" for students with disabilities, designed to their individualized needs in the Least Restricted Environment.
Antipsychotic	The term antipsychotic is applied to a group of drugs used to treat psychosis.
Least restrictive environment	The concept that a child with a disability must be educated in a setting that is as similar as possible to the one in which children who do not have a disability are educated is called least restrictive environment.
Stereotype	A stereotype is considered to be a group concept, held by one social group about another.They are often used in a negative or prejudicial sense and are frequently used to justify certain discriminatory behaviors. This allows powerful social groups to legitimize and protect their dominant position
Neurologist	A physician who studies the nervous system, especially its structure, functions, and abnormalities is referred to as neurologist.
Convergent thinking	Convergent thinking is a thought process that attempts to gradually narrow in on the single best solution to a problem.
Divergent thinking	A thought process that attempts to generate multiple solutions to problems is called divergent thinking.
Guilford	Guilford observed that most individuals display a preference for either convergent or

	divergent thinking. Scientists and engineers typically prefer the former and artists and performers, the latter.
Enrichment	Deliberately making an environment more novel, complex, and perceptually or intellectually stimulating is referred to as enrichment.
Eating disorders	Psychological disorders characterized by distortion of the body image and gross disturbances in eating patterns are called eating disorders.
Selective attention	Selective attention is a type of attention which involves focusing on a specific aspect of a scene while ignoring other aspects.
Socioeconomic	Socioeconomic pertains to the study of the social and economic impacts of any product or service offering, market intervention or other activity on an economy as a whole and on the companies, organization and individuals who are its main economic actors.
Culture-fair	An intelligence test that does not discriminate against members of any minority group is called culture-fair.
Triarchic theory	Sternberg's theory that there are three main types of intelligence: analytical, creative, and practical is called the triarchic theory of intelligence.
Pragmatics	Pragmatics is generally the study of natural language understanding, and specifically the study of how context influences the interpretation of meanings. It is a subfield of linguistics.
Self-fulfilling prophecy	A self-fulfilling prophecy is a prediction that, in being made, actually causes itself to become true.
Perception	Perception is the process of acquiring, interpreting, selecting, and organizing sensory information.
Terman	Terman revised the Stanford-Binet Intelligence Scale in 1916, commonly used to measure intelligence (or I.Q.) in the United States. William Stern's suggestion that mental age/chronological age times 100 (to get rid of the decimal) be made the "intelligence quotient" or I.Q. This apparent mathematization of the measurement gave it an air of scientific accuracy and detachment which contributed greatly to its acceptance among educators and the broad public.
Reading comprehension	Reading comprehension can be defined as the level of understanding of a passage or text. For normal reading rates (around 200-220 words per minute) an acceptable level of comprehension is above 75%.
Metacognition	Metacognition refers to thinking about cognition (memory, perception, calculation, association, etc.) itself. Metacognition can be divided into two types of knowledge: explicit, conscious, factual knowledge; and implicit, unconscious, procedural knowledge.
Validity	The extent to which a test measures what it is intended to measure is called validity.

Representational systems	Representational systems in Neo-Piagetian terminology, is the third stage in the development of self-definition. It is characterized by breadth, balance, and the integration and assessment of various aspects of the self.
Self-concept	Self-concept refers to domain-specific evaluations of the self where a domain may be academics, athletics, etc.
Self-esteem	Self-esteem refers to a person's subjective appraisal of himself or herself as intrinsically positive or negative to some degree.
Society	The social sciences use the term society to mean a group of people that form a semi-closed (or semi-open) social system, in which most interactions are with other individuals belonging to the group.
Self-worth	In psychology, self-esteem or self-worth refers to a person's subjective appraisal of himself or herself as intrinsically positive or negative to some degree.
Psychosocial development	Erikson's psychosocial development describe eight developmental stages through which a healthily developing human should pass from infancy to late adulthood. In each stage the person confronts, and hopefully masters, new challenges.
Social support	Social Support is the physical and emotional comfort given by family, friends, co-workers and others. Research has identified three main types of social support: emotional, practical, sharing points of view.
Emotion	An emotion is a mental states that arise spontaneously, rather than through conscious effort. They are often accompanied by physiological changes.
Socioeconomic Status	A family's socioeconomic status is based on family income, parental education level, parental occupation, and social status in the community. Those with high status often have more success in preparing their children for school because they have access to a wide range of resources.
Bioecological theory	Urie Bronfenbrenner's theory, bioecological theory, suggests that human behavioral development is shaped by one's environment. The theory cites "spheres of influence" to show the relevance of social spheres on behavioral development. Key factors include culture, ethnicity, and gender.
Bronfenbrenner	Bronfenbrenner was a co-founder of the U.S. national Head Start program and founder of the Ecological Theory of Development.
Discrimination	In Learning theory, discrimination refers the ability to distinguish between a conditioned stimulus and other stimuli. It can be brought about by extensive training or differential reinforcement. In social terms, it is the denial of privileges to a person or a group on the basis of prejudice.
Coregulation	A gradual transferring of control from parent to child, beginning in middle childhood is referred to as coregulation.
Reasoning	Reasoning is the act of using reason to derive a conclusion from certain premises. There are two main methods to reach a conclusion,deductive reasoning and inductive reasoning.
Affect	A subjective feeling or emotional tone often accompanied by bodily expressions noticeable to others is called affect.
Statistics	Statistics is a type of data analysis which practice includes the planning, summarizing, and interpreting of observations of a system possibly followed by predicting or forecasting of future events based on a mathematical model of the system being observed.
Personality	Personality refers to the pattern of enduring characteristics that differentiates a person, the patterns of behaviors that make each individual unique.

Temperament	Temperament refers to a basic, innate disposition to change behavior. The activity level is an important dimension of temperament.
Role model	A person who serves as a positive example of desirable behavior is referred to as a role model.
Eccles	Eccles was key to a number of important developments in neuroscience. Until around 1949, Eccles believed that synaptic transmission was primarily electrical rather than chemical. Although he was wrong in this hypothesis, his arguments led himself and others to perform some of the experiments which proved chemical synaptic transmission.
Gender difference	A gender difference is a disparity between genders involving quality or quantity. Though some gender differences are controversial, they are not to be confused with sexist stereotypes.
Representative sample	Representative sample refers to a sample of participants selected from the larger population in such a way that important subgroups within the population are included in the sample in the same proportions as they are found in the larger population.
Lesbian	A lesbian is a homosexual woman. They are women who are sexually and romantically attracted to other women.
Infancy	The developmental period that extends from birth to 18 or 24 months is called infancy.
Perception	Perception is the process of acquiring, interpreting, selecting, and organizing sensory information.
Longitudinal study	Longitudinal study is a type of developmental study in which the same group of participants is followed and measured for an extended period of time, often years.
Cohort	A cohort is a group of individuals defined by their date of birth.
Social policy	Social policy is the study of the welfare state, and the range of responses to social need.
Homosexual	Homosexual refers to a sexual orientation characterized by aesthetic attraction, romantic love, and sexual desire exclusively for members of the same sex or gender identity.
Attitude	An enduring mental representation of a person, place, or thing that evokes an emotional response and related behavior is called attitude.
Stereotype	A stereotype is considered to be a group concept, held by one social group about another.They are often used in a negative or prejudicial sense and are frequently used to justify certain discriminatory behaviors. This allows powerful social groups to legitimize and protect their dominant position
Ethnographic study	Ethnographic study is an in-depth study of a culture, which uses a combination of methods including participant observation.
Naturalistic observation	Naturalistic observation is a method of observation that involves observing subjects in their natural habitats. Researchers take great care in avoiding making interferences with the behavior they are observing by using unobtrusive methods.
Attention	Attention is the cognitive process of selectively concentrating on one thing while ignoring other things. Psychologists have labeled three types of attention: sustained attention, selective attention, and divided attention.
Friendship	The essentials of friendship are reciprocity and commitment between individuals who see themselves more or less as equals. Interaction between friends rests on a more equal power base than the interaction between children and adults.
Assertiveness	Assertiveness basically means the ability to express your thoughts and feelings in a way that clearly states your needs and keeps the lines of communication open with the other.

Gender role	A cluster of behaviors that characterizes traditional female or male behaviors within a cultural setting is a gender role.
Self-efficacy	Self-efficacy is the belief that one has the capabilities to execute the courses of actions required to manage prospective situations.
Bandura	Bandura is best known for his work on social learning theory or Social Cognitivism. His famous Bobo doll experiment illustrated that people learn from observing others.
Conformity	Conformity is the degree to which members of a group will change their behavior, views and attitudes to fit the views of the group. The group can influence members via unconscious processes or via overt social pressure on individuals.
Hartup	According to Hartup, the single best childhood predictor of adult adaptation is not school grades, and not classroom behavior, but rather, the adequacy with which the child gets along with other children.
Ethnic group	An ethnic group is a culture or subculture whose members are readily distinguishable by outsiders based on traits originating from a common racial, national, linguistic, or religious source. Members of an ethnic group are often presumed to be culturally or biologically similar, although this is not in fact necessarily the case.
Prejudice	Prejudice in general, implies coming to a judgment on the subject before learning where the preponderance of the evidence actually lies, or formation of a judgement without direct experience.
Social skills	Social skills are skills used to interact and communicate with others to assist status in the social structure and other motivations.
Popular children	Children who are frequently nominated as a best friend and are rarely disliked by their peers are called popular children.
Shyness	A tendency to avoid others plus uneasiness and strain when socializing is called shyness.
Trait	An enduring personality characteristic that tends to lead to certain behaviors is called a trait. The term trait also means a genetically inherited feature of an organism.
Adolescence	The period of life bounded by puberty and the assumption of adult responsibilities is adolescence.
Obedience	Obedience is the willingness to follow the will of others. Humans have been shown to be surprisingly obedient in the presence of perceived legitimate authority figures, as demonstrated by the Milgram experiment in the 1960s.
Depression	In everyday language depression refers to any downturn in mood, which may be relatively transitory and perhaps due to something trivial. This is differentiated from Clinical depression which is marked by symptoms that last two weeks or more and are so severe that they interfere with daily living.
Social learning	Social learning is learning that occurs as a function of observing, retaining and replicating behavior observed in others. Although social learning can occur at any stage in life, it is thought to be particularly important during childhood, particularly as authority becomes important.
Anxiety	Anxiety is a complex combination of the feeling of fear, apprehension and worry often accompanied by physical sensations such as palpitations, chest pain and/or shortness of breath.
Survey	A method of scientific investigation in which a large sample of people answer questions about their attitudes or behavior is referred to as a survey.

Trauma	Trauma refers to a severe physical injury or wound to the body caused by an external force, or a psychological shock having a lasting effect on mental life.
Control group	A group that does not receive the treatment effect in an experiment is referred to as the control group or sometimes as the comparison group.
Relational aggression	Relational Aggression usually stems from miscommunication and the unsynchronisation of feelings between the partners. The unspoken tension between partners in this kind of problematic relationship tends to manifest itself in aggression towards the partner in subtle, but potentially devastating mannerisms.
Punishment	Punishment is the addtion of a stimulus that reduces the frequency of a response, or the removal of a stimulus that results in a reduction of the response.
Conduct disorder	Conduct disorder is the psychiatric diagnostic category for the occurrence of multiple delinquent activities over a 6-month period. These behaviors include truancy, running away, fire setting, cruelty to animals, breaking and entering, and excessive fighting.
Rape	Rape is a crime where the victim is forced into sexual activity, in particular sexual penetration, against his or her will.
Social phobia	An irrational, excessive fear of public scrutiny is referred to as social phobia.
School phobia	An acute, irrational dread of attending school, usually accompanied by somatic complaints is called school phobia.
Separation anxiety	Separation anxiety is a psychological condition in which an individual has excessive anxiety regarding separation from home, or from those with whom the individual has a strong attachment.
Phobia	A persistent, irrational fear of an object, situation, or activity that the person feels compelled to avoid is referred to as a phobia.
Connectedness	Connectedness, according to Cooper, consists of two dimensions: mutuality and permeability. Connectedness involves processes that link the self to others, as seen in acknowledgment of, respect for, and responsiveness to others.
Suicide	Suicide behavior is rare in childhood but escalates in adolescence. The suicide rate increases in a linear fashion from adolescence through late adulthood.
Obsessive-compulsive disorder	Obsessive-compulsive disorder is an anxiety disorder manifested in a variety of forms, but is most commonly characterized by a subject's obsessive drive to perform a particular task or set of tasks, compulsions commonly termed rituals.
Mood disorder	A mood disorder is a condition where the prevailing emotional mood is distorted or inappropriate to the circumstances.
Heritability	Heritability It is that proportion of the observed variation in a particular phenotype within a particular population, that can be attributed to the contribution of genotype. In other words: it measures the extent to which differences between individuals in a population are due their being different genetically.
Substance abuse	Substance abuse refers to the overindulgence in and dependence on a stimulant, depressant, or other chemical substance, leading to effects that are detrimental to the individual's physical or mental health, or the welfare of others.
Major depression	Major depression is characterized by a severely depressed mood that persists for at least two weeks. Episodes of depression may start suddenly or slowly and can occur several times through a person's life. The disorder may be categorized as "single episode" or "recurrent" depending on whether previous episodes have been experienced before.

Psychotherapy — Psychotherapy is a set of techniques based on psychological principles intended to improve mental health, emotional or behavioral issues.

Learning — Learning is a relatively permanent change in behavior that results from experience. Thus, to attribute a behavioral change to learning, the change must be relatively permanent and must result from experience.

Family functioning — Family functioning is often defined in terms of the availability of two types of primary family resources: utilitarian and psychological.

Family therapy — Family therapy is a branch of psychotherapy that treats family problems. Family therapists consider the family as a system of interacting members; as such, the problems in the family are seen to arise as an emergent property of the interactions in the system, rather than ascribed exclusively to the "faults" or psychological problems of individual members.

Behavior modification — Behavior Modification is a technique of altering an individual's reactions to stimuli through positive reinforcement and the extinction of maladaptive behavior.

Behavior therapy — Behavior therapy refers to the systematic application of the principles of learning to direct modification of a client's problem behaviors.

Play therapy — Play therapy is often used to help the diagnostician to try to determine the cause of disturbed behavior in a child. Treatment therapists then used a type of systematic desensitization or relearning therapy to change the disturbing behavior, either systematically or in less formal social settings.

Developmental level — An individual's current state of physical, emotional, and intellectual development is called the developmental level.

Antidepressants — Antidepressants are medications used primarily in the treatment of clinical depression. Antidepressants create little if any immediate change in mood and require between several days and several weeks to take effect.

Antidepressant — An antidepressant is a medication used primarily in the treatment of clinical depression. They are not thought to produce tolerance, although sudden withdrawal may produce adverse effects. They create little if any immediate change in mood and require between several days and several weeks to take effect.

Antipsychotic — The term antipsychotic is applied to a group of drugs used to treat psychosis.

Protective factors — Protective factors are influences that reduce the impact of early stress and tend to lead to positive outcomes.

Child abuse — Child abuse is the physical or psychological maltreatment of a child.

Art therapy — Art therapy is a type of psychotherapy based upon the assumption that with an engagement in life-enhancing creative processes and the analyses of these processes, individuals will increase awareness and empathy with external reality and within one's self. They will improve skills to cope with symptoms, experiences and trauma, and enhance cognitive abilities.

Post-traumatic stress disorder — Post-traumatic stress disorder is a term for the psychological consequences of exposure to or confrontation with stressful experiences, which involve actual or threatened death, serious physical injury or a threat to physical integrity and which the person found highly traumatic.

Nightmare — Nightmare was the original term for the state later known as waking dream, and more currently as sleep paralysis, associated with rapid eye movement (REM) periods of sleep.

Chronic — Chronic refers to a relatively long duration, usually more than a few months.

Norms — In testing, standards of test performance that permit the comparison of one person's score on

	the test to the scores of others who have taken the same test are referred to as norms.
Reinforcement	In operant conditioning, reinforcement is any change in an environment that (a) occurs after the behavior, (b) seems to make that behavior re-occur more often in the future and (c) that reoccurence of behavior must be the result of the change.
Resilient children	Resilient children weather adverse circumstances, function well despite challenges or threats, or bounce back from traumatic events.
Cultural values	The importance and desirability of various objects and activities as defined by people in a given culture are referred to as cultural values.
Overt aggression	Aggression that is openly directed at its target is referred to as overt aggression.
Maturation	The orderly unfolding of traits, as regulated by the genetic code is called maturation.
Cognitive development	The process by which a child's understanding of the world changes as a function of age and experience is called cognitive development.
Puberty	Puberty refers to the process of physical changes by which a child's body becomes an adult body capable of reproduction.
Nearsightedness	A vision deficiency in which close objects are seen clearly but distant objects appear blurry is nearsightedness.

Adolescence | The period of life bounded by puberty and the assumption of adult responsibilities is adolescence.

Puberty | Puberty refers to the process of physical changes by which a child's body becomes an adult body capable of reproduction.

Social construction | Concept about the nature of reality, based on societally shared perceptions or assumptions is a social construction.

Society | The social sciences use the term society to mean a group of people that form a semi-closed (or semi-open) social system, in which most interactions are with other individuals belonging to the group.

Chronological age | Chronological age refers to the number of years that have elapsed since a person's birth.

Pubescence | The two-year span preceding puberty during which the changes leading to physical and sexual maturity take place is referred to as pubescence.

Maturation | The orderly unfolding of traits, as regulated by the genetic code is called maturation.

Statistics | Statistics is a type of data analysis which practice includes the planning, summarizing, and interpreting of observations of a system possibly followed by predicting or forecasting of future events based on a mathematical model of the system being observed.

Marijuana | Marijuana is the dried vegetable matter of the Cannabis sativa plant. It contains large concentrations of compounds that have medicinal and psychoactive effects when consumed, usually by smoking or eating.

Suicide | Suicide behavior is rare in childhood but escalates in adolescence. The suicide rate increases in a linear fashion from adolescence through late adulthood.

Survey | A method of scientific investigation in which a large sample of people answer questions about their attitudes or behavior is referred to as a survey.

Hormone | A hormone is a chemical messenger from one cell (or group of cells) to another. The best known are those produced by endocrine glands, but they are produced by nearly every organ system. The function of hormones is to serve as a signal to the target cells; the action of the hormone is determined by the pattern of secretion and the signal transduction of the receiving tissue.

Estrogen | Estrogen is a group of steroid compounds that function as the primary female sex hormone. They are produced primarily by developing follicles in the ovaries, the corpus luteum and the placenta.

Genitals | Genitals refers to the internal and external reproductive organs.

Testosterone | Testosterone is a steroid hormone from the androgen group. It is the principal male sex hormone and the "original" anabolic steroid.

Androgen | Androgen is the generic term for any natural or synthetic compound, usually a steroid hormone, that stimulates or controls the development and maintenance of masculine characteristics in vertebrates by binding to androgen receptors.

Testes | Testes are the male reproductive glands or gonads; this is where sperm develop and are stored.

Clitoris | Clitoris refers to an external female sex organ that is highly sensitive to sexual stimulation.

Pituitary gland | The pituitary gland is an endocrine gland about the size of a pea that sits in the small, bony cavity at the base of the brain. The pituitary gland secretes hormones regulating a wide

	variety of bodily activities, including trophic hormones that stimulate other endocrine glands.
Hypothalamus	The hypothalamus is a region of the brain located below the thalamus, forming the major portion of the ventral region of the diencephalon and functioning to regulate certain metabolic processes and other autonomic activities.
Obesity	The state of being more than 20 percent above the average weight for a person of one's height is called obesity.
Protein	A protein is a complex, high-molecular-weight organic compound that consists of amino acids joined by peptide bonds. It is essential to the structure and function of all living cells and viruses. Many are enzymes or subunits of enzymes.
Leptin	Leptin refers to a hormone produced by fat cells that acts in the brain to inhibit hunger and regulate body weight.
Brain	The brain controls and coordinates most movement, behavior and homeostatic body functions such as heartbeat, blood pressure, fluid balance and body temperature. Functions of the brain are responsible for cognition, emotion, memory, motor learning and other sorts of learning. The brain is primarily made up of two types of cells: glia and neurons.
Gland	A gland is an organ in an animal's body that synthesizes a substance for release such as hormones, often into the bloodstream or into cavities inside the body or its outer surface.
Adolescent growth spurt	The rapid increase in weight and height that occurs around the onset of puberty is referred to as the adolescent growth spurt.
Ovulation	Ovulation is the process in the menstrual cycle by which a mature ovarian follicle ruptures and discharges an ovum (also known as an oocyte, female gamete, or casually, an egg) that participates in reproduction.
Secular trend	A secular trend is change that occurs with respect to time.
Affect	A subjective feeling or emotional tone often accompanied by bodily expressions noticeable to others is called affect.
Body image	A person's body image is their perception of their physical appearance. It is more than what a person thinks they will see in a mirror, it is inextricably tied to their self-esteem and acceptance by peers.
Fallopian tube	A tube through which the eggs travel from the ovaries to the uterus is a fallopian tube.
Scrotum	The scrotum is an external sack of skin that holds the testes.
Uterus	The uterus or womb is the major female reproductive organ. The main function of the uterus is to accept a fertilized ovum which becomes implanted into the endometrium, and derives nourishment from blood vessels which develop exclusively for this purpose.
Penis	The penis is the external male copulatory organ and the external male organ of urination. In humans, the penis is homologous to the female clitoris, as it develops from the same embryonic structure. It is capable of erection for use in copulation.
Primary sex characteristics	The primary sex characteristics are any of those parts of the body which are involved in sexual reproduction and constitute the reproductive system..
Secondary sex characteristics	Secondary sex characteristics are traits that distinguish the two sexes of a species, but that are not directly part of the reproductive system.
Larynx	The larynx, or voicebox, is an organ in the neck of mammals involved in protection of the trachea and sound production. The larynx houses the vocal cords, and is situated at the point where the upper tract splits into the trachea and the esophagus.

Nocturnal emission	A nocturnal emission is an ejaculation of semen experienced by males during sleep. It is also called a "wet dream", an involuntary orgasm, or simply an orgasm during sleep.
Ejaculation	Ejaculation is the process of ejecting semen from the penis, and is usually accompanied by orgasm as a result of sexual stimulation.
Semen	Semen is a fluid that contains spermatozoa. It is secreted by the gonads of males for the fertilization of female ova.
Spermarche	Spermarche refers to a boy's first ejaculation.
Menarche	Menarche is the first menstrual period as a girl's body progresses through the changes of puberty. Menarche usually occurs about two years after the first changes of breast development.
Longitudinal study	Longitudinal study is a type of developmental study in which the same group of participants is followed and measured for an extended period of time, often years.
Pheromone	A pheromone is any chemical produced by a living organism that transmits a message to other members of the same species. There are alarm pheromones, food trail pheromones, sex pheromones, and many others. Their use among insects has been particularly well documented, although many vertebrates also communicate using pheromones. Their use by humans is controversial.
Gene	A gene is an ultramicroscopic area of the chromosome. It is the smallest physical unit of the DNA molecule that carries a piece of hereditary information.
X chromosome	The sex chromosomes are one of the 23 pairs of human chromosomes. Each person normally has one pair of sex chromosomes in each cell. Females have two X chromosomes, while males have one X and one Y chromosome. The X chromosome carries hundreds of genes but few, if any, of these have anything to do directly with sex determination.
Receptor	A sensory receptor is a structure that recognizes a stimulus in the internal or external environment of an organism. In response to stimuli the sensory receptor initiates sensory transduction by creating graded potentials or action potentials in the same cell or in an adjacent one.
Hypothesis	A specific statement about behavior or mental processes that is testable through research is a hypothesis.
Allele	An allele is any one of a number of alternative forms of the same gene (sometimes the term refers to a non-gene sequence) occupying a given locus (position) on a chromosome.
Eating disorders	Psychological disorders characterized by distortion of the body image and gross disturbances in eating patterns are called eating disorders.
Depression	In everyday language depression refers to any downturn in mood, which may be relatively transitory and perhaps due to something trivial. This is differentiated from Clinical depression which is marked by symptoms that last two weeks or more and are so severe that they interfere with daily living.
Anxiety	Anxiety is a complex combination of the feeling of fear, apprehension and worry often accompanied by physical sensations such as palpitations, chest pain and/or shortness of breath.
Physiological changes	Alterations in heart rate, blood pressure, perspiration, and other involuntary responses are physiological changes.
Sleep cycle	Sleep cycle refers to a cycle of sleep lasting about 90 minutes and including one or more stages of NREM sleep followed by a period of REM sleep.

Biological rhythm — A biological rhythm is a hypothetical cyclic pattern of alterations in physiology, emotions, and/or intellect

Habit — A habit is a response that has become completely separated from its eliciting stimulus. Early learning theorists used the term to describe S-R associations, however not all S-R associations become a habit, rather many are extinguished after reinforcement is withdrawn.

Metabolism — Metabolism is the biochemical modification of chemical compounds in living organisms and cells.

Fat cells — Fat cells serve as storehouses for liquefied fat in the body and that number from 25 to 35 billion in normal weight individuals; with weight loss, they decrease in size but not in number.

Chronic — Chronic refers to a relatively long duration, usually more than a few months.

Perception — Perception is the process of acquiring, interpreting, selecting, and organizing sensory information.

Attitude — An enduring mental representation of a person, place, or thing that evokes an emotional response and related behavior is called attitude.

Cohort — A cohort is a group of individuals defined by their date of birth.

Anorexia — Anorexia nervosa is an eating disorder characterized by voluntary starvation and exercise stress.

Bulimia — Bulimia refers to a disorder in which a person binges on incredibly large quantities of food, then purges by vomiting or by using laxatives. Bulimia is often less about food, and more to do with deep psychological issues and profound feelings of lack of control.

Binge — Binge refers to relatively brief episode of uncontrolled, excessive consumption.

Binge eating disorder — Binge eating disorder is a syndrome in which people feel their eating is out of control; eat what most would think is an unusually large amount of food; eat much more quickly than usual; eat until so full they are uncomfortable; eat large amounts of food, even when they are not really hungry; eat alone because they are embarrassed about the amount of food they eat; feel disgusted, depressed, or guilty after overeating.

Behavioral therapy — The treatment of a mental disorder through the application of basic principles of conditioning and learning is called behavioral therapy.

Behavior therapy — Behavior therapy refers to the systematic application of the principles of learning to direct modification of a client's problem behaviors.

Antidepressant — An antidepressant is a medication used primarily in the treatment of clinical depression. They are not thought to produce tolerance, although sudden withdrawal may produce adverse effects. They create little if any immediate change in mood and require between several days and several weeks to take effect.

Psychotherapy — Psychotherapy is a set of techniques based on psychological principles intended to improve mental health, emotional or behavioral issues.

Attention — Attention is the cognitive process of selectively concentrating on one thing while ignoring other things. Psychologists have labeled three types of attention: sustained attention, selective attention, and divided attention.

Serotonin — Serotonin, a neurotransmitter, is believed to play an important part of the biochemistry of depression, bipolar disorder and anxiety. It is also believed to be influential on sexuality and appetite.

Cocaine — Cocaine is a crystalline tropane alkaloid that is obtained from the leaves of the coca plant.

It is a stimulant of the central nervous system and an appetite suppressant, creating what has been described as a euphoric sense of happiness and increased energy.

Anabolic steroid

Anabolic steroids are a class of natural and synthetic steroid hormones that promote cell growth and division, resulting in growth of muscle tissue and sometimes bone size and strength. Testosterone is the best known natural anabolic steroid, as well as the best known natural androgen.

Ecstasy

Ecstasy as an emotion is to be outside oneself, in a trancelike state in which an individual transcends ordinary consciousness and as a result has a heightened capacity for exceptional thought or experience. Ecstasy also refers to a relatively new hallucinogen that is chemically similar to mescaline and the amphetamines.

MDMA

MDMA, most commonly known today by the street name ecstasy, is a synthetic entactogen of the phenethylamine family whose primary effect is to stimulate the secretion of large amounts of serotonin as well as dopamine and noradrenaline in the brain, causing a general sense of openness, empathy, energy, euphoria, and well-being.

Impulse control

Deferred gratification is the ability of a person to wait for things they want. This trait is critical for life success. Those who lack this trait are said to suffer from poor impulse control, and often become criminals, as they are unwilling to work and wait for their paycheck.

Predisposition

Predisposition refers to an inclination or diathesis to respond in a certain way, either inborn or acquired. In abnormal psychology, it is a factor that lowers the ability to withstand stress and inclines the individual toward pathology.

Temperament

Temperament refers to a basic, innate disposition to change behavior. The activity level is an important dimension of temperament.

Alcoholism

A disorder that involves long-term, repeated, uncontrolled, compulsive, and excessive use of alcoholic beverages and that impairs the drinker's health and work and social relationships is called alcoholism.

Sensation

Sensation is the first stage in the chain of biochemical and neurologic events that begins with the impinging of a stimulus upon the receptor cells of a sensory organ, which then leads to perception, the mental state that is reflected in statements like "I see a uniformly blue wall."

Peer pressure

Peer pressure comprises a set of group dynamics whereby a group of people in which one feels comfortable may override the sexual personal habits, individual moral inhibitions or idiosyncratic desires to impose a group norm of attitudes or behaviors.

Heroin

Heroin is widely and illegally used as a powerful and addictive drug producing intense euphoria, which often disappears with increasing tolerance. Heroin is a semi-synthetic opioid. It is the 3,6-diacetyl derivative of morphine and is synthesised from it by acetylation.

Authoritative parenting

Authoritative parenting encourages children to be independent but still places limits and controls on their actions. Extensive verbal give-and-take is allowed, and parents are warm and nurturant toward the child.

Gender difference

A gender difference is a disparity between genders involving quality or quantity. Though some gender differences are controversial, they are not to be confused with sexist stereotypes.

Major depression

Major depression is characterized by a severely depressed mood that persists for at least two weeks. Episodes of depression may start suddenly or slowly and can occur several times through a person's life. The disorder may be categorized as "single episode" or "recurrent" depending on whether previous episodes have been experienced before.

Addictive drugs	Addictive drugs produce a biological or psychological dependence in the user; withdrawal from them leads to a craving for the drug that in some cases can be nearly irresistible.
Early-maturing	Early-maturing girls tend to be more likely than their peers to engage in a number of deviant behaviors, such as being truant from school, getting drunk, and stealing.
Addiction	Addiction is an uncontrollable compulsion to repeat a behavior regardless of its consequences. Many drugs or behaviors can precipitate a pattern of conditions recognized as addiction, which include a craving for more of the drug or behavior, increased physiological tolerance to exposure, and withdrawal symptoms in the absence of the stimulus.
Ethnic group	An ethnic group is a culture or subculture whose members are readily distinguishable by outsiders based on traits originating from a common racial, national, linguistic, or religious source. Members of an ethnic group are often presumed to be culturally or biologically similar, although this is not in fact necessarily the case.
Homosexual	Homosexual refers to a sexual orientation characterized by aesthetic attraction, romantic love, and sexual desire exclusively for members of the same sex or gender identity.
Personality	Personality refers to the pattern of enduring characteristics that differentiates a person, the patterns of behaviors that make each individual unique.
Counselor	A counselor is a mental health professional who specializes in helping people with problems not involving serious mental disorders.
Substance abuse	Substance abuse refers to the overindulgence in and dependence on a stimulant, depressant, or other chemical substance, leading to effects that are detrimental to the individual's physical or mental health, or the welfare of others.
Hyperactivity	Hyperactivity can be described as a state in which a individual is abnormally easily excitable and exuberant. Strong emotional reactions and a very short span of attention is also typical for the individual.
Cognitive development	The process by which a child's understanding of the world changes as a function of age and experience is called cognitive development.
Formal operations	Formal operations in Piaget's theory is the final stage of cognitive development, in which children are able to apply abstract logical rules. Not everyone reaches the formal operations stage of development.
Piaget	Piaget argued that young children's answers were qualitatively different than older children rather than quantitative. There are two major aspects to his theory: the process of coming to know and the stages we move through as we gradually acquire this ability.
Concrete operations	In Piaget's theory, the third major stage of cognitive development, in which children can decenter their perception, are less egocentric, and can think logically about concrete objects is called concrete operations.
Hypothetical-deductive reasoning	In Piaget's last stage of development, the formal operational stage, adolescents have the cognitive ability to develop hypotheses, or best guesses, about ways to solve problems. This is called hypothetical-deductive reasoning.
Formal reasoning	The type of reasoning in which the form of an argument, not its semantic content, is crucial is referred to as formal reasoning.
Variable	A variable refers to a measurable factor, characteristic, or attribute of an individual or a system.
Reasoning	Reasoning is the act of using reason to derive a conclusion from certain premises. There are two main methods to reach a conclusion,deductive reasoning and inductive reasoning.

Formal operational	According to Piaget, the period from age 12 to adulthood, which is characterized by abstract thought is referred to as the formal operational stage.
Developmental psychology	The branch of psychology that studies the patterns of growth and change occurring throughout life is referred to as developmental psychology.
Aristotle	Aristotle can be credited with the development of the first theory of learning. He concluded that ideas were generated in consciousness based on four principlesof association: contiguity, similarity, contrast, and succession. In contrast to Plato, he believed that knowledge derived from sensory experience and was not inherited.
Stages	Stages represent relatively discrete periods of time in which functioning is qualitatively different from functioning at other periods.
Individual differences	Individual differences psychology studies the ways in which individual people differ in their behavior. This is distinguished from other aspects of psychology in that although psychology is ostensibly a study of individuals, modern psychologists invariably study groups.
Intuition	Quick, impulsive thought that does not make use of formal logic or clear reasoning is referred to as intuition.
Wisdom	Wisdom is the ability to make correct judgments and decisions. It is an intangible quality gained through experience. Whether or not something is wise is determined in a pragmatic sense by its popularity, how long it has been around, and its ability to predict against future events.
Learning	Learning is a relatively permanent change in behavior that results from experience. Thus, to attribute a behavioral change to learning, the change must be relatively permanent and must result from experience.
Intonation	The use of pitches of varying levels to help communicate meaning is called intonation.
Subculture	As understood in sociology, anthropology and cultural studies, a subculture is a set of people with a distinct set of behavior and beliefs that differentiate them from a larger culture of which they are a part.
Ethnicity	Ethnicity refers to a characteristic based on cultural heritage, nationality characteristics, race, religion, and language.
Clique	A clique is an informal and restricted social group formed by a number of people who share common. Social roles vary, but two roles commonly associated with a female clique is notably applicable to most - that of the "queen bee" and that of the "outcast".
Hypocrisy	Publicly advocating some attitude or behavior and then acting in a way that is inconsistent with this espoused attitude or behavior is called hypocrisy.
Imaginary audience	Imaginary audience refers to an aspect of adolescent egocentrism; the belief that other people are as concerned with our thoughts and behaviors as we are.
Personal fable	Personal fable refers to an aspect of adolescent egocentrism, the belief that our feelings and ideas are special and unique and that we are invulnerable.
Validity	The extent to which a test measures what it is intended to measure is called validity.
Kohlberg	Kohlberg believed that people progressed in their moral reasoning through a series of developmental stages.
Moral development	Development regarding rules and conventions about what people should do in their interactions with other people is called moral development.
Postconventi-nal morality	The third level in Kohlberg's theory of moral reasoning, postconventional morality, suggests individuals can follow internally held moral principles and are able to decide among

	conflicting moral standards.
Moral reasoning	Moral reasoning involves concepts of justice, whereas social conventional judgments are concepts of social organization.
Punishment	Punishment is the addtion of a stimulus that reduces the frequency of a response, or the removal of a stimulus that results in a reduction of the response.
Obedience	Obedience is the willingness to follow the will of others. Humans have been shown to be surprisingly obedient in the presence of perceived legitimate authority figures, as demonstrated by the Milgram experiment in the 1960s.
Universal ethical principles	In Kohlberg's sixth stage, universal ethical principles, moral reasoning is based on the use of abstract reasoning using universal ethical principles.
Conventional morality	Conventional morality is the second level in Kohlberg's theory of moral reasoning. The standards of authority figures are internalized in this stage.
Moral judgment	Making decisions about which actions are right and which are wrong is a moral judgment.
Postconventional level	According to Kohlberg, a period during which moral judgments are derived from moral principles and people look to themselves to set moral standards is the postconventional level.
Cognitive approach	A cognitive approach focuses on the mental processes involved in knowing: how we direct our attention, perceive, remember, think, and solve problems.
Emotion	An emotion is a mental states that arise spontaneously, rather than through conscious effort. They are often accompanied by physiological changes.
Empathy	Empathy is the recognition and understanding of the states of mind, including beliefs, desires and particularly emotions of others without injecting your own.
Guilt	Guilt describes many concepts related to a negative emotion or condition caused by actions which are believed to be, morally wrong. According to Freud, the avoidance of guilt is the basis for moral behavior.
Carol Gilligan	Carol Gilligan is best known for her work on the ethics of care, a theory that contrasts ethics of care to so-called ethics of justice. She claimed that the results of Kohlberg were biased because the participants in the basic study were largely male, and that the scoring method subsequently used tended to favor a principled way of reasoning that was more common to boys, over a moral argumentation concentrating on relations, which would be more amenable to girls.
Cross-cultural studies	Cross-cultural studies are comparisons of a culture with one or more other cultures, which provides information about the degree to which behavior is similar across cultures or the degree to which it is culture specific .
Cultural values	The importance and desirability of various objects and activities as defined by people in a given culture are referred to as cultural values.
Reflection	Reflection is the process of rephrasing or repeating thoughts and feelings expressed, making the person more aware of what they are saying or thinking.
Self-efficacy	Self-efficacy is the belief that one has the capabilities to execute the courses of actions required to manage prospective situations.
Motivation	In psychology, motivation is the driving force (desire) behind all actions of an organism.
Bandura	Bandura is best known for his work on social learning theory or Social Cognitivism. His famous Bobo doll experiment illustrated that people learn from observing others.

Socioeconomic Status	A family's socioeconomic status is based on family income, parental education level, parental occupation, and social status in the community. Those with high status often have more success in preparing their children for school because they have access to a wide range of resources.
Questionnaire	A self-report method of data collection or clinical assessment method in which the individual being studied checks off items on a printed list, answers multiple-choice questions, or writes out answers to essay questions aimed at producing a selfdescription is called questionnaire.
Social capital	Family and community resources upon which a person or family can draw is called social capital.
Authoritative parents	Authoritative parents are strict and warm. Authoritative parents demand mature behavior but use reason rather than force in discipline.
Authoritarian parents	Parents who are rigid in their rules and who demand obedience for the sake of obedience are called authoritarian parents.
Permissive parents	Parents who impose few, if any, rules and who do not supervise their children closely are called permissive parents.
Achievement test	A test designed to determine a person's level of knowledge in a given subject area is referred to as an achievement test.
Authoritarian	The term authoritarian is used to describe a style that enforces strong and sometimes oppressive measures against those in its sphere of influence, generally without attempts at gaining their consent.
Triarchic Theory of Intelligence	The Triarchic Theory of Intelligence was formulated by Robert J. Sternberg. It proposes that intelligence consists of componential intelligence, experiential intelligence, and contextual intelligence.
Sternberg	Sternberg proposed the triarchic theory of intelligence: componential, experiential, and practical. His notion of general intelligence or the g-factor, is a composite of intelligence scores across multiple modalities.
Critical thinking	Critical thinking is a mental process of analyzing or evaluating information, particularly statements or propositions that are offered as true.
Socioeconomic	Socioeconomic pertains to the study of the social and economic impacts of any product or service offering, market intervention or other activity on an economy as a whole and on the companies, organization and individuals who are its main economic actors.
Intelligence test	An intelligence test is a standardized means of assessing a person's current mental ability, for example, the Stanford-Binet test and the Wechsler Adult Intelligence Scale.
Mentoring	Mentoring refers to a developmental relationship between a more experienced individual and a less experienced partner sometimes referred to as a protégé. In well-designed formal mentoring programs, there are program goals, schedules, and training.
Self-esteem	Self-esteem refers to a person's subjective appraisal of himself or herself as intrinsically positive or negative to some degree.
Metacognition	Metacognition refers to thinking about cognition (memory, perception, calculation, association, etc.) itself. Metacognition can be divided into two types of knowledge: explicit, conscious, factual knowledge; and implicit, unconscious, procedural knowledge.
Socialization	Social rules and social relations are created, communicated, and changed in verbal and nonverbal ways creating social complexity useful in identifying outsiders and intelligent breeding partners. The process of learning these skills is called socialization.

Gender stereotypes	Broad categories that reflect our impressions and beliefs about typical females and males are referred to as gender stereotypes.
Marcia	Marcia argued that identity could be viewed as a structure of beliefs, abilities and past experiences regarding the self. Identity is a dynamic, not static structure. At least three aspects of the adolescent's development are important in identity formation: must be confident that they have parental support, must have an established sense of industry, and must be able to adopt a self-reflective stance toward the future.
Juvenile delinquency	Juvenile delinquency refers to a broad range of child and adolescent behaviors, including socially unacceptable behavior, status offenses, and criminal acts.
Juvenile delinquent	An adolescent who breaks the law or engages in behavior that is considered illegal is referred to as a juvenile delinquent.
Threshold	In general, a threshold is a fixed location or value where an abrupt change is observed. In the sensory modalities, it is the minimum amount of stimulus energy necessary to elicit a sensory response.

Cognitive development	The process by which a child's understanding of the world changes as a function of age and experience is called cognitive development.
Construct	A generalized concept, such as anxiety or gravity, is a construct.
Autonomy	Autonomy is the condition of something that does not depend on anything else.
Stages	Stages represent relatively discrete periods of time in which functioning is qualitatively different from functioning at other periods.
Identity versus identity confusion	Identity versus identity confusion is Erikson's fifth developmental stage, which individuals experience during the adolescent years. At this time, individuals are faced with finding out who they are, what they re all about, and where they are going in life.
Identity versus role confusion	Identity versus role confusion, Erikson's fifth psychosocial stage, shows adolescents needing to establish their own identity and to form values to live by. Failure at this stage can lead to an identity crisis.
Adolescence	The period of life bounded by puberty and the assumption of adult responsibilities is adolescence.
Society	The social sciences use the term society to mean a group of people that form a semi-closed (or semi-open) social system, in which most interactions are with other individuals belonging to the group.
Psychosocial development	Erikson's psychosocial development describe eight developmental stages through which a healthily developing human should pass from infancy to late adulthood. In each stage the person confronts, and hopefully masters, new challenges.
Industry versus inferiority	Erikson's fourth stage of development, industry versus inferiority, develops in the elementary school years. Initiative brings children into contact with a new experiences. They direct their energy toward mastering knowledge and intellectual skills.
Psychosocial moratorium	Erikson's term for the gap between childhood security and adult autonomy that adolescents experience as part of their identity exploration is psychosocial moratorium. The individual is actively exploring alternatives in an attempt to form an identity.
Identity crisis	Erikson coinded the term identity crisis: "...a psychosocial state or condition of disorientation and role confusion occurring especially in adolescents as a result of conflicting internal and external experiences, pressures, and expectations and often producing acute anxiety."
Ethnic group	An ethnic group is a culture or subculture whose members are readily distinguishable by outsiders based on traits originating from a common racial, national, linguistic, or religious source. Members of an ethnic group are often presumed to be culturally or biologically similar, although this is not in fact necessarily the case.
Ideology	An ideology can be thought of as a comprehensive vision, as a way of looking at things, as in common sense and several philosophical tendencies, or a set of ideas proposed by the dominant class of a society to all members of this society.
Infancy	The developmental period that extends from birth to 18 or 24 months is called infancy.
Marcia	Marcia argued that identity could be viewed as a structure of beliefs, abilities and past experiences regarding the self. Identity is a dynamic, not static structure. At least three aspects of the adolescent's development are important in identity formation: must be confident that they have parental support, must have an established sense of industry, and must be able to adopt a self-reflective stance toward the future.
Identity statuses	The states of ego development that depend on the presence or absence of crisis and commitment are called identity statuses.

Personality	Personality refers to the pattern of enduring characteristics that differentiates a person, the patterns of behaviors that make each individual unique.
Ego	In Freud's view the Ego serves to balance our primitive needs and our moral beliefs and taboos. Relying on experience, a healthy Ego provides the ability to adapt to reality and interact with the outside world.
Moral reasoning	Moral reasoning involves concepts of justice, whereas social conventional judgments are concepts of social organization.
Self-esteem	Self-esteem refers to a person's subjective appraisal of himself or herself as intrinsically positive or negative to some degree.
Anxiety	Anxiety is a complex combination of the feeling of fear, apprehension and worry often accompanied by physical sensations such as palpitations, chest pain and/or shortness of breath.
Identity diffusion	Identity diffusion is Marcia's term for adolescents who have not yet experienced a crisis or made any commitments.
Identity Achievement	Identity achievement is Marcia's term for an adolescent's having undergone a crisis and made a commitment.
Obedience	Obedience is the willingness to follow the will of others. Humans have been shown to be surprisingly obedient in the presence of perceived legitimate authority figures, as demonstrated by the Milgram experiment in the 1960s.
Reasoning	Reasoning is the act of using reason to derive a conclusion from certain premises. There are two main methods to reach a conclusion,deductive reasoning and inductive reasoning.
Late adolescence	Late adolescence refers to approximately the latter half of the second decade of life. Career interests, dating, and identity exploration are often more pronounced in late adolescence than in early adolescence.
Gender difference	A gender difference is a disparity between genders involving quality or quantity. Though some gender differences are controversial, they are not to be confused with sexist stereotypes.
Carol Gilligan	Carol Gilligan is best known for her work on the ethics of care, a theory that contrasts ethics of care to so-called ethics of justice. She claimed that the results of Kohlberg were biased because the participants in the basic study were largely male, and that the scoring method subsequently used tended to favor a principled way of reasoning that was more common to boys, over a moral argumentation concentrating on relations, which would be more amenable to girls.
Individual differences	Individual differences psychology studies the ways in which individual people differ in their behavior. This is distinguished from other aspects of psychology in that although psychology is ostensibly a study of individuals, modern psychologists invariably study groups.
Psychosocial stages	Erikson's eight developmental stages through the life span, each defined by a conflict that must be resolved satisfactorily in order for healthy personality development to occur are called psychosocial stages.
Connectedness	Connectedness, according to Cooper, consists of two dimensions: mutuality and permeability. Connectedness involves processes that link the self to others, as seen in acknowledgment of, respect for, and responsiveness to others.
Longitudinal study	Longitudinal study is a type of developmental study in which the same group of participants is followed and measured for an extended period of time, often years.
Self-concept	Self-concept refers to domain-specific evaluations of the self where a domain may be academics, athletics, etc.

Attitude	An enduring mental representation of a person, place, or thing that evokes an emotional response and related behavior is called attitude.
Ethnic identity	An enduring, basic aspect of the self that includes a sense of membership in an ethnic group and the attitudes and feelings related to that membership is called an ethnic identity.
Ethnicity	Ethnicity refers to a characteristic based on cultural heritage, nationality characteristics, race, religion, and language.
Questionnaire	A self-report method of data collection or clinical assessment method in which the individual being studied checks off items on a printed list, answers multiple-choice questions, or writes out answers to essay questions aimed at producing a selfdescription is called questionnaire.
Prejudice	Prejudice in general, implies coming to a judgment on the subject before learning where the preponderance of the evidence actually lies, or formation of a judgement without direct experience.
Discrimination	In Learning theory, discrimination refers the ability to distinguish between a conditioned stimulus and other stimuli. It can be brought about by extensive training or differential reinforcement. In social terms, it is the denial of privileges to a person or a group on the basis of prejudice.
Sexual orientation	Sexual orientation refers to the sex or gender of people who are the focus of a person's amorous or erotic desires, fantasies, and spontaneous feelings, the gender(s) toward which one is primarily "oriented".
Attachment	Attachment is the tendency to seek closeness to another person and feel secure when that person is present.
Self-image	A person's self-image is the mental picture, generally of a kind that is quite resistant to change, that depicts not only details that are potentially available to objective investigation by others, but also items that have been learned by that person about himself or herself.
Homosexuality	Homosexuality refers to a sexual orientation characterized by aesthetic attraction, romantic love, and sexual desire exclusively for members of the same sex or gender identity.
Social stigma	A social stigma a distinctive characteristic in a person which can cause or be the result of marginalization when used as an insult by individuals or groups.
Homosexual	Homosexual refers to a sexual orientation characterized by aesthetic attraction, romantic love, and sexual desire exclusively for members of the same sex or gender identity.
Bisexuality	Bisexuality is a sexual orientation characterized by aesthetic attraction, romantic love and sexual desire for both males and females.
American Psychological Association	The American Psychological Association is a professional organization representing psychology in the US. The mission statement is to "advance psychology as a science and profession and as a means of promoting health, education , and human welfare".
Mental disorder	Mental disorder refers to a disturbance in a person's emotions, drives, thought processes, or behavior that involves serious and relatively prolonged distress and/or impairment in ability to function, is not simply a normal response to some event or set of events in the person's environment.
Mental illness	Mental illness is the term formerly used to mean psychological disorder but less preferred because it implies that the causes of the disorder can be found in a medical disease process.
Learning	Learning is a relatively permanent change in behavior that results from experience. Thus, to attribute a behavioral change to learning, the change must be relatively permanent and must

result from experience.

Hormone A hormone is a chemical messenger from one cell (or group of cells) to another. The best known are those produced by endocrine glands, but they are produced by nearly every organ system. The function of hormones is to serve as a signal to the target cells; the action of the hormone is determined by the pattern of secretion and the signal transduction of the receiving tissue.

Puberty Puberty refers to the process of physical changes by which a child's body becomes an adult body capable of reproduction.

Fetus A fetus develops from the end of the 8th week of pregnancy (when the major structures have formed), until birth.

Affect A subjective feeling or emotional tone often accompanied by bodily expressions noticeable to others is called affect.

Brain The brain controls and coordinates most movement, behavior and homeostatic body functions such as heartbeat, blood pressure, fluid balance and body temperature. Functions of the brain are responsible for cognition, emotion, memory, motor learning and other sorts of learning. The brain is primarily made up of two types of cells: glia and neurons.

X chromosome The sex chromosomes are one of the 23 pairs of human chromosomes. Each person normally has one pair of sex chromosomes in each cell. Females have two X chromosomes, while males have one X and one Y chromosome. The X chromosome carries hundreds of genes but few, if any, of these have anything to do directly with sex determination.

Concordance Concordance as used in genetics means the presence of the same trait in both members of a pair of twins, or in sets of individuals. A twin study examines the concordance rates of twins having the same trait, especially a disease, which can help determine how much the disease is affected by genetics versus environment.

Monozygotic Identical twins occur when a single egg is fertilized to form one zygote, calld monozygotic, but the zygote then divides into two separate embryos. The two embryos develop into foetuses sharing the same womb. Monozygotic twins are genetically identical unless there has been a mutation in development, and they are almost always the same gender.

Dizygotic Fraternal twins (commonly known as "non-identical twins") usually occur when two fertilized eggs are implanted in the uterine wall at the same time. The two eggs form two zygotes, and these twins are therefore also known as dizygotic.

Survey A method of scientific investigation in which a large sample of people answer questions about their attitudes or behavior is referred to as a survey.

Social influence Social influence is when the actions or thoughts of individual(s) are changed by other individual(s). Peer pressure is an example of social influence.

Population Population refers to all members of a well-defined group of organisms, events, or things.

Evolution Commonly used to refer to gradual change, evolution is the change in the frequency of alleles within a population from one generation to the next. This change may be caused by different mechanisms, including natural selection, genetic drift, or changes in population (gene flow).

Sexually Transmitted Disease Sexually transmitted disease is commonly transmitted between partners through some form of sexual activity, most commonly vaginal intercourse, oral sex, or anal sex.

Statistics Statistics is a type of data analysis which practice includes the planning, summarizing, and interpreting of observations of a system possibly followed by predicting or forecasting of future events based on a mathematical model of the system being observed.

Gender role	A cluster of behaviors that characterizes traditional female or male behaviors within a cultural setting is a gender role.
Lesbian	A lesbian is a homosexual woman. They are women who are sexually and romantically attracted to other women.
Social skills	Social skills are skills used to interact and communicate with others to assist status in the social structure and other motivations.
Perception	Perception is the process of acquiring, interpreting, selecting, and organizing sensory information.
Norms	In testing, standards of test performance that permit the comparison of one person's score on the test to the scores of others who have taken the same test are referred to as norms.
Sexual abuse	Sexual abuse is a term used to describe non- consentual sexual relations between two or more parties which are considered criminally and/or morally offensive.
Genitals	Genitals refers to the internal and external reproductive organs.
Genital herpes	Genital herpes refers to a sexually transmitted disease caused by a large family of viruses of different strains. These strains also produce other, nonsexually transmitted diseases such as chicken pox and mononucleosis.
Chronic	Chronic refers to a relatively long duration, usually more than a few months.
Chlamydia	Chlamydia is currently one of the most common sexually transmitted disease. It can cause genital infections, conjunctivitis, pelvic inflammatory disease, pneumonia, urethritis, Fitz-Hugh-Curtis syndrome, Reiter's syndrome and lymphogranuloma venereum.
Gonorrhea	Gonorrhea is among the most common curable sexually transmitted diseases in the world. In men, epididymitis, prostatitis and urethral stricture can result from untreated gonorrhoea.In women, Bartholinitis and abscess formation, pelvic inflammatory disease and Fitz-Hugh-Curtis syndrome can occur.
Wisdom	Wisdom is the ability to make correct judgments and decisions. It is an intangible quality gained through experience. Whether or not something is wise is determined in a pragmatic sense by its popularity, how long it has been around, and its ability to predict against future events.
Human immunodefici-ncy virus	The human immunodeficiency virus is a retrovirus that primarily infects vital components of the human immune system. It is transmitted through penetrative and oral sex; blood transfusion; the sharing of contaminated needles in health care settings and through drug injection; and, between mother and infant, during pregnancy, childbirth and breastfeeding.
Semen	Semen is a fluid that contains spermatozoa. It is secreted by the gonads of males for the fertilization of female ova.
Immune system	The most important function of the human immune system occurs at the cellular level of the blood and tissues. The lymphatic and blood circulation systems are highways for specialized white blood cells. These cells include B cells, T cells, natural killer cells, and macrophages. All function with the primary objective of recognizing, attacking and destroying bacteria, viruses, cancer cells, and all substances seen as foreign.
Early childhood	Early childhood refers to the developmental period extending from the end of infancy to about 5 or 6 years of age; sometimes called the preschool years.
Prenatal	Prenatal period refers to the time from conception to birth.
Adolescent rebellion	Pattern of emotional turmoil, characteristic of a minority of adolescents, which may involve conflict with family, alienation from adult society, reckless behavior, and rejection of

adult values is an adolescent rebellion.

Stanley Hall — His laboratory at Johns Hopkins is considered to be the first American laboratory of psychology. In 1887 Stanley Hall founded the American Journal of Psychology. His interests centered around child development and evolutionary theory

Sigmund Freud — Sigmund Freud was the founder of the psychoanalytic school, based on his theory that unconscious motives control much behavior, that particular kinds of unconscious thoughts and memories are the source of neurosis, and that neurosis could be treated through bringing these unconscious thoughts and memories to consciousness in psychoanalytic treatment.

Resurgence — Resurgence refers to the reappearance during extinction, of a previously reinforced behavior.

Life span — Life span refers to the upper boundary of life, the maximum number of years an individual can live. The maximum life span of human beings is about 120 years of age. Females live an average of 6 years longer than males.

Eccles — Eccles was key to a number of important developments in neuroscience. Until around 1949, Eccles believed that synaptic transmission was primarily electrical rather than chemical. Although he was wrong in this hypothesis, his arguments led himself and others to perform some of the experiments which proved chemical synaptic transmission.

Emotion — An emotion is a mental states that arise spontaneously, rather than through conscious effort. They are often accompanied by physiological changes.

Authoritative parenting — Authoritative parenting encourages children to be independent but still places limits and controls on their actions. Extensive verbal give-and-take is allowed, and parents are warm and nurturant toward the child.

Authoritarian parenting — Authoritarian parenting is a restrictive punitive style in which parents urge the child to follow their directions and to respect work and effort. Authoritarian parenting places firm limits and controls on the child and allows little verbal exchange.

Authoritative parents — Authoritative parents are strict and warm. Authoritative parents demand mature behavior but use reason rather than force in discipline.

Habit — A habit is a response that has become completely separated from its eliciting stimulus. Early learning theorists used the term to describe S-R associations, however not all S-R associations become a habit, rather many are extinguished after reinforcement is withdrawn.

Prospective study — Prospective study is a long-term study of a group of people, beginning before the onset of a common disorder. It allows investigators to see how the disorder develops.

Peer pressure — Peer pressure comprises a set of group dynamics whereby a group of people in which one feels comfortable may override the sexual personal habits, individual moral inhibitions or idiosyncratic desires to impose a group norm of attitudes or behaviors.

Role model — A person who serves as a positive example of desirable behavior is referred to as a role model.

Marijuana — Marijuana is the dried vegetable matter of the Cannabis sativa plant. It contains large concentrations of compounds that have medicinal and psychoactive effects when consumed, usually by smoking or eating.

Gender-typing — The process by which people acquire a sense of being female or male and acquire the traits considered typical of females or males within a cultural setting is referred to as gender-typing.

Sears — Sears focused on the application of the social learning theory (SLT) to socialization processes, and how children internalize the values, attitudes, and behaviors predominant in their culture. He articulated the place of parents in fostering internalization. In addition,

	he was among the first social learning theorists to officially acknowledge the reciprocal interaction on an individual's behavior and their environment
Depression	In everyday language depression refers to any downturn in mood, which may be relatively transitory and perhaps due to something trivial. This is differentiated from Clinical depression which is marked by symptoms that last two weeks or more and are so severe that they interfere with daily living.
Social capital	Family and community resources upon which a person or family can draw is called social capital.
Lorenz	Lorenz demonstrated how incubator-hatched geese would imprint on the first suitable moving stimulus they saw within what he called a "critical period" of about 36 hours shortly after hatching. Most famously, the goslings would imprint on Lorenz himself .
Social support	Social Support is the physical and emotional comfort given by family, friends, co-workers and others. Research has identified three main types of social support: emotional, practical, sharing points of view.
Positive relationship	Statistically, a positive relationship refers to a mathematical relationship in which increases in one measure are matched by increases in the other.
Clique	A clique is an informal and restricted social group formed by a number of people who share common. Social roles vary, but two roles commonly associated with a female clique is notably applicable to most - that of the "queen bee" and that of the "outcast".
Friendship	The essentials of friendship are reciprocity and commitment between individuals who see themselves more or less as equals. Interaction between friends rests on a more equal power base than the interaction between children and adults.
Gene	A gene is an ultramicroscopic area of the chromosome. It is the smallest physical unit of the DNA molecule that carries a piece of hereditary information.
Variance	The degree to which scores differ among individuals in a distribution of scores is the variance.
Self-worth	In psychology, self-esteem or self-worth refers to a person's subjective appraisal of himself or herself as intrinsically positive or negative to some degree.
Attention	Attention is the cognitive process of selectively concentrating on one thing while ignoring other things. Psychologists have labeled three types of attention: sustained attention, selective attention, and divided attention.
Juvenile delinquent	An adolescent who breaks the law or engages in behavior that is considered illegal is referred to as a juvenile delinquent.
Socialization	Social rules and social relations are created, communicated, and changed in verbal and nonverbal ways creating social complexity useful in identifying outsiders and intelligent breeding partners. The process of learning these skills is called socialization.
Graham	Graham has conducted a number of studies that reveal stronger socioeconomic-status influences rather than ethnic influences in achievement.
Hartup	According to Hartup, the single best childhood predictor of adult adaptation is not school grades, and not classroom behavior, but rather, the adequacy with which the child gets along with other children.
Reid	Reid was the founder of the Scottish School of Common Sense, and played an integral role in the Scottish Enlightenment. He advocated direct realism, or common sense realism, and argued strongly against the Theory of Ideas advocated by John Locke and René Descartes.

Child development — Scientific study of the processes of change from conception through adolescence is called child development.

Bronfenbrenner — Bronfenbrenner was a co-founder of the U.S. national Head Start program and founder of the Ecological Theory of Development.

Mesosystem — Relationships between microsystems or connections between contexts, such as the connection between family experience and the school experience are referred to as a mesosystem.

Exosystem — The level at which experiences in another social setting, in which the individual does not have an active role, influence what the individual experiences in an immediate context is referred to as the exosystem.

Early Intervention — Early intervention is a process used to recognize warning signs for mental health problems and to take early action against factors that put individuals at risk.

Prefrontal cortex — The prefrontal cortex is the anterior part of the frontal lobes of the brain, lying in front of the motor and associative areas. It has been implicated in planning complex cognitive behaviors, personality expression and moderating correct social behavior. The prefrontal cortex continues to develop until around age 6.

Conduct disorder — Conduct disorder is the psychiatric diagnostic category for the occurrence of multiple delinquent activities over a 6-month period. These behaviors include truancy, running away, fire setting, cruelty to animals, breaking and entering, and excessive fighting.

Punishment — Punishment is the addtion of a stimulus that reduces the frequency of a response, or the removal of a stimulus that results in a reduction of the response.

Kohlberg — Kohlberg believed that people progressed in their moral reasoning through a series of developmental stages.

Social norm — A social norm, is a rule that is socially enforced. In social situations, such as meetings, they are unwritten and often unstated rules that govern individuals' behavior. A social norm is most evident when not followed or broken.

Toddler — A toddler is a child between the ages of one and three years old. During this period, the child learns a great deal about social roles and develops motor skills; to toddle is to walk unsteadily.

Erik Erikson — Erik Erikson conceived eight stages of development, each confronting the individual with its own psychosocial demands, that continued into old age. Personality development, according to Erikson, takes place through a series of crises that must be overcome and internalized by the individual in preparation for the next developmental stage. Such crisis are not catastrophes but vulnerabilities.

Socioeconomic — Socioeconomic pertains to the study of the social and economic impacts of any product or service offering, market intervention or other activity on an economy as a whole and on the companies, organization and individuals who are its main economic actors.

Moral development — Development regarding rules and conventions about what people should do in their interactions with other people is called moral development.

Life stages — Widely recognized periods of life corresponding to broad phases of development are called life stages. They may cross-culturally or socially defined.

Emotional intelligence — The expression emotional intelligence indicates a kind of intelligence or skill that involves the ability to perceive, assess and positively influence one's own and other people's emotions.

Postformal thought — Postformal thought refers to a form of thought, proposed as a fifth stage, that is qualitatively different from Piaget's formal operational thought. Thinking that is

	reflective, relative, and contextual: provisional; realistic; and open to emotions and subjective.
Deprivation	Deprivation, is the loss or withholding of normal stimulation, nutrition, comfort, love, and so forth; a condition of lacking. The level of stimulation is less than what is required.
Cognition	The intellectual processes through which information is obtained, transformed, stored, retrieved, and otherwise used is cognition.
Sternberg	Sternberg proposed the triarchic theory of intelligence: componential, experiential, and practical. His notion of general intelligence or the g-factor, is a composite of intelligence scores across multiple modalities.
Syndrome	The term syndrome is the association of several clinically recognizable features, signs, symptoms, phenomena or characteristics which often occur together, so that the presence of one feature indicates the presence of the others.
Insight	Insight refers to a sudden awareness of the relationships among various elements that had previously appeared to be independent of one another.
Piaget	Piaget argued that young children's answers were qualitatively different than older children rather than quantitative. There are two major aspects to his theory: the process of coming to know and the stages we move through as we gradually acquire this ability.
Launching	The process in which youths move into adulthood and exit their family of origin is called launching. It can be a time to formulate life goals, to develop an identity, and to become more independent before joining with another person to form a new family.

Visual acuity	Visual acuity is the eye's ability to detect fine details and is the quantitative measure of the eye's ability to see an in-focus image at a certain distance.
Adolescence	The period of life bounded by puberty and the assumption of adult responsibilities is adolescence.
Chronic	Chronic refers to a relatively long duration, usually more than a few months.
Suicide	Suicide behavior is rare in childhood but escalates in adolescence. The suicide rate increases in a linear fashion from adolescence through late adulthood.
Stroke	A stroke occurs when the blood supply to a part of the brain is suddenly interrupted by occlusion, by hemorrhage, or other causes
Life span	Life span refers to the upper boundary of life, the maximum number of years an individual can live. The maximum life span of human beings is about 120 years of age. Females live an average of 6 years longer than males.
Chromosome	The DNA which carries genetic information in biological cells is normally packaged in the form of one or more large macromolecules called a chromosome. Humans normally have 46.
Diabetes	Diabetes is a medical disorder characterized by varying or persistent elevated blood sugar levels, especially after eating. All types of diabetes share similar symptoms and complications at advanced stages: dehydration and ketoacidosis, cardiovascular disease, chronic renal failure, retinal damage which can lead to blindness, nerve damage which can lead to erectile dysfunction, gangrene with risk of amputation of toes, feet, and even legs.
Obesity	The state of being more than 20 percent above the average weight for a person of one's height is called obesity.
Gene	A gene is an ultramicroscopic area of the chromosome. It is the smallest physical unit of the DNA molecule that carries a piece of hereditary information.
Triglycerides	Triglycerides are glycerides in which the glycerol is esterified with three fatty acids. They are the main constituent of vegetable oil and animal fats. They play an important role in metabolism as energy sources. They contain a bit more than twice as much energy as carbohydrates and proteins.
Cholesterol	Cholesterol is a steroid, a lipid, and an alcohol, found in the cell membranes of all body tissues, and transported in the blood plasma of all animals. Cholesterol is an important component of the membranes of cells, providing stability; it makes the membrane's fluidity stable over a bigger temperature interval.
Protein	A protein is a complex, high-molecular-weight organic compound that consists of amino acids joined by peptide bonds. It is essential to the structure and function of all living cells and viruses. Many are enzymes or subunits of enzymes.
Longitudinal study	Longitudinal study is a type of developmental study in which the same group of participants is followed and measured for an extended period of time, often years.
Habit	A habit is a response that has become completely separated from its eliciting stimulus. Early learning theorists used the term to describe S-R associations, however not all S-R associations become a habit, rather many are extinguished after reinforcement is withdrawn.
Stages	Stages represent relatively discrete periods of time in which functioning is qualitatively different from functioning at other periods.
Syndrome	The term syndrome is the association of several clinically recognizable features, signs, symptoms, phenomena or characteristics which often occur together, so that the presence of one feature indicates the presence of the others.

Affect	A subjective feeling or emotional tone often accompanied by bodily expressions noticeable to others is called affect.
Personality	Personality refers to the pattern of enduring characteristics that differentiates a person, the patterns of behaviors that make each individual unique.
Emotion	An emotion is a mental states that arise spontaneously, rather than through conscious effort. They are often accompanied by physiological changes.
Circadian rhythm	The circadian rhythm is a name given to the "internal body clock" that regulates the (roughly) 24 hour cycle of biological processes in animals and plants.
Deprivation	Deprivation, is the loss or withholding of normal stimulation, nutrition, comfort, love, and so forth; a condition of lacking. The level of stimulation is less than what is required.
Learning	Learning is a relatively permanent change in behavior that results from experience. Thus, to attribute a behavioral change to learning, the change must be relatively permanent and must result from experience.
Brain	The brain controls and coordinates most movement, behavior and homeostatic body functions such as heartbeat, blood pressure, fluid balance and body temperature. Functions of the brain are responsible for cognition, emotion, memory, motor learning and other sorts of learning. The brain is primarily made up of two types of cells: glia and neurons.
Brain imaging	Brain imaging is a fairly recent discipline within medicine and neuroscience. Brain imaging falls into two broad categories -- structural imaging and functional imaging.
Motivation	In psychology, motivation is the driving force (desire) behind all actions of an organism.
Metamemory	Metamemory refers to self-awareness of the ways in which memory functions, allowing the person to encode, store, and retrieve information effectively.
Prefrontal cortex	The prefrontal cortex is the anterior part of the frontal lobes of the brain, lying in front of the motor and associative areas. It has been implicated in planning complex cognitive behaviors, personality expression and moderating correct social behavior. The prefrontal cortex continues to develop until around age 6.
Coronary heart disease	Coronary heart disease is the end result of the accumulation of atheromatous plaques within the walls of the arteries that supply the myocardium (the muscle of the heart).
Body mass index	The body mass index is a calculated number, used to compare and analyse the health effects of body weight on human bodies of all heights. It is equal to the weight, divided by the square of the height.
Mutation	Mutation is a permanent, sometimes transmissible (if the change is to a germ cell) change to the genetic material (usually DNA or RNA) of a cell. They can be caused by copying errors in the genetic material during cell division and by exposure to radiation, chemicals, or viruses, or can occur deliberately under cellular control during the processes such as meiosis or hypermutation.
Society	The social sciences use the term society to mean a group of people that form a semi-closed (or semi-open) social system, in which most interactions are with other individuals belonging to the group.
Leptin	Leptin refers to a hormone produced by fat cells that acts in the brain to inhibit hunger and regulate body weight.
Gall	Gall most noted for introducing phrenology, was correct in assigning the brain the role of the seat of mental activities, and although he was wrong in detail due to a faulty methodology, the possibility of the localization of brain functions is widely accepted today.

Cardiovascular disease	Cardiovascular disease refers to afflictions in the mechanisms, including the heart, blood vessels, and their controllers, that are responsible for transporting blood to the body's tissues and organs. Psychological factors may play important roles in such diseases and their treatments.
Osteoporosis	Osteoporosis refers to a disorder of aging that involves an extensive loss of bone tissue and is the main reason many older adults walk with a marked stoop. Women are especially vulnerable to osteoporosis.
Depression	In everyday language depression refers to any downturn in mood, which may be relatively transitory and perhaps due to something trivial. This is differentiated from Clinical depression which is marked by symptoms that last two weeks or more and are so severe that they interfere with daily living.
Anxiety	Anxiety is a complex combination of the feeling of fear, apprehension and worry often accompanied by physical sensations such as palpitations, chest pain and/or shortness of breath.
Lungs	The lungs are the essential organs of respiration. Its principal function is to transport oxygen from the atmosphere into the bloodstream, and excrete carbon dioxide from the bloodstream into the atmosphere.
Substance abuse	Substance abuse refers to the overindulgence in and dependence on a stimulant, depressant, or other chemical substance, leading to effects that are detrimental to the individual's physical or mental health, or the welfare of others.
Population	Population refers to all members of a well-defined group of organisms, events, or things.
Nicotine	Nicotine is an organic compound, an alkaloid found naturally throughout the tobacco plant, with a high concentration in the leaves. It is a potent nerve poison and is included in many insecticides. In lower concentrations, the substance is a stimulant and is one of the main factors leading to the pleasure and habit-forming qualities of tobacco smoking.
Secondhand smoke	Also referred to as sidestream smoke, the smoke from the burning end of a cigarette, which contains higher concentrations of ammonia, carbon monoxide, nicotine, and tar than does the smoke inhaled by the smoker is called secondhand smoke.
Carcinogen	A carcinogen is any substance or agent that promotes cancer. A carcinogen is often, but not necessarily, a mutagen or teratogen.
Pancreas	The pancreas is a retroperitoneal organ that serves two functions: it produces juice containing digestive enzymes; and it produces several important hormones including insulin, glucagon, and several other hormones.
Larynx	The larynx, or voicebox, is an organ in the neck of mammals involved in protection of the trachea and sound production. The larynx houses the vocal cords, and is situated at the point where the upper tract splits into the trachea and the esophagus.
Cervix	The cervix is the lower end of the uterus that joins with the top portion of the vaginia.
Liver	The liver plays a major role in metabolism and has a number of functions in the body including detoxification, glycogen storage and plasma protein synthesis. It also produces bile, which is important for digestion. The liver converts most carbohydrates, proteing, and fats into glucose.
Addiction	Addiction is an uncontrollable compulsion to repeat a behavior regardless of its consequences. Many drugs or behaviors can precipitate a pattern of conditions recognized as addiction, which include a craving for more of the drug or behavior, increased physiological tolerance to exposure, and withdrawal symptoms in the absence of the stimulus.

Alcoholism	A disorder that involves long-term, repeated, uncontrolled, compulsive, and excessive use of alcoholic beverages and that impairs the drinker's health and work and social relationships is called alcoholism.
Binge	Binge refers to relatively brief episode of uncontrolled, excessive consumption.
Date rape	Date rape refers to non-consensual sexual activity between people who are already acquainted, or who know each other socially where it is alleged that consent for sexual activity was not given, or was given under duress.
Nervous system	The body's electrochemical communication circuitry, made up of billions of neurons is a nervous system.
Cirrhosis	Cirrhosis is a chronic disease of the liver in which liver tissue is replaced by connective tissue, resulting in the loss of liver function. Cirrhosis is caused by damage from toxins (including alcohol), metabolic problems, chronic viral hepatitis or other causes
Dementia	Dementia is progressive decline in cognitive function due to damage or disease in the brain beyond what might be expected from normal aging.
Adaptation	Adaptation is a lowering of sensitivity to a stimulus following prolonged exposure to that stimulus. Behavioral adaptations are special ways a particular organism behaves to survive in its natural habitat.
Withdrawal symptoms	Withdrawal symptoms are physiological changes that occur when the use of a drug is stopped or dosage decreased.
Detoxification	Detoxification in general is the removal of toxic substances from the body. It is one of the functions of the liver and kidneys, but can also be achieved artificially by techniques such as dialysis and (in a very limited number of cases) chelation therapy.
Psychotherapy	Psychotherapy is a set of techniques based on psychological principles intended to improve mental health, emotional or behavioral issues.
Alcoholic	An alcoholic is dependent on alcohol as characterized by craving, loss of control, physical dependence and withdrawal symptoms, and tolerance.
Seizure	A seizure is a temporary alteration in brain function expressed as a changed mental state, tonic or clonic movements and various other symptoms. They are due to temporary abnormal electrical activity of a group of brain cells.
Tremor	Tremor is the rhythmic, oscillating shaking movement of the whole body or just a certain part of it, caused by problems of the neurons responsible from muscle action.
Cohort	A cohort is a group of individuals defined by their date of birth.
Marijuana	Marijuana is the dried vegetable matter of the Cannabis sativa plant. It contains large concentrations of compounds that have medicinal and psychoactive effects when consumed, usually by smoking or eating.
Hallucinogen	Certain drugs can affect the subjective qualities of perception, thought or emotion, resulting in altered interpretations of sensory input, alternate states of consciousness, or hallucinations. The term hallucinogen is often broadly applied, especially in current scientific literature, to some or all of these substances.
Cocaine	Cocaine is a crystalline tropane alkaloid that is obtained from the leaves of the coca plant. It is a stimulant of the central nervous system and an appetite suppressant, creating what has been described as a euphoric sense of happiness and increased energy.
Attention	Attention is the cognitive process of selectively concentrating on one thing while ignoring other things. Psychologists have labeled three types of attention: sustained attention,

	selective attention, and divided attention.
Socioeconomic Status	A family's socioeconomic status is based on family income, parental education level, parental occupation, and social status in the community. Those with high status often have more success in preparing their children for school because they have access to a wide range of resources.
Adler	Adler argued that human personality could be explained teleologically, separate strands dominated by the guiding purpose of the individual's unconscious self ideal to convert feelings of inferiority to superiority (or rather completeness). The desires of the self ideal were countered by social and ethical demands.
Ethnic group	An ethnic group is a culture or subculture whose members are readily distinguishable by outsiders based on traits originating from a common racial, national, linguistic, or religious source. Members of an ethnic group are often presumed to be culturally or biologically similar, although this is not in fact necessarily the case.
Prostate	The prostate is a gland that supplies most of the fluid that makes up semen, it is located at the base of the uninary bladder.
Random sample	A sample drawn so that each member of a population has an equal chance of being selected to participate is referred to as a random sample.
Survey	A method of scientific investigation in which a large sample of people answer questions about their attitudes or behavior is referred to as a survey.
Sexually Transmitted Disease	Sexually transmitted disease is commonly transmitted between partners through some form of sexual activity, most commonly vaginal intercourse, oral sex, or anal sex.
Infertility	Infertility is the inability to naturally conceive a child or the inability to carry a pregnancy to term.
Reid	Reid was the founder of the Scottish School of Common Sense, and played an integral role in the Scottish Enlightenment. He advocated direct realism, or common sense realism, and argued strongly against the Theory of Ideas advocated by John Locke and René Descartes.
Progesterone	A female sex hormone that promotes growth of the sex organs and helps maintain pregnancy is called progesterone.
Placebo	Placebo refers to a bogus treatment that has the appearance of being genuine.
Genital herpes	Genital herpes refers to a sexually transmitted disease caused by a large family of viruses of different strains. These strains also produce other, nonsexually transmitted diseases such as chicken pox and mononucleosis.
Gonorrhea	Gonorrhea is among the most common curable sexually transmitted diseases in the world. In men, epididymitis, prostatitis and urethral stricture can result from untreated gonorrhoea.In women, Bartholinitis and abscess formation, pelvic inflammatory disease and Fitz-Hugh-Curtis syndrome can occur.
Syphilis	Syphilis is a sexually transmitted disease that is caused by a spirochaete bacterium, Treponema pallidum. If not treated, syphilis can cause serious effects such as damage to the nervous system, heart, or brain. Untreated syphilis can be ultimately fatal.
Social support	Social Support is the physical and emotional comfort given by family, friends, co-workers and others. Research has identified three main types of social support: emotional, practical, sharing points of view.
Self-efficacy	Self-efficacy is the belief that one has the capabilities to execute the courses of actions required to manage prospective situations.

Perception	Perception is the process of acquiring, interpreting, selecting, and organizing sensory information.
Ejaculation	Ejaculation is the process of ejecting semen from the penis, and is usually accompanied by orgasm as a result of sexual stimulation.
Ovum	Ovum is a female sex cell or gamete.
Fallopian tube	A tube through which the eggs travel from the ovaries to the uterus is a fallopian tube.
Uterus	The uterus or womb is the major female reproductive organ. The main function of the uterus is to accept a fertilized ovum which becomes implanted into the endometrium, and derives nourishment from blood vessels which develop exclusively for this purpose.
Ovulation	Ovulation is the process in the menstrual cycle by which a mature ovarian follicle ruptures and discharges an ovum (also known as an oocyte, female gamete, or casually, an egg) that participates in reproduction.
Hormone	A hormone is a chemical messenger from one cell (or group of cells) to another. The best known are those produced by endocrine glands, but they are produced by nearly every organ system. The function of hormones is to serve as a signal to the target cells; the action of the hormone is determined by the pattern of secretion and the signal transduction of the receiving tissue.
In vitro fertilization	In vitro fertilization is a technique in which egg cells are fertilized outside the woman's body. It is a major treatment in infertility where other methods of achieving conception have failed.
Embryo	A developed zygote that has a rudimentary heart, brain, and other organs is referred to as an embryo.
Artificial insemination	Artificial insemination is when sperm is placed into a female's ovarian follicle (intrafollicular), uterus (intrauterine), cervix (intracervical), or fallopian tubes (intratubal) using artificial means rather than by sexual intercourse.
Semen	Semen is a fluid that contains spermatozoa. It is secreted by the gonads of males for the fertilization of female ova.
Cognitive development	The process by which a child's understanding of the world changes as a function of age and experience is called cognitive development.
Cognition	The intellectual processes through which information is obtained, transformed, stored, retrieved, and otherwise used is cognition.
Piaget	Piaget argued that young children's answers were qualitatively different than older children rather than quantitative. There are two major aspects to his theory: the process of coming to know and the stages we move through as we gradually acquire this ability.
Postformal thought	Postformal thought refers to a form of thought, proposed as a fifth stage, that is qualitatively different from Piaget's formal operational thought. Thinking that is reflective, relative, and contextual: provisional; realistic; and open to emotions and subjective.
Formal operations	Formal operations in Piaget's theory is the final stage of cognitive development, in which children are able to apply abstract logical rules. Not everyone reaches the formal operations stage of development.
Formal reasoning	The type of reasoning in which the form of an argument, not its semantic content, is crucial is referred to as formal reasoning.
Individualistic	Cultures have been classified as individualistic, which means having a set of values that

	give priority to personal goals rather than group goals.
Intuition	Quick, impulsive thought that does not make use of formal logic or clear reasoning is referred to as intuition.
Reasoning	Reasoning is the act of using reason to derive a conclusion from certain premises. There are two main methods to reach a conclusion,deductive reasoning and inductive reasoning.
Social dilemma	Social dilemma refers to a situation in which a particular action will benefit the individual who takes it, harm the individuals who don't, and cause more harm than benefit to everyone if everyone takes it.
Subjective experience	Subjective experience refers to reality as it is perceived and interpreted, not as it exists objectively.
Late adolescence	Late adolescence refers to approximately the latter half of the second decade of life. Career interests, dating, and identity exploration are often more pronounced in late adolescence than in early adolescence.
Early adulthood	The developmental period beginning in the late teens or early twenties and lasting into the thirties is called early adulthood; characterized by an increasing self-awareness.
Late adulthood	The developmental period that lasts from about 60 to 70 years of age until death is referred to as late adulthood.
Sternberg	Sternberg proposed the triarchic theory of intelligence: componential, experiential, and practical. His notion of general intelligence or the g-factor, is a composite of intelligence scores across multiple modalities.
Insight	Insight refers to a sudden awareness of the relationships among various elements that had previously appeared to be independent of one another.
Triarchic Theory of Intelligence	The Triarchic Theory of Intelligence was formulated by Robert J. Sternberg. It proposes that intelligence consists of componential intelligence, experiential intelligence, and contextual intelligence.
Practical intelligence	Practical intelligence focuses on the ability to use, apply, implement, and put into practice.
Psychometric	Psychometric study is concerned with the theory and technique of psychological measurement, which includes the measurement of knowledge, abilities, attitudes, and personality traits. The field is primarily concerned with the study of differences between individuals
Hypoglycemia	Hypoglycemia is a medical term referring to a pathologic state produced by a lower than normal amount of sugar (glucose) in the blood. Derangements of function can range from vaguely "feeling bad" to coma and (rarely) death.
Trauma	Trauma refers to a severe physical injury or wound to the body caused by an external force, or a psychological shock having a lasting effect on mental life.
Personality test	A personality test aims to describe aspects of a person's character that remain stable across situations.
Variance	The degree to which scores differ among individuals in a distribution of scores is the variance.
Aptitude test	A test designed to predict a person's ability in a particular area or line of work is called an aptitude test.
Emotional intelligence	The expression emotional intelligence indicates a kind of intelligence or skill that involves the ability to perceive, assess and positively influence one's own and other people's emotions.

McClelland	McClelland asserts that human motivation comprises three dominant needs: the need for achievement (N-Ach), the need for power (N-Pow) and the need for affiliation (N-Affil). The subjective importance of each need varies from individual to individual and depends also on an individual's cultural background.
Discrimination	In Learning theory, discrimination refers the ability to distinguish between a conditioned stimulus and other stimuli. It can be brought about by extensive training or differential reinforcement. In social terms, it is the denial of privileges to a person or a group on the basis of prejudice.
Mayer	Mayer developed the concept of emotional intelligence with Peter Salovey. He is one of the authors of the Mayer-Salovey-Caruso Emotional Intelligence Test, and has developed a new, integrated framework for personality psychology, known as the Systems Framework for Pesronality Psychology.
Conscientiou-ness	Conscientiousness is one of the dimensions of the five-factor model of personality and individual differences involving being organized, thorough, and reliable as opposed to careless, negligent, and unreliable.
Daniel Goleman	Daniel Goleman is the best-selling author of several books that describe Emotional Intelligence.
Empathy	Empathy is the recognition and understanding of the states of mind, including beliefs, desires and particularly emotions of others without injecting your own.
Theories	Theories are logically self-consistent models or frameworks describing the behavior of a certain natural or social phenomenon. They are broad explanations and predictions concerning phenomena of interest.
Intrapersonal	Intrapersonal is the ability to recognize, define, and pursue inner feelings and thoughts, as in poetry and self-knowledge.
Personality trait	According to the Diagnostic and Statistical Manual of the American Psychiatric Association, a personality trait is a "prominent aspect of personality that is exhibited in a wide range of important social and personal contexts. ...".
Moral development	Development regarding rules and conventions about what people should do in their interactions with other people is called moral development.
Maturation	The orderly unfolding of traits, as regulated by the genetic code is called maturation.
Kohlberg	Kohlberg believed that people progressed in their moral reasoning through a series of developmental stages.
Moral judgment	Making decisions about which actions are right and which are wrong is a moral judgment.
Postconventi-nal morality	The third level in Kohlberg's theory of moral reasoning, postconventional morality, suggests individuals can follow internally held moral principles and are able to decide among conflicting moral standards.
Moral reasoning	Moral reasoning involves concepts of justice, whereas social conventional judgments are concepts of social organization.
Kibbutz	Kibbutz is an Israeli farming community in which children are reared in group settings.
Generalization	In conditioning, the tendency for a conditioned response to be evoked by stimuli that are similar to the stimulus to which the response was conditioned is a generalization. The greater the similarity among the stimuli, the greater the probability of generalization.
Attitude	An enduring mental representation of a person, place, or thing that evokes an emotional response and related behavior is called attitude.

Carol Gilligan	Carol Gilligan is best known for her work on the ethics of care, a theory that contrasts ethics of care to so-called ethics of justice. She claimed that the results of Kohlberg were biased because the participants in the basic study were largely male, and that the scoring method subsequently used tended to favor a principled way of reasoning that was more common to boys, over a moral argumentation concentrating on relations, which would be more amenable to girls.
Assertiveness	Assertiveness basically means the ability to express your thoughts and feelings in a way that clearly states your needs and keeps the lines of communication open with the other.
Wisdom	Wisdom is the ability to make correct judgments and decisions. It is an intangible quality gained through experience. Whether or not something is wise is determined in a pragmatic sense by its popularity, how long it has been around, and its ability to predict against future events.
Gender difference	A gender difference is a disparity between genders involving quality or quantity. Though some gender differences are controversial, they are not to be confused with sexist stereotypes.
Socioeconomic	Socioeconomic pertains to the study of the social and economic impacts of any product or service offering, market intervention or other activity on an economy as a whole and on the companies, organization and individuals who are its main economic actors.
Variable	A variable refers to a measurable factor, characteristic, or attribute of an individual or a system.
Intuitive-Projective faith	Stage I Intuitive-Projective faith is the fantasy-filled, imitative phase in which the child can be powerfully and permanently influenced by examples, moods, actions and stories of the visible faith of primally related adults. The stage most typical of the child of three to seven.
Mythic-Literal faith	Stage 2, Mythic-Literal faith, is the stage in which the person begins to take on for him- or herself the stories, beliefs and observances that symbolize belonging to his or her community.
Synthetic-Conventional faith	In Stage 3, Synthetic-Conventional faith, a person's experience of the world now extends beyond the family. A number of spheres demand attention: family, school or work, peers, street society and media, and perhaps religion.
Individuative-Reflective faith	The movement from Stage 3 to Stage 4, Individuative-Reflective faith, is particularly critical for it is in this transition that the late adolescent or adult must begin to take seriously the burden of responsibility for his or her own commitments, lifestyle, beliefs and attitudes.
Norms	In testing, standards of test performance that permit the comparison of one person's score on the test to the scores of others who have taken the same test are referred to as norms.
Conjunctive faith	Stage 5 Conjunctive faith involves the integration into self and outlook of much that was suppressed or unrecognized in the interest of Stage 4's self-certainty and conscious cognitive and affective adaptation to reality.
Universalizing faith	Stage 6, Universalizing faith, is exceedingly rare. The persons best described by it have generated faith compositions in which their felt sense of an ultimate environment is inclusive of all being. They have become incarnators and actualizers of the spirit of an inclusive and fulfilled human community.
Introspection	Introspection is the self report or consideration of one's own thoughts, perceptions and mental processes. Classic introspection was done through trained observers.
Role model	A person who serves as a positive example of desirable behavior is referred to as a role model.

Deductive reasoning	Deductive reasoning refers to a form of reasoning about arguments in which conclusions are determined from the premises. The conclusions are true if the premises are true.
Anatomy	Anatomy is the branch of biology that deals with the structure and organization of living things. It can be divided into animal anatomy (zootomy) and plant anatomy (phytonomy). Major branches of anatomy include comparative anatomy, histology, and human anatomy.
Statistics	Statistics is a type of data analysis which practice includes the planning, summarizing, and interpreting of observations of a system possibly followed by predicting or forecasting of future events based on a mathematical model of the system being observed.
Reading comprehension	Reading comprehension can be defined as the level of understanding of a passage or text. For normal reading rates (around 200-220 words per minute) an acceptable level of comprehension is above 75%.
Critical thinking	Critical thinking is a mental process of analyzing or evaluating information, particularly statements or propositions that are offered as true.
Correlation	A statistical technique for determining the degree of association between two or more variables is referred to as correlation.
Hypothesis	A specific statement about behavior or mental processes that is testable through research is a hypothesis.
Frontal lobe	The frontal lobe comprises four major folds of cortical tissue: the precentral gyrus, superior gyrus and the middle gyrus of the frontal gyri, the inferior frontal gyrus. It has been found to play a part in impulse control, judgement, language, memory, motor function, problem solving, sexual behavior, socialization and spontaneity.
Magnetic resonance imaging	Magnetic resonance imaging is a method of creating images of the inside of opaque organs in living organisms as well as detecting the amount of bound water in geological structures. It is primarily used to demonstrate pathological or other physiological alterations of living tissues and is a commonly used form of medical imaging.
Problem solving	An attempt to find an appropriate way of attaining a goal when the goal is not readily available is called problem solving.
Psychosocial development	Erikson's psychosocial development describe eight developmental stages through which a healthily developing human should pass from infancy to late adulthood. In each stage the person confronts, and hopefully masters, new challenges.
Human genome	The complete sequence or mapping of genes in the human body and their locations is the human genome. It is made up of 23 chromosome pairs with a total of about 3 billion DNA base pairs.
Pragmatism	Pragmatism is characterized by the insistence on consequences, utility and practicality as vital components of truth. Pragmatism objects to the view that human concepts and intellect represent reality, and therefore stands in opposition to both formalist and rationalist schools of philosophy.
Intelligence test	An intelligence test is a standardized means of assessing a person's current mental ability, for example, the Stanford-Binet test and the Wechsler Adult Intelligence Scale.
Middle Adulthood	Middle adulthood refers to the developmental period beginning at approximately 40 years of age and extending to about 60. Maximum bone density occurs by the late thirties and begins to degrade.
Validity	The extent to which a test measures what it is intended to measure is called validity.
Lesbian	A lesbian is a homosexual woman. They are women who are sexually and romantically attracted to other women.

Psychosocial development	Erikson's psychosocial development describe eight developmental stages through which a healthily developing human should pass from infancy to late adulthood. In each stage the person confronts, and hopefully masters, new challenges.
Personality	Personality refers to the pattern of enduring characteristics that differentiates a person, the patterns of behaviors that make each individual unique.
Trait	An enduring personality characteristic that tends to lead to certain behaviors is called a trait. The term trait also means a genetically inherited feature of an organism.
Adolescence	The period of life bounded by puberty and the assumption of adult responsibilities is adolescence.
Life span	Life span refers to the upper boundary of life, the maximum number of years an individual can live. The maximum life span of human beings is about 120 years of age. Females live an average of 6 years longer than males.
Personality trait	According to the Diagnostic and Statistical Manual of the American Psychiatric Association, a personality trait is a "prominent aspect of personality that is exhibited in a wide range of important social and personal contexts. ...".
Personality type	A persistent style of complex behaviors defined by a group of related traits is referred to as a personality type. Myer Friedman and his co-workers first defined personality types in the 1950s. Friedman classified people into 2 categories, Type A and Type B.
Erik Erikson	Erik Erikson conceived eight stages of development, each confronting the individual with its own psychosocial demands, that continued into old age. Personality development, according to Erikson, takes place through a series of crises that must be overcome and internalized by the individual in preparation for the next developmental stage. Such crisis are not catastrophes but vulnerabilities.
Population	Population refers to all members of a well-defined group of organisms, events, or things.
Normative	The term normative is used to describe the effects of those structures of culture which regulate the function of social activity.
Stages	Stages represent relatively discrete periods of time in which functioning is qualitatively different from functioning at other periods.
Life structure	Life structure is Daniel Levinson's term for the basic pattern of one's life at any given time, including one's relationships and activities and the significance they have for the individual.
Intimacy versus isolation	The life crisis of young adulthood, which is characterized by the task of developing binding intimate relationships is referred to as Erikson's intimacy versus isolation stage.
Homosexual	Homosexual refers to a sexual orientation characterized by aesthetic attraction, romantic love, and sexual desire exclusively for members of the same sex or gender identity.
Friendship	The essentials of friendship are reciprocity and commitment between individuals who see themselves more or less as equals. Interaction between friends rests on a more equal power base than the interaction between children and adults.
Autonomy	Autonomy is the condition of something that does not depend on anything else.
Anxiety	Anxiety is a complex combination of the feeling of fear, apprehension and worry often accompanied by physical sensations such as palpitations, chest pain and/or shortness of breath.
Personality test	A personality test aims to describe aspects of a person's character that remain stable across situations.

Depression	In everyday language depression refers to any downturn in mood, which may be relatively transitory and perhaps due to something trivial. This is differentiated from Clinical depression which is marked by symptoms that last two weeks or more and are so severe that they interfere with daily living.
Gender role	A cluster of behaviors that characterizes traditional female or male behaviors within a cultural setting is a gender role.
Social clock	The social clock refers to the timetable according to which individuals are expected to accomplish life's tasks, such as getting married, having children, or establishing themselves in a career.
Society	The social sciences use the term society to mean a group of people that form a semi-closed (or semi-open) social system, in which most interactions are with other individuals belonging to the group.
Norms	In testing, standards of test performance that permit the comparison of one person's score on the test to the scores of others who have taken the same test are referred to as norms.
Openness to Experience	Openness to Experience, one of the big-five traits, describes a dimension of cognitive style that distinguishes imaginative, creative people from down-to-earth, conventional people.
Five-factor model	The five-factor model of personality proposes that there are five universal dimensions of personality: Neuroticism, Extraversion, Openness, Conscientiousness, and Agreeableness.
Agreeableness	Agreeableness, one of the big-five personality traits, reflects individual differences in concern with cooperation and social harmony. It is the degree individuals value getting along with others.
Extraversion	Extraversion, one of the big-five personailty traits, is marked by pronounced engagement with the external world. They are people who enjoy being with people, are full of energy, and often experience positive emotions.
Neuroticism	Eysenck's use of the term neuroticism (or Emotional Stability) was proposed as the dimension describing individual differences in the predisposition towards neurotic disorder.
Big five	The big five factors of personality are Openness to experience, Conscientiousness, Extraversion, Agreeableness, and Emotional Stability.
Conscientiou-ness	Conscientiousness is one of the dimensions of the five-factor model of personality and individual differences involving being organized, thorough, and reliable as opposed to careless, negligent, and unreliable.
Assertiveness	Assertiveness basically means the ability to express your thoughts and feelings in a way that clearly states your needs and keeps the lines of communication open with the other.
Emotion	An emotion is a mental states that arise spontaneously, rather than through conscious effort. They are often accompanied by physiological changes.
Fisher	Fisher was a eugenicist, evolutionary biologist, geneticist and statistician. He has been described as "The greatest of Darwin's successors", and a genius who almost single-handedly created the foundations for modern statistical science inventing the techniques of maximum likelihood and analysis of variance.
Longitudinal study	Longitudinal study is a type of developmental study in which the same group of participants is followed and measured for an extended period of time, often years.
Validity	The extent to which a test measures what it is intended to measure is called validity.
Individual differences	Individual differences psychology studies the ways in which individual people differ in their behavior. This is distinguished from other aspects of psychology in that although psychology

	is ostensibly a study of individuals, modern psychologists invariably study groups.
Early adulthood	The developmental period beginning in the late teens or early twenties and lasting into the thirties is called early adulthood; characterized by an increasing self-awareness.
Time-out	Time-out is an operant conditioning punishment procedure in which, after unwanted behavior, the person is temporarily removed from a setting--in theory, a removal of stimuli resulting in an increase in the frequency of wanted behaviors; an example of negative reinforcement.
Affect	A subjective feeling or emotional tone often accompanied by bodily expressions noticeable to others is called affect.
Factor analysis	Factor analysis is a statistical technique that originated in psychometrics. The objective is to explain the most of the variability among a number of observable random variables in terms of a smaller number of unobservable random variables called factors.
Questionnaire	A self-report method of data collection or clinical assessment method in which the individual being studied checks off items on a printed list, answers multiple-choice questions, or writes out answers to essay questions aimed at producing a selfdescription is called questionnaire.
Theories	Theories are logically self-consistent models or frameworks describing the behavior of a certain natural or social phenomenon. They are broad explanations and predictions concerning phenomena of interest.
Attention	Attention is the cognitive process of selectively concentrating on one thing while ignoring other things. Psychologists have labeled three types of attention: sustained attention, selective attention, and divided attention.
Self-concept	Self-concept refers to domain-specific evaluations of the self where a domain may be academics, athletics, etc.
Adaptation	Adaptation is a lowering of sensitivity to a stimulus following prolonged exposure to that stimulus. Behavioral adaptations are special ways a particular organism behaves to survive in its natural habitat.
Sexual orientation	Sexual orientation refers to the sex or gender of people who are the focus of a person's amorous or erotic desires, fantasies, and spontaneous feelings, the gender(s) toward which one is primarily "oriented".
Learning	Learning is a relatively permanent change in behavior that results from experience. Thus, to attribute a behavioral change to learning, the change must be relatively permanent and must result from experience.
Femininity	Femininity is the set of characteristics defined by a culture for idealized females.
Self-disclosure	The process of revealing private thoughts, feelings, and one's personal history to others is referred to as self-disclosure.
Attachment	Attachment is the tendency to seek closeness to another person and feel secure when that person is present.
Middle Adulthood	Middle adulthood refers to the developmental period beginning at approximately 40 years of age and extending to about 60. Maximum bone density occurs by the late thirties and begins to degrade.
Hartup	According to Hartup, the single best childhood predictor of adult adaptation is not school grades, and not classroom behavior, but rather, the adequacy with which the child gets along with other children.
Triangular	The triangular theory of love characterizes love in an interpersonal relationship on three

theory of love | different scales: intimacy, passion and commitment. It was developed by Robert Sternberg.

Sternberg | Sternberg proposed the triarchic theory of intelligence: componential, experiential, and practical. His notion of general intelligence or the g-factor, is a composite of intelligence scores across multiple modalities.

Temperament | Temperament refers to a basic, innate disposition to change behavior. The activity level is an important dimension of temperament.

Individualistic | Cultures have been classified as individualistic, which means having a set of values that give priority to personal goals rather than group goals.

Romantic love | An intense, positive emotion that involves sexual attraction, feelings of caring, and the belief that one is in love is romantic love.

Collectivist | A person who defines the self in terms of relationships to other people and groups and gives priority to group goals is called collectivist.

Social role | Social role refers to expected behavior patterns associated with particular social positions.

Human nature | Human nature is the fundamental nature and substance of humans, as well as the range of human behavior that is believed to be invariant over long periods of time and across very different cultural contexts.

Sensation | Sensation is the first stage in the chain of biochemical and neurologic events that begins with the impinging of a stimulus upon the receptor cells of a sensory organ, which then leads to perception, the mental state that is reflected in statements like "I see a uniformly blue wall."

Prejudice | Prejudice in general, implies coming to a judgment on the subject before learning where the preponderance of the evidence actually lies, or formation of a judgement without direct experience.

Matching hypothesis | The matching hypothesis is a popular theory proposed by Walster in 1966, on what causes people to be attracted to their partners. It claims that people are more likely to form long term relationships with people who are roughly equally as physically attractive as themselves.

Infatuation | The term "infatuation" carries connotations of immaturity or fatuousness, while "limerence" is intended to separate these connotations from the emotion.

Empty love | Empty love consists of the commitment component without intimacy or passion. Sometimes, a stronger love deteriorates into empty love, in which the commitment remains, but the intimacy and passion have died. In cultures in which arranged marriages are common, relationships often begin as empty love.

Attitude | An enduring mental representation of a person, place, or thing that evokes an emotional response and related behavior is called attitude.

Survey | A method of scientific investigation in which a large sample of people answer questions about their attitudes or behavior is referred to as a survey.

Acquaintance rape | Acquaintance rape refers to non-consensual sexual activity between people who are already acquainted, or who know each other socially - friends, acquaintances, people on a date, or even people in an existing romantic relationship, where it is alleged that consent for sexual activity was not given, or was given under duress.

Rape | Rape is a crime where the victim is forced into sexual activity, in particular sexual penetration, against his or her will.

Ethnic group | An ethnic group is a culture or subculture whose members are readily distinguishable by

	outsiders based on traits originating from a common racial, national, linguistic, or religious source. Members of an ethnic group are often presumed to be culturally or biologically similar, although this is not in fact necessarily the case.
Lesbian	A lesbian is a homosexual woman. They are women who are sexually and romantically attracted to other women.
Homosexuality	Homosexuality refers to a sexual orientation characterized by aesthetic attraction, romantic love, and sexual desire exclusively for members of the same sex or gender identity.
Self-image	A person's self-image is the mental picture, generally of a kind that is quite resistant to change, that depicts not only details that are potentially available to objective investigation by others, but also items that have been learned by that person about himself or herself.
Discrimination	In Learning theory, discrimination refers the ability to distinguish between a conditioned stimulus and other stimuli. It can be brought about by extensive training or differential reinforcement. In social terms, it is the denial of privileges to a person or a group on the basis of prejudice.
Self-esteem	Self-esteem refers to a person's subjective appraisal of himself or herself as intrinsically positive or negative to some degree.
Species	Species refers to a reproductively isolated breeding population.
Free choice	Free choice refers to the ability to freely make choices that are not controlled by genetics, learning, or unconscious forces.
Social support	Social Support is the physical and emotional comfort given by family, friends, co-workers and others. Research has identified three main types of social support: emotional, practical, sharing points of view.
Random sample	A sample drawn so that each member of a population has an equal chance of being selected to participate is referred to as a random sample.
Sexually Transmitted Disease	Sexually transmitted disease is commonly transmitted between partners through some form of sexual activity, most commonly vaginal intercourse, oral sex, or anal sex.
Cohort	A cohort is a group of individuals defined by their date of birth.
Domestic violence	Domestic violence is any violence between current or former partners in an intimate relationship, wherever and whenever the violence occurs. The violence may include physical, sexual, emotional or financial abuse.
Statistics	Statistics is a type of data analysis which practice includes the planning, summarizing, and interpreting of observations of a system possibly followed by predicting or forecasting of future events based on a mathematical model of the system being observed.
Socialization	Social rules and social relations are created, communicated, and changed in verbal and nonverbal ways creating social complexity useful in identifying outsiders and intelligent breeding partners. The process of learning these skills is called socialization.
Punishment	Punishment is the addtion of a stimulus that reduces the frequency of a response, or the removal of a stimulus that results in a reduction of the response.
Social class	Social class describes the relationships between people in hierarchical societies or cultures. Those with more power usually subordinate those with less power.
Ethnicity	Ethnicity refers to a characteristic based on cultural heritage, nationality characteristics, race, religion, and language.

Guilt	Guilt describes many concepts related to a negative emotion or condition caused by actions which are believed to be, morally wrong. According to Freud, the avoidance of guilt is the basis for moral behavior.
Gender difference	A gender difference is a disparity between genders involving quality or quantity. Though some gender differences are controversial, they are not to be confused with sexist stereotypes.
Empirical	Empirical means the use of working hypotheses which are capable of being disproved using observation or experiment.
Perception	Perception is the process of acquiring, interpreting, selecting, and organizing sensory information.
Late adulthood	The developmental period that lasts from about 60 to 70 years of age until death is referred to as late adulthood.
Primary caregiver	Primary caregiver refers to a person primarily responsible for the care of an infant, usually the infant's mother or father.
Menopause	Menopause is a stage of the human female reproductive cycle that occurs as the ovaries stop producing estrogen, causing the reproductive system to gradually shut down.
Cognitive development	The process by which a child's understanding of the world changes as a function of age and experience is called cognitive development.
Creativity	Creativity is the ability to think about something in novel and unusual ways and come up with unique solutions to problems. It involves divergent thinking, having many solutions or views to a problem.

Middle Adulthood	Middle adulthood refers to the developmental period beginning at approximately 40 years of age and extending to about 60. Maximum bone density occurs by the late thirties and begins to degrade.
Life span	Life span refers to the upper boundary of life, the maximum number of years an individual can live. The maximum life span of human beings is about 120 years of age. Females live an average of 6 years longer than males.
Life expectancy	The number of years that will probably be lived by the average person born in a particular year is called life expectancy.
Population	Population refers to all members of a well-defined group of organisms, events, or things.
Cohort	A cohort is a group of individuals defined by their date of birth.
Reid	Reid was the founder of the Scottish School of Common Sense, and played an integral role in the Scottish Enlightenment. He advocated direct realism, or common sense realism, and argued strongly against the Theory of Ideas advocated by John Locke and René Descartes.
Norms	In testing, standards of test performance that permit the comparison of one person's score on the test to the scores of others who have taken the same test are referred to as norms.
Maturation	The orderly unfolding of traits, as regulated by the genetic code is called maturation.
Anxiety	Anxiety is a complex combination of the feeling of fear, apprehension and worry often accompanied by physical sensations such as palpitations, chest pain and/or shortness of breath.
Individual differences	Individual differences psychology studies the ways in which individual people differ in their behavior. This is distinguished from other aspects of psychology in that although psychology is ostensibly a study of individuals, modern psychologists invariably study groups.
Socioeconomic Status	A family's socioeconomic status is based on family income, parental education level, parental occupation, and social status in the community. Those with high status often have more success in preparing their children for school because they have access to a wide range of resources.
Ethnicity	Ethnicity refers to a characteristic based on cultural heritage, nationality characteristics, race, religion, and language.
Creativity	Creativity is the ability to think about something in novel and unusual ways and come up with unique solutions to problems. It involves divergent thinking, having many solutions or views to a problem.
Wisdom	Wisdom is the ability to make correct judgments and decisions. It is an intangible quality gained through experience. Whether or not something is wise is determined in a pragmatic sense by its popularity, how long it has been around, and its ability to predict against future events.
Physiological changes	Alterations in heart rate, blood pressure, perspiration, and other involuntary responses are physiological changes.
Affect	A subjective feeling or emotional tone often accompanied by bodily expressions noticeable to others is called affect.
Habit	A habit is a response that has become completely separated from its eliciting stimulus. Early learning theorists used the term to describe S-R associations, however not all S-R associations become a habit, rather many are extinguished after reinforcement is withdrawn.
Farsightedness	Hyperopia, also known as farsightedness, is a defect of vision caused by an imperfection in the eye (often when the eyeball is too short), causing inability to focus on near objects,

	and in extreme cases causing a sufferer to be unable to focus on objects at any distance.
Presbyopia	Presbyopia is the eye's diminished power of accommodation that occurs with aging. Presbyopia is not a disease as such, but a condition that affects everyone at a certain age.
Visual acuity	Visual acuity is the eye's ability to detect fine details and is the quantitative measure of the eye's ability to see an in-focus image at a certain distance.
Brightness	The dimension of visual sensation that is dependent on the intensity of light reflected from a surface and that corresponds to the amplitude of the light wave is called brightness.
Retina	The retina is a thin layer of cells at the back of the eyeball. It is the part of the eye which converts light into nervous signals. The retina contains photoreceptor cells which receive the light; the resulting neural signals then undergo complex processing by other neurons of the retina, and are transformed into action potentials in retinal ganglion cells whose axons form the optic nerve.
Pupil	In the eye, the pupil is the opening in the middle of the iris. It appears black because most of the light entering it is absorbed by the tissues inside the eye. The size of the pupil is controlled by involuntary contraction and dilation of the iris, in order to regulate the intensity of light entering the eye. This is known as the pupillary reflex.
Nearsightedness	A vision deficiency in which close objects are seen clearly but distant objects appear blurry is nearsightedness.
Myopia	Myopia is a refractive defect of the eye in which light focuses in front of the retina. Those with myopia are often described as nearsighted or short-sighted in that they typically can see nearby objects clearly but distant objects appear blurred because the lens cannot flatten enough.
Taste bud	The taste bud (or lingual papillae) is a small structure on the upper surface of the tongue that provides information about the taste of food being eaten. It is known that there are five taste sensations: Sweet, Bitter, Umami, Salty and Sour.
Senses	The senses are systems that consist of a sensory cell type that respond to a specific kind of physical energy, and that correspond to a defined region within the brain where the signals are received and interpreted.
Adolescence	The period of life bounded by puberty and the assumption of adult responsibilities is adolescence.
Metabolism	Metabolism is the biochemical modification of chemical compounds in living organisms and cells.
Spence	Spence attributed improvement in performance to motivational factors rather than habit factors. His Discrimination Learning Theory argued that reinforcement combined with frustration or inhibitors facilitates finding a correct stimulus among a cluster which includes incorrect ones.
Reaction time	The amount of time required to respond to a stimulus is referred to as reaction time.
Stimulus	A change in an environmental condition that elicits a response is a stimulus.
Gland	A gland is an organ in an animal's body that synthesizes a substance for release such as hormones, often into the bloodstream or into cavities inside the body or its outer surface.
Aerobic exercise	Aerobic exercise is a type of exercise in which muscles draw on oxygen in the blood as well as fats and glucose, that increase cardiovascular endurance.
Estrogen	Estrogen is a group of steroid compounds that function as the primary female sex hormone. They are produced primarily by developing follicles in the ovaries, the corpus luteum and the

Go to **Cram101.com** for the Practice Tests for this Chapter.

placenta.

Hormone A hormone is a chemical messenger from one cell (or group of cells) to another. The best known are those produced by endocrine glands, but they are produced by nearly every organ system. The function of hormones is to serve as a signal to the target cells; the action of the hormone is determined by the pattern of secretion and the signal transduction of the receiving tissue.

Climacteric The period between about ages 45 and 60 in which there is a loss of capacity to sexually reproduce in women and a decline in the reproductive capacity of men is called climacteric.

Ovulation Ovulation is the process in the menstrual cycle by which a mature ovarian follicle ruptures and discharges an ovum (also known as an oocyte, female gamete, or casually, an egg) that participates in reproduction.

Menopause Menopause is a stage of the human female reproductive cycle that occurs as the ovaries stop producing estrogen, causing the reproductive system to gradually shut down.

Attitude An enduring mental representation of a person, place, or thing that evokes an emotional response and related behavior is called attitude.

Testosterone Testosterone is a steroid hormone from the androgen group. It is the principal male sex hormone and the "original" anabolic steroid.

Depression In everyday language depression refers to any downturn in mood, which may be relatively transitory and perhaps due to something trivial. This is differentiated from Clinical depression which is marked by symptoms that last two weeks or more and are so severe that they interfere with daily living.

Insanity A legal status indicating that a person cannot be held responsible for his or her actions because of mental illness is called insanity.

Insomnia Insomnia is a sleep disorder characterized by an inability to sleep and/or to remain asleep for a reasonable period during the night.

Sensation Sensation is the first stage in the chain of biochemical and neurologic events that begins with the impinging of a stimulus upon the receptor cells of a sensory organ, which then leads to perception, the mental state that is reflected in statements like "I see a uniformly blue wall."

Coronary heart disease Coronary heart disease is the end result of the accumulation of atheromatous plaques within the walls of the arteries that supply the myocardium (the muscle of the heart).

Osteoporosis Osteoporosis refers to a disorder of aging that involves an extensive loss of bone tissue and is the main reason many older adults walk with a marked stoop. Women are especially vulnerable to osteoporosis.

Double-blind In a double-blind experiment, neither the individuals nor the researchers know who belongs to the control group. Only after all the data are recorded may researchers be permitted to learn which individuals are which. Performing an experiment in double-blind fashion is a way to lessen the influence of prejudices and unintentional physical cues on the results.

Cholesterol Cholesterol is a steroid, a lipid, and an alcohol, found in the cell membranes of all body tissues, and transported in the blood plasma of all animals. Cholesterol is an important component of the membranes of cells, providing stability; it makes the membrane's fluidity stable over a bigger temperature interval.

Placebo Placebo refers to a bogus treatment that has the appearance of being genuine.

Sexual dysfunction Sexual dysfunction or sexual malfunction is difficulty during any stage of the sexual act (which includes desire, arousal, orgasm, and resolution) that prevents the individual or

	couple from enjoying sexual activity.
Ejaculation	Ejaculation is the process of ejecting semen from the penis, and is usually accompanied by orgasm as a result of sexual stimulation.
Representative sample	Representative sample refers to a sample of participants selected from the larger population in such a way that important subgroups within the population are included in the sample in the same proportions as they are found in the larger population.
Erectile dysfunction	Erectile dysfunction, also known as impotence, is the inability to develop or maintain an erection of the penis for satisfactory sexual intercourse regardless of the capability of ejaculation. There are various underlying causes, many of which are medically reversible.
Penis	The penis is the external male copulatory organ and the external male organ of urination. In humans, the penis is homologous to the female clitoris, as it develops from the same embryonic structure. It is capable of erection for use in copulation.
Hypertension	Hypertension is a medical condition where the blood pressure in the arteries is chronically elevated. Persistent hypertension is one of the risk factors for strokes, heart attacks, heart failure and arterial aneurysm, and is a leading cause of chronic renal failure.
Diabetes	Diabetes is a medical disorder characterized by varying or persistent elevated blood sugar levels, especially after eating. All types of diabetes share similar symptoms and complications at advanced stages: dehydration and ketoacidosis, cardiovascular disease, chronic renal failure, retinal damage which can lead to blindness, nerve damage which can lead to erectile dysfunction, gangrene with risk of amputation of toes, feet, and even legs.
Chronic	Chronic refers to a relatively long duration, usually more than a few months.
Penile implant	Penile implant refers to surgical treatment for male erectile disorder involving the insertion of a prosthesis that may be a semirigid silicone rod or an inflatable tube.
Prostaglandin	A prostaglandin is any member of a group of lipid compounds that are derived from fatty acids and have important functions. They act on a variety of cells such as vascular smooth muscle cells causing constriction or dilation, on platelets causing aggregation or disaggregation and on spinal neurons causing pain.
Semen	Semen is a fluid that contains spermatozoa. It is secreted by the gonads of males for the fertilization of female ova.
Psychotherapy	Psychotherapy is a set of techniques based on psychological principles intended to improve mental health, emotional or behavioral issues.
Sex therapy	Sex therapy is the treatment of sexual dysfunction, such as non-consumation, premature ejaculation or erectile dysfunction, problems commonly caused by stress, tiredness and other environmental and relationship factors.
Society	The social sciences use the term society to mean a group of people that form a semi-closed (or semi-open) social system, in which most interactions are with other individuals belonging to the group.
Socioeconomic	Socioeconomic pertains to the study of the social and economic impacts of any product or service offering, market intervention or other activity on an economy as a whole and on the companies, organization and individuals who are its main economic actors.
Stroke	A stroke occurs when the blood supply to a part of the brain is suddenly interrupted by occlusion, by hemorrhage, or other causes
Personality	Personality refers to the pattern of enduring characteristics that differentiates a person, the patterns of behaviors that make each individual unique.

Cognitive development The process by which a child's understanding of the world changes as a function of age and experience is called cognitive development.

Immune system The most important function of the human immune system occurs at the cellular level of the blood and tissues. The lymphatic and blood circulation systems are highways for specialized white blood cells. These cells include B cells, T cells, natural killer cells, and macrophages. All function with the primary objective of recognizing, attacking and destroying bacteria, viruses, cancer cells, and all substances seen as foreign.

Glucose Glucose, a simple monosaccharide sugar, is one of the most important carbohydrates and is used as a source of energy in animals and plants. Glucose is one of the main products of photosynthesis and starts respiration.

Longitudinal study Longitudinal study is a type of developmental study in which the same group of participants is followed and measured for an extended period of time, often years.

Discrimination In Learning theory, discrimination refers the ability to distinguish between a conditioned stimulus and other stimuli. It can be brought about by extensive training or differential reinforcement. In social terms, it is the denial of privileges to a person or a group on the basis of prejudice.

Ethnic group An ethnic group is a culture or subculture whose members are readily distinguishable by outsiders based on traits originating from a common racial, national, linguistic, or religious source. Members of an ethnic group are often presumed to be culturally or biologically similar, although this is not in fact necessarily the case.

Homogeneous In biology homogeneous has a meaning similar to its meaning in mathematics. Generally it means "the same" or "of the same quality or general property".

Prejudice Prejudice in general, implies coming to a judgment on the subject before learning where the preponderance of the evidence actually lies, or formation of a judgement without direct experience.

Prostate The prostate is a gland that supplies most of the fluid that makes up semen, it is located at the base of the uninary bladder.

Menarche Menarche is the first menstrual period as a girl's body progresses through the changes of puberty. Menarche usually occurs about two years after the first changes of breast development.

Gene A gene is an ultramicroscopic area of the chromosome. It is the smallest physical unit of the DNA molecule that carries a piece of hereditary information.

Uterus The uterus or womb is the major female reproductive organ. The main function of the uterus is to accept a fertilized ovum which becomes implanted into the endometrium, and derives nourishment from blood vessels which develop exclusively for this purpose.

Progesterone A female sex hormone that promotes growth of the sex organs and helps maintain pregnancy is called progesterone.

Progestin A hormone used to maintain pregnancy that can cause masculinization of the fetus is progestin.

Validity The extent to which a test measures what it is intended to measure is called validity.

Gall Gall most noted for introducing phrenology, was correct in assigning the brain the role of the seat of mental activities, and although he was wrong in detail due to a faulty methodology, the possibility of the localization of brain functions is widely accepted today.

Predisposition Predisposition refers to an inclination or diathesis to respond in a certain way, either inborn or acquired. In abnormal psychology, it is a factor that lowers the ability to

	withstand stress and inclines the individual toward pathology.
Receptor	A sensory receptor is a structure that recognizes a stimulus in the internal or external environment of an organism. In response to stimuli the sensory receptor initiates sensory transduction by creating graded potentials or action potentials in the same cell or in an adjacent one.
Emotion	An emotion is a mental states that arise spontaneously, rather than through conscious effort. They are often accompanied by physiological changes.
Neuroticism	Eysenck's use of the term neuroticism (or Emotional Stability) was proposed as the dimension describing individual differences in the predisposition towards neurotic disorder.
Attention	Attention is the cognitive process of selectively concentrating on one thing while ignoring other things. Psychologists have labeled three types of attention: sustained attention, selective attention, and divided attention.
Acute ptsd	A Posttraumatic stress disorder that is diagnosed one to three months following the traumatic event is called acute ptsd.
Marijuana	Marijuana is the dried vegetable matter of the Cannabis sativa plant. It contains large concentrations of compounds that have medicinal and psychoactive effects when consumed, usually by smoking or eating.
Survey	A method of scientific investigation in which a large sample of people answer questions about their attitudes or behavior is referred to as a survey.
Major depression	Major depression is characterized by a severely depressed mood that persists for at least two weeks. Episodes of depression may start suddenly or slowly and can occur several times through a person's life. The disorder may be categorized as "single episode" or "recurrent" depending on whether previous episodes have been experienced before.
Stress management	Stress management encompasses techniques intended to equip a person with effective coping mechanisms for dealing with psychological stress.
Social support	Social Support is the physical and emotional comfort given by family, friends, co-workers and others. Research has identified three main types of social support: emotional, practical, sharing points of view.
Group therapy	Group therapy is a form of psychotherapy during which one or several therapists treat a small group of clients together as a group. This may be more cost effective than individual therapy, and possibly even more effective.
Rheumatoid arthritis	Rheumatoid arthritis is a chronic, inflammatory autoimmune disorder that causes the immune system to attack the joints. It is a disabling and painful inflammatory condition, which can lead to substantial loss of mobility due to pain and joint destruction.
Control group	A group that does not receive the treatment effect in an experiment is referred to as the control group or sometimes as the comparison group.
Asthma	Asthma is a complex disease characterized by bronchial hyperresponsiveness (BHR), inflammation, mucus production and intermittent airway obstruction.
Job satisfaction	A person's attitudes and feelings about his or her job and facets of the job is called job satisfaction.
Autonomy	Autonomy is the condition of something that does not depend on anything else.
Field study	Field study refers to any scientific research study in which data are collected in a setting other than the laboratory.
Correlation	A statistical technique for determining the degree of association between two or more

	variables is referred to as correlation.
Syndrome	The term syndrome is the association of several clinically recognizable features, signs, symptoms, phenomena or characteristics which often occur together, so that the presence of one feature indicates the presence of the others.
Statistics	Statistics is a type of data analysis which practice includes the planning, summarizing, and interpreting of observations of a system possibly followed by predicting or forecasting of future events based on a mathematical model of the system being observed.
Mental illness	Mental illness is the term formerly used to mean psychological disorder but less preferred because it implies that the causes of the disorder can be found in a medical disease process.
Suicide	Suicide behavior is rare in childhood but escalates in adolescence. The suicide rate increases in a linear fashion from adolescence through late adulthood.
Motivation	In psychology, motivation is the driving force (desire) behind all actions of an organism.
Spatial orientation	Spatial orientation refers to how people understand the placement of objects in space with themselves as the reference point.
Reasoning	Reasoning is the act of using reason to derive a conclusion from certain premises. There are two main methods to reach a conclusion,deductive reasoning and inductive reasoning.
Inductive reasoning	A form of reasoning in which we reason from individual cases or particular facts to a general conclusion is referred to as inductive reasoning. The conclusion can be said to follow with a probability rather than certainty.
Crystallized intelligence	One's lifetime of intellectual achievement, as and shown largely through vocabulary and knowledge of world affairs is called crystallized intelligence.
Fluid intelligence	Mental flexibility in the ability to reason abstractly is called fluid intelligence. Fluid intelligence tends to decline around middle adulthood.
Inference	Inference is the act or process of drawing a conclusion based solely on what one already knows.
Crystallized abilities	In Cattell's theory of intelligence, crystallized abilities are intellectual abilities that develop from cultural context and learning experience.
Fluid abilities	In Cattell's theory of intelligence, fluid abilities are intellectual abilities that are biologically determined and reflected in tests of memory span and spatial thinking.
Learning	Learning is a relatively permanent change in behavior that results from experience. Thus, to attribute a behavioral change to learning, the change must be relatively permanent and must result from experience.
Psychometric	Psychometric study is concerned with the theory and technique of psychological measurement, which includes the measurement of knowledge, abilities, attitudes, and personality traits. The field is primarily concerned with the study of differences between individuals
Tumor	A tumor is an abnormal growth that when located in the brain can either be malignant and directly destroy brain tissue, or be benign and disrupt functioning by increasing intracranial pressure.
Brain	The brain controls and coordinates most movement, behavior and homeostatic body functions such as heartbeat, blood pressure, fluid balance and body temperature. Functions of the brain are responsible for cognition, emotion, memory, motor learning and other sorts of learning. The brain is primarily made up of two types of cells: glia and neurons.
Information processing	Information processing is an approach to the goal of understanding human thinking. The essence of the approach is to see cognition as being essentially computational in nature,

	with mind being the software and the brain being the hardware.
Cognitive psychology	Cognitive psychology is the psychological science which studies the mental processes that are hypothesised to underlie behavior. This covers a broad range of research domains, examining questions about the workings of memory, attention, perception, knowledge representation, reasoning, creativity and problem solving.
Social psychology	Social psychology is the study of the nature and causes of human social behavior, with an emphasis on how people think towards each other and how they relate to each other.
Postformal thought	Postformal thought refers to a form of thought, proposed as a fifth stage, that is qualitatively different from Piaget's formal operational thought. Thinking that is reflective, relative, and contextual: provisional; realistic; and open to emotions and subjective.
Intuition	Quick, impulsive thought that does not make use of formal logic or clear reasoning is referred to as intuition.
Intelligence test	An intelligence test is a standardized means of assessing a person's current mental ability, for example, the Stanford-Binet test and the Wechsler Adult Intelligence Scale.
Problem solving	An attempt to find an appropriate way of attaining a goal when the goal is not readily available is called problem solving.
Sternberg	Sternberg proposed the triarchic theory of intelligence: componential, experiential, and practical. His notion of general intelligence or the g-factor, is a composite of intelligence scores across multiple modalities.
Kuhn	Kuhn is most famous for his book The Structure of Scientific Revolutions in which he presented the idea that science does not evolve gradually toward truth, but instead undergoes periodic revolutions which he calls "paradigm shifts."
Ego	In Freud's view the Ego serves to balance our primitive needs and our moral beliefs and taboos. Relying on experience, a healthy Ego provides the ability to adapt to reality and interact with the outside world.
Exemplars	Exemplars refer to the individual instances of a concept that are stored in memory from personal experience.
Moral judgment	Making decisions about which actions are right and which are wrong is a moral judgment.
Kohlberg	Kohlberg believed that people progressed in their moral reasoning through a series of developmental stages.
Postconventi-nal level	According to Kohlberg, a period during which moral judgments are derived from moral principles and people look to themselves to set moral standards is the postconventional level.
Conventional level	According to Kohlberg, a period during which moral judgments is largely reflective of social conventions is the conventional level. It is a "law and order" approach to morality.
Stages	Stages represent relatively discrete periods of time in which functioning is qualitatively different from functioning at other periods.
Social influence	Social influence is when the actions or thoughts of individual(s) are changed by other individual(s). Peer pressure is an example of social influence.
Late adulthood	The developmental period that lasts from about 60 to 70 years of age until death is referred to as late adulthood.
Darwin	Darwin achieved lasting fame as originator of the theory of evolution through natural selection. His book Expression of Emotions in Man and Animals is generally considered the

	first text on comparative psychology.
Intrinsic motivation	Intrinsic motivation causes people to engage in an activity for its own sake. They are subjective factors and include self-determination, curiosity, challenge, effort, and others.
Attachment	Attachment is the tendency to seek closeness to another person and feel secure when that person is present.
Acquisition	Acquisition is the process of adapting to the environment, learning or becoming conditioned. In classical conditoning terms, it is the initial learning of the stimulus response link, which involves a neutral stimulus being associated with a unconditioned stimulus and becoming a conditioned stimulus.
Threshold	In general, a threshold is a fixed location or value where an abrupt change is observed. In the sensory modalities, it is the minimum amount of stimulus energy necessary to elicit a sensory response.
Instinct	Instinct is the word used to describe inherent dispositions towards particular actions. They are generally an inherited pattern of responses or reactions to certain kinds of situations.
Divergent thinking	A thought process that attempts to generate multiple solutions to problems is called divergent thinking.
Life structure	Life structure is Daniel Levinson's term for the basic pattern of one's life at any given time, including one's relationships and activities and the significance they have for the individual.
Social role	Social role refers to expected behavior patterns associated with particular social positions.
Motives	Needs or desires that energize and direct behavior toward a goal are motives.
Endometriosis	Endometriosis is a common medical condition where the tissue lining the uterus (the endometrium, from endo, "inside", and metrium, "mother") is found outside of the uterus, typically affecting other organs in the pelvis. The condition can lead to serious health problems, primarily pain and infertility.
Sexual harassment	Deliberate or repeated verbal comments, gestures, or physical contact of a sexual nature that is unwanted by the recipient is called sexual harassment.
Cognition	The intellectual processes through which information is obtained, transformed, stored, retrieved, and otherwise used is cognition.
Social clock	The social clock refers to the timetable according to which individuals are expected to accomplish life's tasks, such as getting married, having children, or establishing themselves in a career.
Meditation	Meditation usually refers to a state in which the body is consciously relaxed and the mind is allowed to become calm and focused.
Self-esteem	Self-esteem refers to a person's subjective appraisal of himself or herself as intrinsically positive or negative to some degree.
Friendship	The essentials of friendship are reciprocity and commitment between individuals who see themselves more or less as equals. Interaction between friends rests on a more equal power base than the interaction between children and adults.
Theories	Theories are logically self-consistent models or frameworks describing the behavior of a certain natural or social phenomenon. They are broad explanations and predictions concerning phenomena of interest.
Lesbian	A lesbian is a homosexual woman. They are women who are sexually and romantically attracted to other women.

Go to **Cram101.com** for the Practice Tests for this Chapter.

Psychosocial development	Erikson's psychosocial development describe eight developmental stages through which a healthily developing human should pass from infancy to late adulthood. In each stage the person confronts, and hopefully masters, new challenges.
Evolution	Commonly used to refer to gradual change, evolution is the change in the frequency of alleles within a population from one generation to the next. This change may be caused by different mechanisms, including natural selection, genetic drift, or changes in population (gene flow).
Middle Adulthood	Middle adulthood refers to the developmental period beginning at approximately 40 years of age and extending to about 60. Maximum bone density occurs by the late thirties and begins to degrade.
Personality	Personality refers to the pattern of enduring characteristics that differentiates a person, the patterns of behaviors that make each individual unique.
Trait	An enduring personality characteristic that tends to lead to certain behaviors is called a trait. The term trait also means a genetically inherited feature of an organism.
Self-actualization	Self-actualization (a term originated by Kurt Goldstein) is the instinctual need of a human to make the most of their unique abilities. Maslow described it as follows: Self Actualization is the intrinsic growth of what is already in the organism, or more accurately, of what the organism is.
Maslow	Maslow is mostly noted today for his proposal of a hierarchy of human needs which he often presented as a pyramid. Maslow was an instrumental player in the formation of the humanistic movement, also known as the third force in psychology.
Population	Population refers to all members of a well-defined group of organisms, events, or things.
Maturation	The orderly unfolding of traits, as regulated by the genetic code is called maturation.
Theories	Theories are logically self-consistent models or frameworks describing the behavior of a certain natural or social phenomenon. They are broad explanations and predictions concerning phenomena of interest.
Stages	Stages represent relatively discrete periods of time in which functioning is qualitatively different from functioning at other periods.
Cohort	A cohort is a group of individuals defined by their date of birth.
Erik Erikson	Erik Erikson conceived eight stages of development, each confronting the individual with its own psychosocial demands, that continued into old age. Personality development, according to Erikson, takes place through a series of crises that must be overcome and internalized by the individual in preparation for the next developmental stage. Such crisis are not catastrophes but vulnerabilities.
Jung	Jung was in some aspects a response to Sigmund Freud's psychoanalysis. He proposed and developed the concepts of the extroverted and introverted personality, archetypes, and the collective unconscious. His work has been influential in psychiatry and in the study of religion, literature, and related fields.
Society	The social sciences use the term society to mean a group of people that form a semi-closed (or semi-open) social system, in which most interactions are with other individuals belonging to the group.
Generativity versus stagnation	Generativity versus stagnation is Erikson's term for the crisis of middle adulthood. The individual is characterized by the task of being productive and contributing to younger generations.
Normative	The term normative is used to describe the effects of those structures of culture which regulate the function of social activity.

Generativity	Generativity refers to an adult's concern for and commitment to the well-being of future generations.
Creativity	Creativity is the ability to think about something in novel and unusual ways and come up with unique solutions to problems. It involves divergent thinking, having many solutions or views to a problem.
Mentoring	Mentoring refers to a developmental relationship between a more experienced individual and a less experienced partner sometimes referred to as a protégé. In well-designed formal mentoring programs, there are program goals, schedules, and training.
Social clock	The social clock refers to the timetable according to which individuals are expected to accomplish life's tasks, such as getting married, having children, or establishing themselves in a career.
Social role	Social role refers to expected behavior patterns associated with particular social positions.
Launching	The process in which youths move into adulthood and exit their family of origin is called launching. It can be a time to formulate life goals, to develop an identity, and to become more independent before joining with another person to form a new family.
Early adulthood	The developmental period beginning in the late teens or early twenties and lasting into the thirties is called early adulthood; characterized by an increasing self-awareness.
Early childhood	Early childhood refers to the developmental period extending from the end of infancy to about 5 or 6 years of age; sometimes called the preschool years.
Infancy	The developmental period that extends from birth to 18 or 24 months is called infancy.
Menopause	Menopause is a stage of the human female reproductive cycle that occurs as the ovaries stop producing estrogen, causing the reproductive system to gradually shut down.
Midlife transition	Levinson's term for the ages from 40 to 45, which are characterized by a shift in psychological perspective from viewing ourselves in terms of years lived to viewing ourselves in terms of the years we have left is called the midlife transition.
Infant mortality	Infant mortality is the death of infants in the first year of life. The leading causes of infant mortality are dehydration and disease. Major causes of infant mortality in more developed countries include congenital malformation, infection and SIDS. Infant mortality rate is the number of newborns dying under a year of age divided by the number of live births during the year.
Midlife crisis	Midlife crisis refers to a period of turmoil usually occurring in a person's 40s and brought on by an awareness of one's mortality; characterized by a reassessment of one's life and a decision to make changes, either drastic or moderate, in order to make the remaining years better.
Adolescence	The period of life bounded by puberty and the assumption of adult responsibilities is adolescence.
Psychoanalyst	A psychoanalyst is a specially trained therapist who attempts to treat the individual by uncovering and revealing to the individual otherwise subconscious factors that are contributing to some undesirable behavor.
Maladaptive	In psychology, a behavior or trait is adaptive when it helps an individual adjust and function well within their social environment. A maladaptive behavior or trait is counterproductive to the individual.
Autonomy	Autonomy is the condition of something that does not depend on anything else.
Insight	Insight refers to a sudden awareness of the relationships among various elements that had

	previously appeared to be independent of one another.
Motives	Needs or desires that energize and direct behavior toward a goal are motives.
Gender identity	Gender identity describes the gender with which a person identifies, but can also be used to refer to the gender that other people attribute to the individual on the basis of what they know from gender role indications.
Affect	A subjective feeling or emotional tone often accompanied by bodily expressions noticeable to others is called affect.
Piaget	Piaget argued that young children's answers were qualitatively different than older children rather than quantitative. There are two major aspects to his theory: the process of coming to know and the stages we move through as we gradually acquire this ability.
Marcia	Marcia argued that identity could be viewed as a structure of beliefs, abilities and past experiences regarding the self. Identity is a dynamic, not static structure. At least three aspects of the adolescent's development are important in identity formation: must be confident that they have parental support, must have an established sense of industry, and must be able to adopt a self-reflective stance toward the future.
Accommodation	Piaget's developmental process of accommodation is the modification of currently held schemes or new schemes so that new information inconsistent with the existing schemes can be integrated and understood.
Assimilation	According to Piaget, assimilation is the process of the organism interacting with the environment given the organism's cognitive structure. Assimilation is reuse of schemas to fit new information.
Self-concept	Self-concept refers to domain-specific evaluations of the self where a domain may be academics, athletics, etc.
Perception	Perception is the process of acquiring, interpreting, selecting, and organizing sensory information.
Personality trait	According to the Diagnostic and Statistical Manual of the American Psychiatric Association, a personality trait is a "prominent aspect of personality that is exhibited in a wide range of important social and personal contexts. ...".
Schema	Schema refers to a way of mentally representing the world, such as a belief or an expectation, that can influence perception of persons, objects, and situations.
Cognitive development	The process by which a child's understanding of the world changes as a function of age and experience is called cognitive development.
Identity statuses	The states of ego development that depend on the presence or absence of crisis and commitment are called identity statuses.
Self-image	A person's self-image is the mental picture, generally of a kind that is quite resistant to change, that depicts not only details that are potentially available to objective investigation by others, but also items that have been learned by that person about himself or herself.
Ethnicity	Ethnicity refers to a characteristic based on cultural heritage, nationality characteristics, race, religion, and language.
Lesbian	A lesbian is a homosexual woman. They are women who are sexually and romantically attracted to other women.
Script	A schema, or behavioral sequence, for an event is called a script. It is a form of schematic organization, with real-world events organized in terms of temporal and causal relations

	between component acts.
Exemplars	Exemplars refer to the individual instances of a concept that are stored in memory from personal experience.
Gender role	A cluster of behaviors that characterizes traditional female or male behaviors within a cultural setting is a gender role.
Motivation	In psychology, motivation is the driving force (desire) behind all actions of an organism.
Androgyny	Androgyny refers to two concepts. The first is the mixing of masculine and feminine characteristics. Secondly it describes something that is neither masculine nor feminine.
Longitudinal study	Longitudinal study is a type of developmental study in which the same group of participants is followed and measured for an extended period of time, often years.
Attitude	An enduring mental representation of a person, place, or thing that evokes an emotional response and related behavior is called attitude.
Mental illness	Mental illness is the term formerly used to mean psychological disorder but less preferred because it implies that the causes of the disorder can be found in a medical disease process.
Social support	Social Support is the physical and emotional comfort given by family, friends, co-workers and others. Research has identified three main types of social support: emotional, practical, sharing points of view.
Late adulthood	The developmental period that lasts from about 60 to 70 years of age until death is referred to as late adulthood.
Empathy	Empathy is the recognition and understanding of the states of mind, including beliefs, desires and particularly emotions of others without injecting your own.
Altruism	Altruism is being helpful to other people with little or no interest in being rewarded for one's efforts. This is distinct from merely helping others.
Socioemotional selectivity theory	Socioemotional selectivity theory suggests that older adults become more selective about their social networks. Because they place a high value on emotional satisfaction, they often spend more time with familiar individuals with whom they have had rewarding relationships.
Life-span perspective	The view that development is lifelong, multidimensional, multidirectional, plastic, contextual, multidisciplinary, and involves growth, maintenance and regulation is referred to as the life-span perspective.
Life span	Life span refers to the upper boundary of life, the maximum number of years an individual can live. The maximum life span of human beings is about 120 years of age. Females live an average of 6 years longer than males.
Cardiovascular disease	Cardiovascular disease refers to afflictions in the mechanisms, including the heart, blood vessels, and their controllers, that are responsible for transporting blood to the body's tissues and organs. Psychological factors may play important roles in such diseases and their treatments.
Suicide	Suicide behavior is rare in childhood but escalates in adolescence. The suicide rate increases in a linear fashion from adolescence through late adulthood.
Representative sample	Representative sample refers to a sample of participants selected from the larger population in such a way that important subgroups within the population are included in the sample in the same proportions as they are found in the larger population.
Depression	In everyday language depression refers to any downturn in mood, which may be relatively transitory and perhaps due to something trivial. This is differentiated from Clinical depression which is marked by symptoms that last two weeks or more and are so severe that

	they interfere with daily living.
Homosexuality	Homosexuality refers to a sexual orientation characterized by aesthetic attraction, romantic love, and sexual desire exclusively for members of the same sex or gender identity.
Homosexual	Homosexual refers to a sexual orientation characterized by aesthetic attraction, romantic love, and sexual desire exclusively for members of the same sex or gender identity.
Cohort effect	Similarities in behavior among a group of peers that stem from the fact that group members are approximately of the same age are referred to as the cohort effect.
Friendship	The essentials of friendship are reciprocity and commitment between individuals who see themselves more or less as equals. Interaction between friends rests on a more equal power base than the interaction between children and adults.
Hartup	According to Hartup, the single best childhood predictor of adult adaptation is not school grades, and not classroom behavior, but rather, the adequacy with which the child gets along with other children.
Stereotype	A stereotype is considered to be a group concept, held by one social group about another.They are often used in a negative or prejudicial sense and are frequently used to justify certain discriminatory behaviors. This allows powerful social groups to legitimize and protect their dominant position
Attachment	Attachment is the tendency to seek closeness to another person and feel secure when that person is present.
Life expectancy	The number of years that will probably be lived by the average person born in a particular year is called life expectancy.
Dementia	Dementia is progressive decline in cognitive function due to damage or disease in the brain beyond what might be expected from normal aging.
Sandwich generation	The sandwich generation are people caught between the often conflicting demands of raising children and caring for aging parents.
Psychotherapy	Psychotherapy is a set of techniques based on psychological principles intended to improve mental health, emotional or behavioral issues.
Feedback	Feedback refers to information returned to a person about the effects a response has had.
Milgram	Milgram conducted the Small world experiment (the source of the six degrees of separation concept) and the experiment on obedience to authority.
Survey	A method of scientific investigation in which a large sample of people answer questions about their attitudes or behavior is referred to as a survey.
Primary caregiver	Primary caregiver refers to a person primarily responsible for the care of an infant, usually the infant's mother or father.
Construct	A generalized concept, such as anxiety or gravity, is a construct.
Humanistic	Humanistic refers to any system of thought focused on subjective experience and human problems and potentials.
Adaptation	Adaptation is a lowering of sensitivity to a stimulus following prolonged exposure to that stimulus. Behavioral adaptations are special ways a particular organism behaves to survive in its natural habitat.
Socioeconomic Status	A family's socioeconomic status is based on family income, parental education level, parental occupation, and social status in the community. Those with high status often have more success in preparing their children for school because they have access to a wide range of

resources.

Brain The brain controls and coordinates most movement, behavior and homeostatic body functions such as heartbeat, blood pressure, fluid balance and body temperature. Functions of the brain are responsible for cognition, emotion, memory, motor learning and other sorts of learning. The brain is primarily made up of two types of cells: glia and neurons.

Intelligence test An intelligence test is a standardized means of assessing a person's current mental ability, for example, the Stanford-Binet test and the Wechsler Adult Intelligence Scale.

Conscientiousness Conscientiousness is one of the dimensions of the five-factor model of personality and individual differences involving being organized, thorough, and reliable as opposed to careless, negligent, and unreliable.

Cognitive appraisal Lazarus' term for individuals' interpretation of events in their lives as threatening, harmful, or challenging and their determination of whether they have the resources to effectively cope with the events is referred to as cognitive appraisal.

Case study A carefully drawn biography that may be obtained through interviews, questionnaires, and psychological tests is called a case study.

Learning Learning is a relatively permanent change in behavior that results from experience. Thus, to attribute a behavioral change to learning, the change must be relatively permanent and must result from experience.

Wisdom Wisdom is the ability to make correct judgments and decisions. It is an intangible quality gained through experience. Whether or not something is wise is determined in a pragmatic sense by its popularity, how long it has been around, and its ability to predict against future events.

Mental Tests The term "Mental Tests" was invented by James Cattell, beginning the specialization in psychology known as psychological assessment.

Discrimination	In Learning theory, discrimination refers the ability to distinguish between a conditioned stimulus and other stimuli. It can be brought about by extensive training or differential reinforcement. In social terms, it is the denial of privileges to a person or a group on the basis of prejudice.
Prejudice	Prejudice in general, implies coming to a judgment on the subject before learning where the preponderance of the evidence actually lies, or formation of a judgement without direct experience.
Ageism	Ageism is bias against a person or group on the grounds of age. When that bias is the primary motivation behind acts of discrimination against that person or group, then those acts constitute age discrimination..
Population	Population refers to all members of a well-defined group of organisms, events, or things.
Relative size	Relative size is a monocular cue where an an automobile that is close to us seems larger than one that is far away. The visual system exploits the relative size of similar (or familiar) objects to judge distance.
Late adulthood	The developmental period that lasts from about 60 to 70 years of age until death is referred to as late adulthood.
Disuse	Disuse refers to theory that memory traces weaken when memories are not periodically used or retrieved.
Longitudinal study	Longitudinal study is a type of developmental study in which the same group of participants is followed and measured for an extended period of time, often years.
Body mass index	The body mass index is a calculated number, used to compare and analyse the health effects of body weight on human bodies of all heights. It is equal to the weight, divided by the square of the height.
Gene	A gene is an ultramicroscopic area of the chromosome. It is the smallest physical unit of the DNA molecule that carries a piece of hereditary information.
Chronological age	Chronological age refers to the number of years that have elapsed since a person's birth.
Gerontology	Gerontology is the study of the elderly, and of the aging process itself. It is to be distinguished from geriatrics, which is the study of the diseases of the elderly. Gerontology covers the social, psychological and biology aspects of aging.
Life expectancy	The number of years that will probably be lived by the average person born in a particular year is called life expectancy.
Cohort	A cohort is a group of individuals defined by their date of birth.
Life span	Life span refers to the upper boundary of life, the maximum number of years an individual can live. The maximum life span of human beings is about 120 years of age. Females live an average of 6 years longer than males.
Species	Species refers to a reproductively isolated breeding population.
Stroke	A stroke occurs when the blood supply to a part of the brain is suddenly interrupted by occlusion, by hemorrhage, or other causes
Affect	A subjective feeling or emotional tone often accompanied by bodily expressions noticeable to others is called affect.
Depression	In everyday language depression refers to any downturn in mood, which may be relatively transitory and perhaps due to something trivial. This is differentiated from Clinical depression which is marked by symptoms that last two weeks or more and are so severe that

	they interfere with daily living.
Coronary heart disease	Coronary heart disease is the end result of the accumulation of atheromatous plaques within the walls of the arteries that supply the myocardium (the muscle of the heart).
Gender difference	A gender difference is a disparity between genders involving quality or quantity. Though some gender differences are controversial, they are not to be confused with sexist stereotypes.
Middle Adulthood	Middle adulthood refers to the developmental period beginning at approximately 40 years of age and extending to about 60. Maximum bone density occurs by the late thirties and begins to degrade.
Social support	Social Support is the physical and emotional comfort given by family, friends, co-workers and others. Research has identified three main types of social support: emotional, practical, sharing points of view.
Ethnic group	An ethnic group is a culture or subculture whose members are readily distinguishable by outsiders based on traits originating from a common racial, national, linguistic, or religious source. Members of an ethnic group are often presumed to be culturally or biologically similar, although this is not in fact necessarily the case.
Hormone	A hormone is a chemical messenger from one cell (or group of cells) to another. The best known are those produced by endocrine glands, but they are produced by nearly every organ system. The function of hormones is to serve as a signal to the target cells; the action of the hormone is determined by the pattern of secretion and the signal transduction of the receiving tissue.
Immune system	The most important function of the human immune system occurs at the cellular level of the blood and tissues. The lymphatic and blood circulation systems are highways for specialized white blood cells. These cells include B cells, T cells, natural killer cells, and macrophages. All function with the primary objective of recognizing, attacking and destroying bacteria, viruses, cancer cells, and all substances seen as foreign.
Theories	Theories are logically self-consistent models or frameworks describing the behavior of a certain natural or social phenomenon. They are broad explanations and predictions concerning phenomena of interest.
Programmed senescence	The view that aging is determined by a biological clock that ticks at a rate governed by genes is called programmed senescence.
Telomeres	A telomere is a region of highly repetitive DNA at the end of a chromosome. Every time linear eukaryotic chromosomes are replicated, the DNA polymerase complex stops several hundred bases before the end; if it were not for telomeres, this would quickly result in the loss of useful genetic information. The loss of telomeres has been suggested as a cause of "aging."
Wear-and-Tear theory	The view that factors such as pollution, disease, and ultraviolet light contribute to degrade the body, so that the body gradually loses the ability to repair itself is called the Wear-and-Tear theory.
Metabolism	Metabolism is the biochemical modification of chemical compounds in living organisms and cells.
Protein	A protein is a complex, high-molecular-weight organic compound that consists of amino acids joined by peptide bonds. It is essential to the structure and function of all living cells and viruses. Many are enzymes or subunits of enzymes.
Free-radical theory	Free-radical theory of aging that states that people age because inside their cells normal metabolism produces unstable oxygen molecules known as free radicals. These molecules ricochet around inside cells, damaging DNA and other cellular structures.

Muscular dystrophy — Muscular dystrophy is a chronic disease characterized by progressive skeletal muscle weakness, defects in muscle proteins, and the death of muscle cells and tissue. In some forms of muscular dystrophy, cardiac and smooth muscles are affected. It is the most common hereditary diseases.

Mitochondria — Mitochondria are sometimes described as "cellular power plants", because their primary function is to convert organic materials into energy in the form of ATP.

Arthritis — Arthritis is a group of conditions that affect the health of the bone joints in the body. Arthritis can be caused from strains and injuries caused by repetitive motion, sports, overexertion, and falls. Unlike the autoimmune diseases, it largely affects older people and results from the degeneration of joint cartilage.

Cataracts — A cataract is any opacity which develops in the crystalline lens of the eye or in its envelope. Cataracts form for a variety of reasons, including long term ultraviolet exposure, secondary effects of diseases such as diabetes, or simply due to advanced age.

Mutation — Mutation is a permanent, sometimes transmissible (if the change is to a germ cell) change to the genetic material (usually DNA or RNA) of a cell. They can be caused by copying errors in the genetic material during cell division and by exposure to radiation, chemicals, or viruses, or can occur deliberately under cellular control during the processes such as meiosis or hypermutation.

Diabetes — Diabetes is a medical disorder characterized by varying or persistent elevated blood sugar levels, especially after eating. All types of diabetes share similar symptoms and complications at advanced stages: dehydration and ketoacidosis, cardiovascular disease, chronic renal failure, retinal damage which can lead to blindness, nerve damage which can lead to erectile dysfunction, gangrene with risk of amputation of toes, feet, and even legs.

Chemotherapy — Chemotherapy is the use of chemical substances to treat disease. In its modern-day use, it refers almost exclusively to cytostatic drugs used to treat cancer.In its non-oncological use, the term may also refer to antibiotics.

T cells — T cells are a subset of lymphocytes that play a large role in the immune response. Some attack antigens directly while others help regulate the system.

Allele — An allele is any one of a number of alternative forms of the same gene (sometimes the term refers to a non-gene sequence) occupying a given locus (position) on a chromosome.

Variable — A variable refers to a measurable factor, characteristic, or attribute of an individual or a system.

Interaction effect — The situation in a factorial design whereby one variable influences another variable differently at different levels is an interaction effect.

Cognition — The intellectual processes through which information is obtained, transformed, stored, retrieved, and otherwise used is cognition.

Steroid — A steroid is a lipid characterized by a carbon skeleton with four fused rings. Different steroids vary in the functional groups attached to these rings. Hundreds of distinct steroids have been identified in plants and animals. Their most important role in most living systems is as hormones.

Osteoporosis — Osteoporosis refers to a disorder of aging that involves an extensive loss of bone tissue and is the main reason many older adults walk with a marked stoop. Women are especially vulnerable to osteoporosis.

Brain — The brain controls and coordinates most movement, behavior and homeostatic body functions such as heartbeat, blood pressure, fluid balance and body temperature. Functions of the brain are responsible for cognition, emotion, memory, motor learning and other sorts of learning.

	The brain is primarily made up of two types of cells: glia and neurons.
Chronic	Chronic refers to a relatively long duration, usually more than a few months.
Glucose	Glucose, a simple monosaccharide sugar, is one of the most important carbohydrates and is used as a source of energy in animals and plants. Glucose is one of the main products of photosynthesis and starts respiration.
Aerobic exercise	Aerobic exercise is a type of exercise in which muscles draw on oxygen in the blood as well as fats and glucose, that increase cardiovascular endurance.
Cerebral cortex	The cerebral cortex is the outermost layer of the cerebrum and has a grey color. It is made up of four lobes and it is involved in many complex brain functions including memory, perceptual awareness, "thinking", language and consciousness. The cerebral cortex receives sensory information from many different sensory organs eg: eyes, ears, etc. and processes the information.
White matter	White matter is one of the two main solid components of the central nervous system. It is composed of axons which connect various grey matter areas of the brain to each other and carry nerve impulses between neurons.
Dendrite	A dendrite is a slender, typically branched projection of a nerve cell, or "neuron," which conducts the electrical stimulation received from other cells to the body or soma of the cell from which it projects. This stimulation arrives through synapses, which typically are located near the tips of the dendrites and away from the soma.
Synapse	A synapse is specialized junction through which cells of the nervous system signal to one another and to non-neuronal cells such as muscles or glands.
Neuron	The neuron is the primary cell of the nervous system. They are found in the brain, the spinal cord, in the nerves and ganglia of the peripheral nervous system. It is a specialized cell that conducts impulses through the nervous system and contains three major parts: cell body, dendrites, and an axon. It can have many dendrites but only one axon.
Lesion	A lesion is a non-specific term referring to abnormal tissue in the body. It can be caused by any disease process including trauma (physical, chemical, electrical), infection, neoplasm, metabolic and autoimmune.
Axon	An axon, or "nerve fiber," is a long slender projection of a nerve cell, or "neuron," which conducts electrical impulses away from the neuron's cell body or soma.
Nerve	A nerve is an enclosed, cable-like bundle of nerve fibers or axons, which includes the glia that ensheath the axons in myelin. Neurons are sometimes called nerve cells, though this term is technically imprecise since many neurons do not form nerves.
Hippocampus	The hippocampus is a part of the brain located inside the temporal lobe. It forms a part of the limbic system and plays a part in memory and navigation.
Learning	Learning is a relatively permanent change in behavior that results from experience. Thus, to attribute a behavioral change to learning, the change must be relatively permanent and must result from experience.
Cochlear implant	A cochlear implant is a hearing device that can help people with certain kinds of hearing impairment or who have a severe to profound hearing loss. The implant works by using the tonotopic organization of the basilar membrane of the inner ear.
Information processing	Information processing is an approach to the goal of understanding human thinking. The essence of the approach is to see cognition as being essentially computational in nature, with mind being the software and the brain being the hardware.
Perception	Perception is the process of acquiring, interpreting, selecting, and organizing sensory

	information.
Visual acuity	Visual acuity is the eye's ability to detect fine details and is the quantitative measure of the eye's ability to see an in-focus image at a certain distance.
Reaction time	The amount of time required to respond to a stimulus is referred to as reaction time.
Macular degeneration	Macular degeneration is a medical condition where the light sensing cells in the macula malfunction and over time cease to work.
Glaucoma	Glaucoma is a group of diseases of the optic nerve involving loss of retinal ganglion cells. Untreated glaucoma leads to permanent damage of the optic nerve and resultant visual field loss, which can progress to blindness.
Retina	The retina is a thin layer of cells at the back of the eyeball. It is the part of the eye which converts light into nervous signals. The retina contains photoreceptor cells which receive the light; the resulting neural signals then undergo complex processing by other neurons of the retina, and are transformed into action potentials in retinal ganglion cells whose axons form the optic nerve.
Optic nerve	The optic nerve is the nerve that transmits visual information from the retina to the brain. The optic nerve is composed of retinal ganglion cell axons and support cells.
Senses	The senses are systems that consist of a sensory cell type that respond to a specific kind of physical energy, and that correspond to a defined region within the brain where the signals are received and interpreted.
Taste bud	The taste bud (or lingual papillae) is a small structure on the upper surface of the tongue that provides information about the taste of food being eaten. It is known that there are five taste sensations: Sweet, Bitter, Umami, Salty and Sour.
Receptor	A sensory receptor is a structure that recognizes a stimulus in the internal or external environment of an organism. In response to stimuli the sensory receptor initiates sensory transduction by creating graded potentials or action potentials in the same cell or in an adjacent one.
Olfactory bulb	The olfactory bulb is a part of the brain that is a distinct outgrowth from the forebrain. It plays a major role in olfaction, which is the perception of smells. The olfactory bulb receives direct input from olfactory nerve, made up of the axons from approximately 10 million olfactory receptor neurons in the olfactory mucosa, a region of the nasal cavity.
Plasticity	The capacity for modification and change is referred to as plasticity.
Control group	A group that does not receive the treatment effect in an experiment is referred to as the control group or sometimes as the comparison group.
Erectile dysfunction	Erectile dysfunction, also known as impotence, is the inability to develop or maintain an erection of the penis for satisfactory sexual intercourse regardless of the capability of ejaculation. There are various underlying causes, many of which are medically reversible.
Orthopedic Impairments	Orthopedic impairments involve restricted movement or lack of control over movement due to muscle, bone, or joint problems.
Rheumatoid arthritis	Rheumatoid arthritis is a chronic, inflammatory autoimmune disorder that causes the immune system to attack the joints. It is a disabling and painful inflammatory condition, which can lead to substantial loss of mobility due to pain and joint destruction.
Physical therapy	Physical therapy is a health profession concerned with the assessment, diagnosis, and treatment of disease and disability through physical means. It is based upon principles of medical science, and is generally held to be within the sphere of conventional medicine.

Obesity	The state of being more than 20 percent above the average weight for a person of one's height is called obesity.
Lungs	The lungs are the essential organs of respiration. Its principal function is to transport oxygen from the atmosphere into the bloodstream, and excrete carbon dioxide from the bloodstream into the atmosphere.
Hypertension	Hypertension is a medical condition where the blood pressure in the arteries is chronically elevated. Persistent hypertension is one of the risk factors for strokes, heart attacks, heart failure and arterial aneurysm, and is a leading cause of chronic renal failure.
Anxiety	Anxiety is a complex combination of the feeling of fear, apprehension and worry often accompanied by physical sensations such as palpitations, chest pain and/or shortness of breath.
Dementia	Dementia is progressive decline in cognitive function due to damage or disease in the brain beyond what might be expected from normal aging.
Tremor	Tremor is the rhythmic, oscillating shaking movement of the whole body or just a certain part of it, caused by problems of the neurons responsible from muscle action.
Socioeconomic Status	A family's socioeconomic status is based on family income, parental education level, parental occupation, and social status in the community. Those with high status often have more success in preparing their children for school because they have access to a wide range of resources.
Malnutrition	Malnutrition is a general term for the medical condition in a person or animal caused by an unbalanced diet—either too little or too much food, or a diet missing one or more important nutrients.
Atherosclerosis	Process by which a fatty substance or plaque builds up inside arteries to form obstructions is called atherosclerosis.
Neurofibrillary tangles	Neurofibrillary tangles are pathological protein aggregates found within neurons in cases of Alzheimer's disease.
Plaques	Plaques refer to small, round areas composed of remnants of lost neurons and beta-amyloid, a waxy protein deposit; present in the brains of patients with Alzheimer's disease.
Long-term memory	Long-term memory is memory that lasts from over 30 seconds to years.
Stages	Stages represent relatively discrete periods of time in which functioning is qualitatively different from functioning at other periods.
Cerebrospinal fluid	A solution that fills the hollow cavities of the brain and circulates around the brain and spinal cord is called cerebrospinal fluid.
Brain imaging	Brain imaging is a fairly recent discipline within medicine and neuroscience. Brain imaging falls into two broad categories -- structural imaging and functional imaging.
Identical twins	Identical twins occur when a single egg is fertilized to form one zygote (monozygotic) but the zygote then divides into two separate embryos. The two embryos develop into foetuses sharing the same womb. Monozygotic twins are genetically identical unless there has been a mutation in development, and they are almost always the same gender.
Concordance	Concordance as used in genetics means the presence of the same trait in both members of a pair of twins, or in sets of individuals. A twin study examines the concordance rates of twins having the same trait, especially a disease, which can help determine how much the disease is affected by genetics versus environment.
Working Memory	Working memory is the collection of structures and processes in the brain used for

	temporarily storing and manipulating information. Working memory consists of both memory for items that are currently being processed, and components governing attention and directing the processing itself.
Chromosome	The DNA which carries genetic information in biological cells is normally packaged in the form of one or more large macromolecules called a chromosome. Humans normally have 46.
Attention	Attention is the cognitive process of selectively concentrating on one thing while ignoring other things. Psychologists have labeled three types of attention: sustained attention, selective attention, and divided attention.
Genetic testing	Genetic testing allows the genetic diagnosis of vulnerabilities to inherited diseases, and can also be used to determine a person's ancestry. Every person carries two copies of every gene, one inherited from their mother, one inherited from their father.
Cholesterol	Cholesterol is a steroid, a lipid, and an alcohol, found in the cell membranes of all body tissues, and transported in the blood plasma of all animals. Cholesterol is an important component of the membranes of cells, providing stability; it makes the membrane's fluidity stable over a bigger temperature interval.
Sleep apnea	Sleep apnea refers to a sleep disorder involving periods during sleep when breathing stops and the person must awaken briefly in order to breathe; major symptoms are excessive daytime sleepiness and loud snoring.
Amyloid precursor protein	Amyloid beta is a protein fragment of 39-42 amino acids that is the main constituent of amyloid plaques in various neurological disorders, most prominently Alzheimer's disease. It is the product of protease activity of the secretase enzymes on amyloid precursor protein.
Amino acid	Amino acid is the basic structural building unit of proteins. They form short polymer chains called peptides or polypeptides which in turn form structures called proteins.
Enzyme	An enzyme is a protein that catalyzes, or speeds up, a chemical reaction. Enzymes are essential to sustain life because most chemical reactions in biological cells would occur too slowly, or would lead to different products, without enzymes.
Antioxidants	Antioxidants are chemicals that prevent the oxidation of other chemicals. The normal processes of oxidation produce highly reactive free radicals. These can readily react with and damage other molecules. The presence of extremely easily oxidisable compounds in the system can "mop up" free radicals before they damage other essential molecules.
Suicide	Suicide behavior is rare in childhood but escalates in adolescence. The suicide rate increases in a linear fashion from adolescence through late adulthood.
Chemical imbalance	Chemical imbalance refers to relative excess or deficit in brain chemicals, such as neurotransmitters, that may be implicated in some psychological disorders.
Neurotransmitter	A neurotransmitter is a chemical that is used to relay, amplify and modulate electrical signals between a neurons and another cell.
Interpersonal therapy	A brief psychotherapy designed to help depressed people better understand and cope with problems relating to their interpersonal relationships is referred to as interpersonal therapy.
Psychotherapy	Psychotherapy is a set of techniques based on psychological principles intended to improve mental health, emotional or behavioral issues.
Antidepressant	An antidepressant is a medication used primarily in the treatment of clinical depression. They are not thought to produce tolerance, although sudden withdrawal may produce adverse effects. They create little if any immediate change in mood and require between several days and several weeks to take effect.

Serotonin	Serotonin, a neurotransmitter, is believed to play an important part of the biochemistry of depression, bipolar disorder and anxiety. It is also believed to be influential on sexuality and appetite.
Reuptake	Reuptake is the reabsorption of a neurotransmitter by the molecular transporter of a pre-synaptic neuron after it has performed its function of transmitting a neural impulse.
Cognitive development	The process by which a child's understanding of the world changes as a function of age and experience is called cognitive development.
Baltes	Baltes describes the life-span perspective as one that sees hurman development as lifelong, multidimensional, multidirectional, plastic, contextual, and multidisciplinary, and as involving growth, maintenance, and regulation.
Wisdom	Wisdom is the ability to make correct judgments and decisions. It is an intangible quality gained through experience. Whether or not something is wise is determined in a pragmatic sense by its popularity, how long it has been around, and its ability to predict against future events.
Mental processes	The thoughts, feelings, and motives that each of us experiences privately but that cannot be observed directly are called mental processes.
Sternberg	Sternberg proposed the triarchic theory of intelligence: componential, experiential, and practical. His notion of general intelligence or the g-factor, is a composite of intelligence scores across multiple modalities.
Reasoning	Reasoning is the act of using reason to derive a conclusion from certain premises. There are two main methods to reach a conclusion,deductive reasoning and inductive reasoning.
Intelligence test	An intelligence test is a standardized means of assessing a person's current mental ability, for example, the Stanford-Binet test and the Wechsler Adult Intelligence Scale.
Test anxiety	High levels of arousal and worry that seriously impair test performance is referred to as test anxiety.
Wechsler Adult Intelligence Scale	Wechsler adult intelligence scale is an individual intelligence test for adults that yields separate verbal and performance IQ scores as well as an overall IQ score.
Crystallized abilities	In Cattell's theory of intelligence, crystallized abilities are intellectual abilities that develop from cultural context and learning experience.
Fluid abilities	In Cattell's theory of intelligence, fluid abilities are intellectual abilities that are biologically determined and reflected in tests of memory span and spatial thinking.
Crystallized intelligence	One's lifetime of intellectual achievement, as and shown largely through vocabulary and knowledge of world affairs is called crystallized intelligence.
Pragmatics	Pragmatics is generally the study of natural language understanding, and specifically the study of how context influences the interpretation of meanings. It is a subfield of linguistics.
Compensation	In personaility, compensation, according to Adler, is an effort to overcome imagined or real inferiorities by developing one's abilities.
Fluid intelligence	Mental flexibility in the ability to reason abstractly is called fluid intelligence. Fluid intelligence tends to decline around middle adulthood.
Central nervous system	The vertebrate central nervous system consists of the brain and spinal cord.
Individual	Individual differences psychology studies the ways in which individual people differ in their

differences	behavior. This is distinguished from other aspects of psychology in that although psychology is ostensibly a study of individuals, modern psychologists invariably study groups.
Electrode	Any device used to electrically stimulate nerve tissue or to record its activity is an electrode.
Primary mental abilities	According to Thurstone, the basic abilities that make up intelligence are called primary mental abilities.
Inductive reasoning	A form of reasoning in which we reason from individual cases or particular facts to a general conclusion is referred to as inductive reasoning. The conclusion can be said to follow with a probability rather than certainty.
Spatial orientation	Spatial orientation refers to how people understand the placement of objects in space with themselves as the reference point.
Cognitive skills	Cognitive skills such as reasoning, attention, and memory can be advanced and sustained through practice and training.
Hypothesis	A specific statement about behavior or mental processes that is testable through research is a hypothesis.
Causation	Causation concerns the time order relationship between two or more objects such that if a specific antecendent condition occurs the same consequent must always follow.
Enrichment	Deliberately making an environment more novel, complex, and perceptually or intellectually stimulating is referred to as enrichment.
Sensory memory	Sensory memory is our ability to retain impressions of sensory information after the original stimulus has ceased.
Limited capacity	Limited capacity refers to the concept that one's information processing ability is restricted. Metaphors for capacity include mental space, mental energy or effort, and time.
Elaboration	The extensiveness of processing at any given level of memory is called elaboration. The use of elaboration changes developmentally. Adolescents are more likely to use elaboration spontaneously than children.
Procedural memory	Procedural memory is the long-term memory of skills and procedures, or "how to" knowledge.
Episodic memory	Episodic memory is the explicit memory of events. It includes time, place, and associated emotions (which affect the quality of the memorization).
Semantic memory	Semantic memory refers to the memory of meanings, understandings, and other knowledge.
Tip-of-the-tongue	Tip-of-the-tongue phenomenon is the feeling that information is in memory although it cannot be retrieved.
Implicit memory	Implicit memory is the long-term memory of skills and procedures, or "how to" knowledge. It is often not easily verbalized, but can be used without consciously thinking about it.
Habit	A habit is a response that has become completely separated from its eliciting stimulus. Early learning theorists used the term to describe S-R associations, however not all S-R associations become a habit, rather many are extinguished after reinforcement is withdrawn.
Priming	A phenomenon in which exposure to a word or concept later makes it easier to recall related information, even when one has no conscious memory of the word or concept is called priming.
Retrieval	Retrieval is the location of stored information and its subsequent return to consciousness. It is the third stage of information processing.
Encoding	Encoding refers to interpreting; transforming; modifying information so that it can be placed

	in memory. It is the first stage of information processing.
Source monitoring	The process of making attributions about the origins of memories is called source monitoring.
Prefrontal cortex	The prefrontal cortex is the anterior part of the frontal lobes of the brain, lying in front of the motor and associative areas. It has been implicated in planning complex cognitive behaviors, personality expression and moderating correct social behavior. The prefrontal cortex continues to develop until around age 6.
Corpus callosum	The corpus callosum is the largest white matter structure in the brain. It consists of mostly of contralateral axon projections. The corpus callosum connects the left and right cerebral hemispheres. Most communication between regions in different halves of the brain are carried over the corpus callosum.
Right hemisphere	The brain is divided into left and right cerebral hemispheres. The right hemisphere of the cortex controls the left side of the body.
Left hemisphere	The left hemisphere of the cortex controls the right side of the body, coordinates complex movements, and, in 95% of people, controls the production of speech and written language.
Questionnaire	A self-report method of data collection or clinical assessment method in which the individual being studied checks off items on a printed list, answers multiple-choice questions, or writes out answers to essay questions aimed at producing a selfdescription is called questionnaire.
Metamemory	Metamemory refers to self-awareness of the ways in which memory functions, allowing the person to encode, store, and retrieve information effectively.
Mnemonic	A mnemonic is a memory aid. They are often verbal, are sometimes in verse form, and are often used to remember lists.
Personality	Personality refers to the pattern of enduring characteristics that differentiates a person, the patterns of behaviors that make each individual unique.
Illusion	An illusion is a distortion of a sensory perception.
Jung	Jung was in some aspects a response to Sigmund Freud's psychoanalysis. He proposed and developed the concepts of the extroverted and introverted personality, archetypes, and the collective unconscious. His work has been influential in psychiatry and in the study of religion, literature, and related fields.
Practical intelligence	Practical intelligence focuses on the ability to use, apply, implement, and put into practice.
Openness to Experience	Openness to Experience, one of the big-five traits, describes a dimension of cognitive style that distinguishes imaginative, creative people from down-to-earth, conventional people.
Motivation	In psychology, motivation is the driving force (desire) behind all actions of an organism.
Creativity	Creativity is the ability to think about something in novel and unusual ways and come up with unique solutions to problems. It involves divergent thinking, having many solutions or views to a problem.
Motives	Needs or desires that energize and direct behavior toward a goal are motives.
Clinical psychologist	A psychologist, usually with a Ph.D, whose training is in the diagnosis, treatment, or research of psychological and behavioral disorders is a clinical psychologist.
Generalization	In conditioning, the tendency for a conditioned response to be evoked by stimuli that are similar to the stimulus to which the response was conditioned is a generalization. The greater the similarity among the stimuli, the greater the probability of generalization.

Normative	The term normative is used to describe the effects of those structures of culture which regulate the function of social activity.
Society	The social sciences use the term society to mean a group of people that form a semi-closed (or semi-open) social system, in which most interactions are with other individuals belonging to the group.
Alcoholism	A disorder that involves long-term, repeated, uncontrolled, compulsive, and excessive use of alcoholic beverages and that impairs the drinker's health and work and social relationships is called alcoholism.
Major depressive disorder	The diagnosis of a major depressive disorder occurs when an individual experiences a major depressive episode and depressed characteristics, such as lethargy and depression, last for 2 weeks or longer and daily functioning becomes impaired.
Cross-sectional research	A research method in which people of different ages are compared at the same point in time is called cross-sectional research.
Stereotype	A stereotype is considered to be a group concept, held by one social group about another.They are often used in a negative or prejudicial sense and are frequently used to justify certain discriminatory behaviors. This allows powerful social groups to legitimize and protect their dominant position

Psychosocial development	Erikson's psychosocial development describe eight developmental stages through which a healthily developing human should pass from infancy to late adulthood. In each stage the person confronts, and hopefully masters, new challenges.
Life span	Life span refers to the upper boundary of life, the maximum number of years an individual can live. The maximum life span of human beings is about 120 years of age. Females live an average of 6 years longer than males.
Adaptation	Adaptation is a lowering of sensitivity to a stimulus following prolonged exposure to that stimulus. Behavioral adaptations are special ways a particular organism behaves to survive in its natural habitat.
Baltes	Baltes describes the life-span perspective as one that sees hurman development as lifelong, multidimensional, multidirectional, plastic, contextual, and multidisciplinary, and as involving growth, maintenance, and regulation.
Trait	An enduring personality characteristic that tends to lead to certain behaviors is called a trait. The term trait also means a genetically inherited feature of an organism.
Socioemotional selectivity theory	Socioemotional selectivity theory suggests that older adults become more selective about their social networks. Because they place a high value on emotional satisfaction, they often spend more time with familiar individuals with whom they have had rewarding relationships.
Longitudinal study	Longitudinal study is a type of developmental study in which the same group of participants is followed and measured for an extended period of time, often years.
Depression	In everyday language depression refers to any downturn in mood, which may be relatively transitory and perhaps due to something trivial. This is differentiated from Clinical depression which is marked by symptoms that last two weeks or more and are so severe that they interfere with daily living.
Emotion	An emotion is a mental states that arise spontaneously, rather than through conscious effort. They are often accompanied by physiological changes.
Personality trait	According to the Diagnostic and Statistical Manual of the American Psychiatric Association, a personality trait is a "prominent aspect of personality that is exhibited in a wide range of important social and personal contexts. ...".
Big five	The big five factors of personality are Openness to experience, Conscientiousness, Extraversion, Agreeableness, and Emotional Stability.
Cross-sectional research	A research method in which people of different ages are compared at the same point in time is called cross-sectional research.
Ego integrity versus despair	Erikson's term for the crisis of late adulthood, characterized by the task of maintaining one's sense of identity despite physical deterioration is called ego integrity versus despair.
Late adulthood	The developmental period that lasts from about 60 to 70 years of age until death is referred to as late adulthood.
Personality	Personality refers to the pattern of enduring characteristics that differentiates a person, the patterns of behaviors that make each individual unique.
Normative	The term normative is used to describe the effects of those structures of culture which regulate the function of social activity.
Terman	Terman revised the Stanford-Binet Intelligence Scale in 1916, commonly used to measure intelligence (or I.Q.) in the United States. William Stern's suggestion that mental age/chronological age times 100 (to get rid of the decimal) be made the "intelligence quotient" or I.Q. This apparent mathematization of the measurement gave it an air of

	scientific accuracy and detachment which contributed greatly to its acceptance among educators and the broad public.
Stages	Stages represent relatively discrete periods of time in which functioning is qualitatively different from functioning at other periods.
Conscientiou-ness	Conscientiousness is one of the dimensions of the five-factor model of personality and individual differences involving being organized, thorough, and reliable as opposed to careless, negligent, and unreliable.
Habit	A habit is a response that has become completely separated from its eliciting stimulus. Early learning theorists used the term to describe S-R associations, however not all S-R associations become a habit, rather many are extinguished after reinforcement is withdrawn.
Variable	A variable refers to a measurable factor, characteristic, or attribute of an individual or a system.
Wisdom	Wisdom is the ability to make correct judgments and decisions. It is an intangible quality gained through experience. Whether or not something is wise is determined in a pragmatic sense by its popularity, how long it has been around, and its ability to predict against future events.
Ego	In Freud's view the Ego serves to balance our primitive needs and our moral beliefs and taboos. Relying on experience, a healthy Ego provides the ability to adapt to reality and interact with the outside world.
Social support	Social Support is the physical and emotional comfort given by family, friends, co-workers and others. Research has identified three main types of social support: emotional, practical, sharing points of view.
Social class	Social class describes the relationships between people in hierarchical societies or cultures. Those with more power usually subordinate those with less power.
Sublimation	Sublimation is a coping mechanism. It refers to rechanneling sexual or aggressive energy into pursuits that society considers acceptable or admirable.
Altruism	Altruism is being helpful to other people with little or no interest in being rewarded for one's efforts. This is distinct from merely helping others.
Perception	Perception is the process of acquiring, interpreting, selecting, and organizing sensory information.
Post-traumatic stress disorder	Post-traumatic stress disorder is a term for the psychological consequences of exposure to or confrontation with stressful experiences, which involve actual or threatened death, serious physical injury or a threat to physical integrity and which the person found highly traumatic.
Emotion-focused coping	Lazarus' emotion-focused coping describes individuals' response to stress demonstrated in an emotional manner, especially using defensive methods.
Attention	Attention is the cognitive process of selectively concentrating on one thing while ignoring other things. Psychologists have labeled three types of attention: sustained attention, selective attention, and divided attention.
Cardiovascular disease	Cardiovascular disease refers to afflictions in the mechanisms, including the heart, blood vessels, and their controllers, that are responsible for transporting blood to the body's tissues and organs. Psychological factors may play important roles in such diseases and their treatments.
Empirical	Empirical means the use of working hypotheses which are capable of being disproved using observation or experiment.

Suicide	Suicide behavior is rare in childhood but escalates in adolescence. The suicide rate increases in a linear fashion from adolescence through late adulthood.
Self-esteem	Self-esteem refers to a person's subjective appraisal of himself or herself as intrinsically positive or negative to some degree.
Subjective experience	Subjective experience refers to reality as it is perceived and interpreted, not as it exists objectively.
Theories	Theories are logically self-consistent models or frameworks describing the behavior of a certain natural or social phenomenon. They are broad explanations and predictions concerning phenomena of interest.
Disengagement theory	Disengagement theory of aging suggests that aging is a gradual withdrawal from the world on physical, psychological, and social levels.
Activity theory	Activity theory states that the more active and involved older adults are, the more likely they are to be satisfied with their lives.
Gerontology	Gerontology is the study of the elderly, and of the aging process itself. It is to be distinguished from geriatrics, which is the study of the diseases of the elderly. Gerontology covers the social, psychological and biology aspects of aging.
Introspection	Introspection is the self report or consideration of one's own thoughts, perceptions and mental processes. Classic introspection was done through trained observers.
Jung	Jung was in some aspects a response to Sigmund Freud's psychoanalysis. He proposed and developed the concepts of the extroverted and introverted personality, archetypes, and the collective unconscious. His work has been influential in psychiatry and in the study of religion, literature, and related fields.
Social role	Social role refers to expected behavior patterns associated with particular social positions.
Hypothesis	A specific statement about behavior or mental processes that is testable through research is a hypothesis.
Self-efficacy	Self-efficacy is the belief that one has the capabilities to execute the courses of actions required to manage prospective situations.
Affect	A subjective feeling or emotional tone often accompanied by bodily expressions noticeable to others is called affect.
Continuity Theory	Continuity Theory states for behavior based on a disorderly perceptual process, subjects learn simultaneously about all the stimuli that are present and then respond when stimuli resemble any from the original training session.
Compensation	In personaility, compensation, according to Adler, is an effort to overcome imagined or real inferiorities by developing one's abilities.
Society	The social sciences use the term society to mean a group of people that form a semi-closed (or semi-open) social system, in which most interactions are with other individuals belonging to the group.
Life expectancy	The number of years that will probably be lived by the average person born in a particular year is called life expectancy.
Norms	In testing, standards of test performance that permit the comparison of one person's score on the test to the scores of others who have taken the same test are referred to as norms.
Population	Population refers to all members of a well-defined group of organisms, events, or things.
Representative	Representative sample refers to a sample of participants selected from the larger population

sample	in such a way that important subgroups within the population are included in the sample in the same proportions as they are found in the larger population.
Socioeconomic Status	A family's socioeconomic status is based on family income, parental education level, parental occupation, and social status in the community. Those with high status often have more success in preparing their children for school because they have access to a wide range of resources.
Social capital	Family and community resources upon which a person or family can draw is called social capital.
Autonomy	Autonomy is the condition of something that does not depend on anything else.
Corporal punishment	Corporal punishment is the use of physical force with the intention of causing pain, but not injury.
Accommodation	Piaget's developmental process of accommodation is the modification of currently held schemes or new schemes so that new information inconsistent with the existing schemes can be integrated and understood.
Emotional abuse	There is no single accepted definition of emotional abuse which, like other forms of violence in a relationship, is based on power and domination.
Domestic violence	Domestic violence is any violence between current or former partners in an intimate relationship, wherever and whenever the violence occurs. The violence may include physical, sexual, emotional or financial abuse.
Nerve	A nerve is an enclosed, cable-like bundle of nerve fibers or axons, which includes the glia that ensheath the axons in myelin. Neurons are sometimes called nerve cells, though this term is technically imprecise since many neurons do not form nerves.
Cultural values	The importance and desirability of various objects and activities as defined by people in a given culture are referred to as cultural values.
Individualism	Individualism refers to putting personal goals ahead of group goals and defining one's identity in terms of personal attributes rather than group memberships.
Assimilation	According to Piaget, assimilation is the process of the organism interacting with the environment given the organism's cognitive structure. Assimilation is reuse of schemas to fit new information.
Cohort	A cohort is a group of individuals defined by their date of birth.
Gender difference	A gender difference is a disparity between genders involving quality or quantity. Though some gender differences are controversial, they are not to be confused with sexist stereotypes.
Friendship	The essentials of friendship are reciprocity and commitment between individuals who see themselves more or less as equals. Interaction between friends rests on a more equal power base than the interaction between children and adults.
Gender role	A cluster of behaviors that characterizes traditional female or male behaviors within a cultural setting is a gender role.
Homosexual	Homosexual refers to a sexual orientation characterized by aesthetic attraction, romantic love, and sexual desire exclusively for members of the same sex or gender identity.
Lesbian	A lesbian is a homosexual woman. They are women who are sexually and romantically attracted to other women.
Reid	Reid was the founder of the Scottish School of Common Sense, and played an integral role in the Scottish Enlightenment. He advocated direct realism, or common sense realism, and argued strongly against the Theory of Ideas advocated by John Locke and René Descartes.

Life satisfaction	A person's attitudes about his or her overall life are referred to as life satisfaction.
Discrimination	In Learning theory, discrimination refers the ability to distinguish between a conditioned stimulus and other stimuli. It can be brought about by extensive training or differential reinforcement. In social terms, it is the denial of privileges to a person or a group on the basis of prejudice.
Attitude	An enduring mental representation of a person, place, or thing that evokes an emotional response and related behavior is called attitude.
Stereotype	A stereotype is considered to be a group concept, held by one social group about another.They are often used in a negative or prejudicial sense and are frequently used to justify certain discriminatory behaviors. This allows powerful social groups to legitimize and protect their dominant position
Self-disclosure	The process of revealing private thoughts, feelings, and one's personal history to others is referred to as self-disclosure.
Socioeconomic	Socioeconomic pertains to the study of the social and economic impacts of any product or service offering, market intervention or other activity on an economy as a whole and on the companies, organization and individuals who are its main economic actors.
Problem-focused coping	Lazarus' problem-focused coping is a strategy used by individuals who face their troubles and try to solve them.
Individual differences	Individual differences psychology studies the ways in which individual people differ in their behavior. This is distinguished from other aspects of psychology in that although psychology is ostensibly a study of individuals, modern psychologists invariably study groups.
Generativity	Generativity refers to an adult's concern for and commitment to the well-being of future generations.

Attitude	An enduring mental representation of a person, place, or thing that evokes an emotional response and related behavior is called attitude.
Affect	A subjective feeling or emotional tone often accompanied by bodily expressions noticeable to others is called affect.
Society	The social sciences use the term society to mean a group of people that form a semi-closed (or semi-open) social system, in which most interactions are with other individuals belonging to the group.
Anchor	An anchor is a sample of work or performance used to set the specific performance standard for a rubric level .
Population	Population refers to all members of a well-defined group of organisms, events, or things.
Late adulthood	The developmental period that lasts from about 60 to 70 years of age until death is referred to as late adulthood.
Stroke	A stroke occurs when the blood supply to a part of the brain is suddenly interrupted by occlusion, by hemorrhage, or other causes
Hospice	Hospice is program committed to making the end of life as free from pain, anxiety, and depression as possible. The goals of hospice contrast with those of a hospital, which are to cure disease and prolong life.
Anxiety	Anxiety is a complex combination of the feeling of fear, apprehension and worry often accompanied by physical sensations such as palpitations, chest pain and/or shortness of breath.
Stages	Stages represent relatively discrete periods of time in which functioning is qualitatively different from functioning at other periods.
Psychotherapy	Psychotherapy is a set of techniques based on psychological principles intended to improve mental health, emotional or behavioral issues.
Social support	Social Support is the physical and emotional comfort given by family, friends, co-workers and others. Research has identified three main types of social support: emotional, practical, sharing points of view.
Psychiatrist	A psychiatrist is a physician who specializes in the diagnosis and treatment of psychological disorders.
Kubler-Ross	Kubler-Ross proposed the now famous Five Stages of Grief as a pattern of phases, most or all of which people tend to go through, in sequence, after being faced with tragedy such as death of a loved one or their own impending death. The five stages of grief, in sequential order, are denial, anger, bargaining, depression, and acceptance.
Depression	In everyday language depression refers to any downturn in mood, which may be relatively transitory and perhaps due to something trivial. This is differentiated from Clinical depression which is marked by symptoms that last two weeks or more and are so severe that they interfere with daily living.
Denial	Denial is a psychological defense mechanism in which a person faced with a fact that is uncomfortable or painful to accept rejects it instead, insisting that it is not true despite what may be overwhelming evidence.
Emotion	An emotion is a mental states that arise spontaneously, rather than through conscious effort. They are often accompanied by physiological changes.
Spinal cord	The spinal cord is a part of the vertebrate nervous system that is enclosed in and protected by the vertebral column (it passes through the spinal canal). It consists of nerve cells. The

	spinal cord carries sensory signals and motor innervation to most of the skeletal muscles in the body.
Guilt	Guilt describes many concepts related to a negative emotion or condition caused by actions which are believed to be, morally wrong. According to Freud, the avoidance of guilt is the basis for moral behavior.
Individual differences	Individual differences psychology studies the ways in which individual people differ in their behavior. This is distinguished from other aspects of psychology in that although psychology is ostensibly a study of individuals, modern psychologists invariably study groups.
Counselor	A counselor is a mental health professional who specializes in helping people with problems not involving serious mental disorders.
Personality	Personality refers to the pattern of enduring characteristics that differentiates a person, the patterns of behaviors that make each individual unique.
Arthritis	Arthritis is a group of conditions that affect the health of the bone joints in the body. Arthritis can be caused from strains and injuries caused by repetitive motion, sports, overexertion, and falls. Unlike the autoimmune diseases, it largely affects older people and results from the degeneration of joint cartilage.
Cognitive development	The process by which a child's understanding of the world changes as a function of age and experience is called cognitive development.
Life span	Life span refers to the upper boundary of life, the maximum number of years an individual can live. The maximum life span of human beings is about 120 years of age. Females live an average of 6 years longer than males.
Normative	The term normative is used to describe the effects of those structures of culture which regulate the function of social activity.
Adolescence	The period of life bounded by puberty and the assumption of adult responsibilities is adolescence.
Suicide	Suicide behavior is rare in childhood but escalates in adolescence. The suicide rate increases in a linear fashion from adolescence through late adulthood.
Mental illness	Mental illness is the term formerly used to mean psychological disorder but less preferred because it implies that the causes of the disorder can be found in a medical disease process.
Drug addiction	Drug addiction, or substance dependence is the compulsive use of drugs, to the point where the user has no effective choice but to continue use.
Chronic	Chronic refers to a relatively long duration, usually more than a few months.
Concrete operational	According to Piaget, the period from 7 to 12 years of age, which is characterized by logical thought and a loss of egocentrism, is referred to as concrete operational stage. Conservation skills are formed - understanding that quantity, length or number of items is unrelated to the appearance of the object or items.
Irreversibility	Irreversibility in psychology is the inability of an individual to envision reversing an action.
Causation	Causation concerns the time order relationship between two or more objects such that if a specific antecendent condition occurs the same consequent must always follow.
Piaget	Piaget argued that young children's answers were qualitatively different than older children rather than quantitative. There are two major aspects to his theory: the process of coming to know and the stages we move through as we gradually acquire this ability.
Integrity	Erikson's eighth and final stage of development is Integrity Versus Despair. In late

versus despair	adulthood individuals reflect on the past and either piece together a positive review or conclude that one's life has not been well spent.
Friendship	The essentials of friendship are reciprocity and commitment between individuals who see themselves more or less as equals. Interaction between friends rests on a more equal power base than the interaction between children and adults.
Self-esteem	Self-esteem refers to a person's subjective appraisal of himself or herself as intrinsically positive or negative to some degree.
Attention	Attention is the cognitive process of selectively concentrating on one thing while ignoring other things. Psychologists have labeled three types of attention: sustained attention, selective attention, and divided attention.
Infant mortality	Infant mortality is the death of infants in the first year of life. The leading causes of infant mortality are dehydration and disease. Major causes of infant mortality in more developed countries include congenital malformation, infection and SIDS. Infant mortality rate is the number of newborns dying under a year of age divided by the number of live births during the year.
Life expectancy	The number of years that will probably be lived by the average person born in a particular year is called life expectancy.
Fetus	A fetus develops from the end of the 8th week of pregnancy (when the major structures have formed), until birth.
Euthanasia	Euthanasia is the practice of killing a person or animal, in a painless or minimally painful way, for merciful reasons, usually to end their suffering.
Passive euthanasia	The withholding of available treatments, such as life-sustaining devices, allowing the person to die is passive euthanasia.
Brain	The brain controls and coordinates most movement, behavior and homeostatic body functions such as heartbeat, blood pressure, fluid balance and body temperature. Functions of the brain are responsible for cognition, emotion, memory, motor learning and other sorts of learning. The brain is primarily made up of two types of cells: glia and neurons.
Advance directive	An advance directive is a written document that lets you specify what type of medical care you want in the future, should you lose the ability to make those decisions and communicate them for yourself. It also allows you to appoint an "agent," someone you choose to speak on your behalf.
Liver	The liver plays a major role in metabolism and has a number of functions in the body including detoxification, glycogen storage and plasma protein synthesis. It also produces bile, which is important for digestion. The liver converts most carbohydrates, proteing, and fats into glucose.
Ethnicity	Ethnicity refers to a characteristic based on cultural heritage, nationality characteristics, race, religion, and language.
Pancreas	The pancreas is a retroperitoneal organ that serves two functions: it produces juice containing digestive enzymes; and it produces several important hormones including insulin, glucagon, and several other hormones.
Brain death	Brain death is defined as a complete and irreversible cessation of brain activity. A brain-dead individual has no electrical activity (EEG) and no clinical evidence of brain function. Absence of apparent brain function is not enough. Evidence of irreversibility is also required.
Ethnic group	An ethnic group is a culture or subculture whose members are readily distinguishable by

outsiders based on traits originating from a common racial, national, linguistic, or religious source. Members of an ethnic group are often presumed to be culturally or biologically similar, although this is not in fact necessarily the case.

Acute | Acute means sudden, sharp, and abrupt. Usually short in duration.

Stereotype | A stereotype is considered to be a group concept, held by one social group about another.They are often used in a negative or prejudicial sense and are frequently used to justify certain discriminatory behaviors. This allows powerful social groups to legitimize and protect their dominant position

Prostate | The prostate is a gland that supplies most of the fluid that makes up semen, it is located at the base of the uninary bladder.

Survey | A method of scientific investigation in which a large sample of people answer questions about their attitudes or behavior is referred to as a survey.

Barbiturate | A barbiturate is a drug that acts as a central nervous system (CNS) depressant, and by virtue of this produces a wide spectrum of effects, from mild sedation to anesthesia.

Death with Dignity Act | Oregon's Death with Dignity Act legalizes physician-assisted suicide with certain restrictions, making Oregon the first U.S. state and one of the first jurisdictions in the world to officially do so.

Sullivan | Sullivan developed the Self System, a configuration of the personality traits developed in childhood and reinforced by positive affirmation and the security operations developed in childhood to avoid anxiety and threats to self-esteem.

Motivation | In psychology, motivation is the driving force (desire) behind all actions of an organism.

Life review | Life review refers to the process in which people in late adulthood examine and evaluate their lives.

Self-understanding | Self-understanding is a child's cognitive representation of the self, the substance and content of the child's self-conceptions.

Ego | In Freud's view the Ego serves to balance our primitive needs and our moral beliefs and taboos. Relying on experience, a healthy Ego provides the ability to adapt to reality and interact with the outside world.

Printed in the United Kingdom
by Lightning Source UK Ltd.
113783UKS00001B/19